PROMISES TO KEEP

The Mutual of America Story

PROMISES TO KEEP

The Mutual of America Story

JOHN BAIRD

New York
1989

This book is dedicated to the people we serve,
the men and women of the not-for-profit world.

About the Author

John Baird is vice president of Eastern College in suburban Philadelphia, Pennsylvania. He is a graduate of Princeton University and serves on the boards of numerous organizations including America's oldest life insurance company, The Presbyterian Ministers' Fund, organized in 1717. His seven published books include *Horn of Plenty,* the history of that corporation.

Contents

Illustrations

PHOTOGRAPHS

Acknowledgments

Books need lead time. *Promises to Keep* began in 1984 with a phone call to the author from William J. Flynn. Soon other people became involved, and this page provides the place to thank them for their assistance. Some are named. Others, owing to the constraints of space, remain unnamed, but my sincere appreciation is hereby expressed to all who had a part in making me knowledgeable about Mutual of America and its role in the insurance industry.

Mutual of America made records available to me, granted me access to employees and clients, and encouraged my complete freedom of thought and expression. All the company executives and other employees with whom I have talked have been generous with facts and forthright in their opinions. Isadore Feferman, Howard H. Hennington, Daniel J. Robins, Linda DeHooge, John Cerrato, Jr., and Helmut Frick merit individual mention for their significant contributions of time and effort. Special thanks go to Executive Vice President and Secretary Stephanie J. Kopp for her unfailing efficiency and enthusiasm.

Members of the board of directors, both past and present, made valuable contributions. Richard C. Brockway, Leland S. Brown, and C. Virgil Martin proved particularly helpful. Lewis D. Cole, C. Paul Hulten, George E. Johnson, and Dolores J. Morrissey added distinctive viewpoints.

Support also came from William H. Hackett, the late Earl T. Helsel, William Kaufman, Clement R. McCormack, Frank P. Montgomery, Christopher W. Stanwood, and Mary D. Stander. Mention should also be made of Grace G. Blanchard, Susan Blanchard Bliss, Sally Blanchard Erickson, Daniel Bliss, Susan Ellsworth Glover, Jane Glover Gorman, Gordon Gray

Glover, and Ruth Glover Smith who provided information and insight as members of these important families.

The American College of Life Underwriters, through the interest of its former president, David W. Gregg, and Marjorie A. Fletcher proved invaluable. The American Council of Life Insurance also helped with the cooperation of Vice President Carl Appelquist and Kim Elizabeth Lowry.

Interesting incidents and background data were contributed by a number of other people including Thomas C. Cochran, Ostrum Enders, David C. Hewitt, George P. Jenkins, Robert L. Newell, John P. McGuinn, James W. Toren, and J. Robert Wilhelm.

David C. Harrop earns my deepest appreciation for his editorial role in the final preparation of the manuscript. He not only closely reviewed the entire text but also conducted over 35 interviews with people involved in the history of the company. He interwove excerpts from these interviews throughout the account to provide an additional personal flavor to the book.

Last but not least, profound gratitude must be expressed for the intellectual and spiritual support of Dan M. McGill, who supported the project and offered valuable advice from start to finish. In this way, he sustained my efforts over the past few years.

John Baird

Preface

The history of Mutual of America is a history of caring. It is the story of men and women who recognized an urgent need in the not-for-profit community and responded with an unstinting measure of dedication and wisdom.

It is hard to believe that there was a time when nurses, social workers, and all those who work for all of us were not covered by a pension plan. They could not even look forward to the benefits of Social Security. They could expect nothing when it came time to retire. These people who gave so generously were left dependent on the charity of others. Their need gave rise to the company known today as Mutual of America.

Ralph H. Blanchard was the founder and early vitalizing force of the movement that created solutions for these problems. Under his guidance, a group of extraordinary individuals, accomplished in their own professions and dedicated to the cause, gathered to volunteer their talents and time.

Pioneers such as Gerard Swope, chairman of the General Electric Company and the first chairman of the board of the company that became Mutual of America, his successor Henry Bruère, chairman of the Bowery Savings Bank in New York, and all those who worked with them envisioned a national retirement system that would not only provide for the future security of not-for-profit professionals, but also give them the flexibility to move from one agency to another without loss of benefits. How well they succeeded in their efforts is recorded here.

A debt of gratitude is owed to the men and women of the New York State Insurance Department, who throughout the years assisted management with its task of developing pension services for the not-for-profit sector. Also, we offer a special thank you to the management of the John Hancock Mutual Life Insurance Company, who provided much needed help in the formative years.

Today, Mutual of America is a major force in the insurance industry, but this has not always been the case. In the early years, it was a struggle to survive. Pinching pennies was a way of life, and the addition of a few more people to the staff was a cause for celebration. But the company prospered under the steady guidance of many exceptional leaders and went from success to success.

Mutual of America has traveled a long way and sees no end to the road before it. The company has moved from card files to computerization and stands on the brink of the age of telecommunications. Clearly, a company is not just ledgers and records, it is people; and the unsung professionals who have contributed their talents and efforts to the growth of Mutual of America have earned our appreciation and admiration.

Though Mutual of America has mushroomed in size, it never forgets its roots or its original purpose. The company's success is not just counted in numbers, but also in the quality of its service to the not-for-profit community. History is not a static record, but a living thing, and in the years to come, Mutual of America, through a constant rededication, will remain true to its goals.

PART ONE

THE BEGINNING
(1945–1951)

Milton H. Glover
President, 1945–1951
Chairman, 1955–1962

INTRODUCTION TO PART ONE

Mutual of America was originally called the National Health & Welfare Retirement Association (NHWRA), and under that name, first began business on October 1, 1945, offering employer retirement plans and insurance coverages. In that year, slightly more than 5,000 workers in 400 small not-for-profit health and welfare agencies received at least a small measure of retirement and insurance coverage from one company for the first time in America's history.

NHWRA was unique in setting up a retirement system for not-for-profit health and welfare organizations. Such groups had been generally unable to obtain coverage from insurance carriers due to the small number of people that typically were employed. Furthermore, their employees were not eligible to participate in Social Security under the original Social Security Act of 1935. This had excluded several categories of workers, among them, those in most not-for-profit organizations.

The idea for this company, clearly, has proven to be a good one, and the management and directors of the company have demonstrated great success over the years in offering better and more complete coverage and services to not-for-profit employees.

The growth and expansion of Mutual of America have been remarkable. This is true not only in the numbers of people covered and in the increase in types of products and services available, but also in the developed capital resources. NHWRA began in 1945 with several loans from Community Chests and Councils, Inc. (CCC, known today as the United Way of America), which provided an initial grant of $10,000 and then a loan of $25,000 for working capital. By the end of 1988, the assets of Mutual of America and its subsidiaries totaled more than $4.8 billion.

The following history relies upon numerous documents detailing the company's progress. It also quotes extensively from interviews that were held with over 35 people currently or formerly associated with the organization. The people who were interviewed include employees, officers, trustees, and others who are personally acquainted with the company's story. In this way, many of the individuals who devoted their energies and working lives to Mutual of America have been able to contribute directly to the unfolding of their story.

This history is one of people whose dedication, perseverance, and courage in taking risks have developed the company from its modest origins to the effective and influential insurance enterprise that it is today. Two of these individuals have been described by many as having been indispensable in the remarkable growth of the company, and it is quite proper to identify them at the outset.

As George E. Johnson, once acting president of the company, trustee, and consultant has said: "The amazing success of Mutual of America was largely the result of two remarkable men, Ralph Blanchard and Bill Flynn. They sold the idea and they're very unique people. Without either of them the company would never be where it is today" *(George E. Johnson Interview, May 13, 1988)*.

These sentiments are expressed in varying ways by everyone who is or has been connected with Mutual of America. There are few left who can say that they have known both men intimately, but one who does is William Kaufman, chairman emeritus of the Mobile Community Foundation in Mobile, Alabama. He has contributed to the company's development in several capacities over thirty years. He recently said: "If Ralph Blanchard (who would not fly) had not gotten on those trains and taken all those trips and made this available... and then, of course, if Bill Flynn hadn't come along and improved the program to where it's much more meaningful now.... Let's just say that I'm eternally grateful to them" *(William Kaufman Interview, April 28, 1988)*.

4

Chapter One
IN SEARCH OF SECURITY

"Ralph Blanchard had a general humanitarian interest as well as a desire to take care of his own people. He intended to help those workers not under any pension plan and who, at that point, were not eligible for Social Security" *(C. Virgil Martin Interview, April 5, 1988).*

On October 7, 1945, a maintenance worker at St. Vincent's Hospital, Erie, Pennsylvania, died suddenly of a cerebral hemorrhage. His death came just days after his employer had contracted for retirement and death benefits from a new organization called the National Health & Welfare Retirement Association, Inc. (NHWRA), which had just begun business on October 1. He had paid a single $3.25 contribution that was matched by his employer. As a result of a modest term insurance program associated with the retirement plan, his daughter received $1,305, then a significant sum.

Few such survivors were so fortunate. In those days most social workers knew financial double jeopardy. They were without retirement protection and lacked life insurance as well. The economic plight of health and welfare employees involved not only poor pay and scant safeguards against disability or sickness, but also the prospect of poverty in old age. NHWRA came into being that year as the culmination of efforts begun in 1937 to do something definite about the economic vulnerability of those men and women who worked in the service sector of American society. These efforts stemmed from the shock of the Great Depression, which had begun with the collapse of the values of traded securities on "Black Friday," October 29, 1929. The stock market crash started a financial paralysis which attacked every sector of national life.

5

By 1935 per capita income had dropped to $474 from its 1929 level of $705. In the three years between 1929 and 1932, unemployment had jumped from 1.6 million to 12.1 million people.[1] Bank closings, the use of scrip as a substitute for money, an epidemic of bankruptcies, and mass layoffs of workers marked these desperate years.

Unemployment was the worst part. So many men and women without work brought home the true dimensions of the disaster and made the national problem both immediate and personal. Prosperity proved not to be just around the corner, and jobless men lived in clumps of shacks called Hoovervilles. For those with jobs, wages hit unbelievably low levels. Fringe benefits ranged from modest for a fortunate few to non-existent for most employees.

Social workers fared even worse. Rarely well paid in the best of times, and without retirement protection, most people employed in the humanitarian agencies—those who tried to improve life for others—faced fewer jobs, even lower-than-usual salaries, and an impecunious status when they became senior citizens. On the other hand, the professional staffs of some private schools and colleges enjoyed protection through the Teachers Insurance & Annuity Association (TIAA), active since 1918, and ministers of various Protestant denominations were covered by the pension plans of their own denominations.

These examples were exceptional. In those days, most men and women whose life work consisted of helping others through not-for-profit organizations received meager financial help from their employers during their active years and could anticipate none at retirement. On the death of an employee, it was not uncommon for the agency executive or a fellow worker to pass the hat for the purpose of helping to defray the burial expenses. The economic devastation and starkness of the years following 1929 cut through what one social work leader termed inertia, indifference, and even downright hostility. The grimness of the times forced improvements in workers' conditions throughout American employment.

A breakthrough finally came in 1935, when Congress passed

6

the Social Security Act. The bill was sponsored by New York Senator Robert F. Wagner. Although a significant first step for the United States, the beginnings of Social Security left much to be desired. Actual benefits ranged from $10 to $85 per month. The new law, however, did not cover all workers. It excluded agricultural workers, domestic employees, governmental employees, and employees of "certain religious, charitable, humane and educational institutions not organized or operated for profit."[2]

Social workers were excluded from the Act for several reasons. There was great inertia on the part of the not-for-profit field itself to take action to have social workers included. Second, the money that would have been required to establish and operate such plans was scarce. And finally, there was some concern that making tax-exempt organizations subject to Social Security payroll taxes might raise questions as to the propriety or legality of their tax-exempt status.

As a result, many members of the health and welfare community actively opposed inclusion in the new insurance scheme. They wrote letters, they lobbied against being included, and they succeeded in escaping the government net. Ironically, they also succeeded in depriving their employees of even this meager protection for their old age.

Nevertheless, the enactment of Social Security started an intellectual and spiritual chain reaction within the national labor force. The profit sector achieved certain immediate benefits. The not-for-profit part split off and was forced to face the need to find commensurate worker protection from other sources. No ready solution became apparent, and social workers began to leave their calling to seek jobs in business and industry. Agencies found it difficult to replace them.[3] Without money to fund their own retirement programs, the not-for-profit community turned to certain national foundations for grants to initiate such plans but without success.

The life insurance industry also declined to offer encouragement to not-for-profit agencies. Life insurance companies believed that the financial and fiduciary burdens of operating such a plan for the health and welfare world would be enormous. The majority of social work agencies employed few people. Most fell below the 50-person minimum considered economically viable by the large insurance companies. Along with the dollar risk of this mass protection for low-income people stood the probability of an awesome management work load. A typical agency would need the insurer to collect premiums, keep all records, and distribute benefits.

Community Chests and Councils (CCC) had formed through a gradual aggregation of the strong individual Community Chests, which had developed across the country, and CCC had not opposed Social Security. When the new law took effect on January 1, 1937, CCC renewed its efforts to secure retirement rights for social workers. With almost 500 local Community Chests representing thousands of individual agencies in agreement, CCC took action. It went on record favoring Social Security coverage for its people through amendment of the original law. It also appointed a preliminary committee to study the problem of retirement plans and other fringe benefits for health and welfare employees and to recommend a course of future action.

Federal initiatives and programs in the 1930's had reduced the need for Community Chests to raise money for relief. These private agencies were then able to concentrate upon family service and related social programs. Regardless of emphasis, however, the unique concept of the Community Chest gained increasing acceptance in most major cities. In addition, the combined fund-raising approach brought more money to most of the individual agencies. At the same time, a larger national interest in and concern for community social benefit was being created.

The board of directors of the Community Chests and Councils created its Social Security committee on March 5, 1937.[4] Chaired by attorney Walter A. Edwards from Providence, Rhode Island, this group consulted TIAA, which had been providing retirement benefit plans in the field of higher education, to ask if that experienced group would make its retirement plan available to health and welfare agencies.

TIAA considered the request, but decided against offering their plans to employees outside the education field. They agreed, however, to help CCC in its quest for retirement coverage for social workers and appointed their executive vice president, Dr. Rainard B. Robbins, as technical consultant to the committee.

For two years, the committee worked on a suggested set of retirement plans. During this time, Congress considered amendments to the Social Security Act but took no action despite the urging of many not-for-profit organizations including churches, colleges, hospitals, and social welfare agencies. Before the proposed plan of the CCC committee could be approved and implemented, the Second World War absorbed the energies of everyone including the Community Chest movement and forced the suspension of the committee's exploratory activities.[5] Retirement protection for social workers had to wait.

At the end of 1942, Allen T. Burns retired as the executive director of Community Chests and Councils. His successor was Ralph Harris Blanchard, who had been part of the movement since 1923. Mr. Blanchard began his new assignment with a statement typical of the man: "The way is pointed to a future in which Councils of Social Agencies will operate on a much broader scope than before the war."[6]

Ralph H. Blanchard had risen to the top of his vocation after an early career in banking. Born on June 27, 1895, in Niagara Falls, New York, he grew up in a family of eight children, the first four of whom died during a diphtheria epidemic. His father was an electroplater. He attended the public schools of his city and graduated from Cornell University in 1917.

During the five years at his first job with Peoples Bank of Niagara Falls, he developed an interest in the local Chamber of Commerce and Community Chest. In 1923 he began to manage the latter. He moved five years later to New York City, where he joined the CCC staff as an administrative director and field consultant. In the early 1930's, Mr. Blanchard helped local Community Chests achieve budget reductions. He also served on CCC rescue squads to help their fund campaigns.

9

As new executive director of the national organization, Mr. Blanchard assumed office on January 1, 1943. Sensing that a congressional amendment to the Social Security Act would not come soon, he moved in a different direction. With consummate skill he assembled a committee to study a retirement plan for health and welfare workers.

As Leland Brown, a former chairman of the board of NHWRA and a man with many years of involvement with the company's affairs, says: "Ralph was not only a very forward-looking man, he was a very jovial man, and a man of great ability to bind people to him and to get them interested in helping him in a cause in which he greatly believed. And Ralph was a good arm twister. He knew how to approach anybody at any level to get things done, and he did it in such a nice way you didn't quite realize your arm was hurting until later" *(Leland S. Brown Interview, April 6, 1988).*

Tom K. Smith, chairman of the Boatmen's National Bank, St. Louis, led the committee. Allen T. Burns, Mr. Blanchard's predecessor, acted as secretary, and TIAA's Dr. Rainard B. Robbins once again proved to be an invaluable consultant. Milton H. Glover, a Hartford National Bank and Trust Company vice president, served as a member and thus began his 29-year relationship with the organization that ensued.

The group had the backing of two other men who were both captains of industry and national Community Chests and Councils leaders: E.A. Roberts and Gerard Swope. Mr. Roberts, president of Fidelity Mutual Insurance Company, Philadelphia, was also president of CCC.

Mr. Swope, president of General Electric, was a former national chairman of Mobilization for Human Needs and later chairman of the National War Fund. He was an international business figure and had extensive experience with United States advisory boards and commissions. Because he enjoyed contacts with numerous domestic corporations, including New York's National City Bank where he served as a member of the board of directors, Mr. Swope was able to open many doors for the committee. "If there were a 'top five' powerful, non-political figures in America then, Gerard Swope would be one of them" *(C. Virgil Martin Interview, April 5, 1988).*

Virgil Martin, at the time one of Ralph Blanchard's vice presidents and the executive director of the New York War Fund, provided staff assistance for the committee. Mr. Martin later became chairman of Carson Pirie Scott & Company in Chicago. Messrs. Martin and Glover enjoyed long and productive relationships as board members with the retirement organization that was soon to be formed.

July 1, 1943, marked the start of compulsory withholding of federal income tax payments from employees' pay. The event was far-reaching, for soon thereafter, local Community Chests and Councils persuaded many employers to authorize simultaneous payroll deductions for the benefit of the Community Chest. The results of this development were spectacular, for "instead of a cash handout of a dollar or less, an employee might pledge 15 cents per week...making a total gift of $7.80 for the year."[7]

On September 9, 1943, the committee's report to CCC was presented. The report recommended that the board approve the development of a retirement plan for health and welfare workers and then put such a plan into effect as soon as possible. Approval came in December 1943, after Community Chests and Councils consulted with representatives of 25 national agencies to secure their suggestions and endorsement.

The study committee found that transferability of retirement benefit credits was essential for any effective pension plan in the welfare field because employees of health and welfare agencies tended to move frequently from one agency to another. Therefore, the plan could not have as long a service requirement for vesting as those of most industrial pension plans. The study committee advised full vesting. In addition, it rejected the concept of fixed benefits because of the unpredictability of costs, proposing instead a money purchase or fixed contribution plan.

The 1943 study committee was followed in January 1944 by an organizing committee which was to create the National Health & Welfare Retirement Association. Funded with an initial grant of $10,000, this organizing committee went right to work with Milton H. Glover as chairman, Homer Wickenden as secretary, and Henry S. Beers, Aetna Life vice president (later CEO of Aetna), as advisor.

Forty-four life insurance companies were approached regarding reinsurance of benefits for the developing organization, but only six offered their services. Some were too small, some were not qualified in all states, others did not handle group coverage, and still others "preferred only industrial plans."[8] Several were cautious about the concept and reluctant to commit their reputation to the fledgling operation.

The John Hancock Mutual Life Insurance Company of Boston finally agreed to be the reinsurer. "...It was the influence of Charles Francis as a member of the board and from the founding group brought in by Blanchard...that got the John Hancock, I think rather reluctantly, to take on the reinsurance and the risk of doing it" *(Leland S. Brown Interview, April 6, 1988).* The John Hancock was a large, conservative, and well-managed company, experienced in group annuities and group insurance.

Guy W. Cox was president of the John Hancock during these conversations with Community Chests and Councils in 1944. The contacts were sustained largely by Ralph H. Blanchard, who earned the title of architect of the Retirement Association that was created during these negotiations. He kept the project moving and was supported by some CCC executives, including Lynn D. Mowatt of Los Angeles, and Kenneth Sturges of Cleveland. Mr. Blanchard faced the indifference of some other professional Community Chest leaders, who lacked his vision and energy, but he never faltered in his determination to see the project through to completion.

In 1944, Mr. Blanchard became one of six members of the National Health & Welfare Retirement Association provisional board. The organization occupied office space at the headquarters of Community Chests and Councils at 155 East 44th Street in New York City. As early as June 1944, Homer Wickenden (recruited by Mr. Blanchard from the New York United Hospital Fund) and his secretary, Mary D. Stander, began work, but the provisional board first met officially on October 27, 1944, at the Commodore Hotel.

Present were four of the appointed members, their lawyer, and the first administrative employee. Two members there were social workers: Ralph H. Blanchard, executive director, Community Chests and Councils; and John B. Dawson, executive director, Philadelphia Health and Welfare Council. Two were bankers: Milton H. Glover, vice president, Connecticut Bank and Trust Company, Hartford; and Hobart M. McPherson, vice president, National City Bank, New York. The two others present were Theodore V. Zavatt, Esq., and Homer Wickenden. Absent were Robert O. Loosley, secretary of Brown University, and John O. Stubbs, a Boston investment banker.

Mr. Dawson served as a temporary chairman and Mr. Wickenden as temporary secretary. Mr. Glover was elected provisional president, and Mr. Wickenden, provisional secretary. These two elected officers were authorized, empowered, and directed to execute the Declaration of Intention, Constitution, and By-Laws on behalf of the Retirement Association and to file them with the superintendent of insurance of the state of New York.

The Retirement Association's first home office
(1945–1947) was at 441 Lexington Avenue.

Chapter Two

GETTING ESTABLISHED

"Unless you were there at the beginning, you can't imagine how enormous the strides have been because when we first had our office on Lexington Avenue (we had this little tiny office) for a while we didn't even have furniture. Homer Wickenden and I had desks, but when we started hiring clerical workers we didn't have enough chairs to go around so we got some boxes that they could sit on until we bought some furniture. We had no money to start with. . . . And looking back on it and seeing what has developed over the years, it's almost fantastic to think that so much gain has been made" *(Mary D. Stander Interview, May 10, 1988)*.

The announcement in January 1945 of the formation of NHWRA elicited considerable interest and press coverage. The *New York Times* ran an article entitled "Security Systems in Welfare Field,"[1] and the *New York World Telegram* printed a piece called "Social Workers to Get Retirement Benefits."[2] Across the country articles appeared, such as "Set Security Plans for 500,000 Now in Welfare Work"[3] and "Plan Will Help Social Workers."[4] Important trade publications, including the *Eastern Underwriter*, *New York Journal of Commerce*, and the *American Banker,* also provided coverage.

Arthur J. Altmeyer, the Social Security board chairman, expressed encouragement, calling NHWRA a "valuable supplement to the basic protection of the old-age and survivors' insurance."[5] Robert E. Dineen, the New York State superintendent of insurance, certified the enterprise on January 3, 1945, by stating that the company was to be incorporated as a retirement system and authorized to transact business in New York State.

The first meeting of the board of trustees was held on January 5, 1945, at the offices of Community Chests and Councils to

Gerard Swope
Chairman, 1945–1947

confirm the names and terms of office for the six original trustees: Ralph H. Blanchard, John B. Dawson, Milton H. Glover, Robert O. Loosley, Hobart M. McPherson, and John O. Stubbs. Gerard Swope became chairman of the board, and Mr. Glover became president. The firm of Satterlee & Warfield was retained as the legal counsel and Haskins & Sells as the certified public accountants. An executive committee was appointed to have all the powers and to exercise the duties of the board of trustees between meetings of the entire group.

In accordance with the By-Laws, Mr. Glover as president became chairman of the executive committee. Chairman Swope became an ex officio member of that body, and the other five original trustees comprised the rest of the committee. The John Hancock Mutual Life Insurance Company agreed to reinsure all benefits provided for in the By-Laws.[6] The Retirement Association accepted this offer with the understanding that the reinsurance terms would be spelled out in the final agreements that were being prepared.

The Chase National Bank and National City Bank, both of Manhattan, were designated as banking institutions for the Retirement Association. The Retirement Association's officers were authorized to borrow up to $10,000 from Community Chests and Councils to be secured by a non-interest-bearing promissory note due not later than January 1, 1946.

CCC had advanced NHWRA $10,000 the previous year for preliminary expenses, but only $1,744 of that sum remained, and it would be months before any actual premium income would be received. The charter trustees went ahead with almost no money but with a desire to do something definite to improve the retirement years of health and welfare employees.

When the Retirement Association was organized, a great deal of thought went into the question of where it should be domiciled and the advantages and disadvantages of organizing it as an insurance company, a trust, or some other legal entity.

Unique to the state of New York was a little-known and seldom used section of the Insurance Law (then Section 200) that authorized the establishment of retirement systems. Section

200 provided that an employer or a group of employers having business interests in common could establish a not-for-profit retirement system as a corporation for the purpose of providing pension benefits for the employees of such employer or group of employers.

Section 200 also provided that such a corporation could be organized without capital, whereas a life insurance company could not commence operations without sizable capital and surplus. As I. Murray Krowitz, then an inspector with the New York State Insurance Department, explained it: "There was no provision in the Insurance Law that would accommodate the need for a not-for-profit organization. If they were going to form a life insurance company, they would have to raise a certain amount of capital which they obviously could not do, or else try to form a mutual life insurance company which had not been done for many years because it required getting thousands of people to buy insurance and pay premiums in advance of the company's formation" (*I. Murray Krowitz Interview, May 10, 1988*).

Under Section 200 the benefits provided by a retirement system could be 100 percent reinsured. That provision enabled the company to commence business in safety, relying upon the expertise and the financial stability of an established life insurance company. A disadvantage was that the Insurance Department determined that under this Section 200, the terms of the plans had to be contained in the By-Laws.

This early decision to incorporate under Section 200 was crucial because it established the structure, operating method, and contracting method of the Retirement Association for years to come. Incorporation under Section 200 made the existence of the NHWRA possible, but "the Insurance Department—and I was the one who did this—pointed out that they had very limited authority under this Section 200, and, therefore, could not act in the same way as a life insurance company might" (*I. Murray Krowitz Interview, May 10, 1988*). Mr. Krowitz further explained that the Insurance Department worked closely with NHWRA through the years because of the unique requirements of Section 200.

In the first six months of NHWRA's existence, the trustees faced many challenges. They needed to find an office that NHWRA could call its own; to employ a staff sufficient to conduct the business; to refine the actual reinsurance agreement with the John Hancock; to enlist a much larger board of trustees; and to secure a tax exemption from the United States Treasury Department. These goals were accomplished while accumulating the minimum 5,000 individual participant constituency base described in the By-Laws as necessary to begin actual operations.

Chairman Gerard Swope, Trustee Ralph Blanchard, and President Milton Glover, all part-time volunteers, formed the inner circle of responsibility. These men carried the major burden, aided by the one full-time paid professional, Homer Wickenden. The dual roles of president and chairman of the executive committee gave Mr. Glover a position of great influence in the early months of 1945. The accomplishments of the board in those exciting days reflected the measure of his involvement.

Mr. Glover was born of Canadian parents on October 10, 1899, in Providence, Rhode Island. Before he finished high school, his father, a building contractor, died. Milton Glover worked his way through Brown University, played halfback on the varsity football team, and graduated with a degree in philosophy in 1922. After seven years with the J. G. White Company in New York City, he joined the Hartford National Bank & Trust Company as an investment officer. He was promoted to vice president in 1939, and eventually some of his responsibilities involved community service. At one time he coached a football team of poor boys known as the "Frog Hollow Echoes." Over the years, he became a director of a dozen corporations including Connecticut General Life Insurance Company and a trustee of numerous cultural and charitable organizations, including the Greater Hartford Young Men's Christian Association (YMCA).

Mr. Glover's interest and experience in community affairs brought him to Ralph Blanchard's attention. As executive director of the Community Chests and Councils, Mr.

19

Vice President Christopher W. Stanwood was originally loaned to the Retirement Association by the John Hancock in 1944.

Mary D. Stander, who in June 1944 became the Retirement Association's first staff employee, attended the dinner celebrating Mutual of America's 40th anniversary.

Blanchard made a point of getting to know local leaders across the country, and this knowledge proved useful when he looked for people who could help him do something about the retirement plight of social workers. He enlisted Mr. Glover for the CCC board of directors and also placed him on the 1943 study committee.

The Retirement Association assembled a team of workers to handle the rapidly-growing administrative detail and to start the sales program. Homer Wickenden and Mary Stander, his secretary, were soon joined by Henry S. Grambor, who was hired to manage the records and given the title of manager of accounting statistics. Christopher W. Stanwood, who had worked with the committee in 1944, was a technical representative. The John Hancock not only furnished Mr. Stanwood, but also initially paid his salary. Mr. Stanwood remained with the company until 1971 and rose to the position of vice president/field director.

As Christopher Stanwood remembers it: "I had been working for the John Hancock and was loaned by them to the Association. I had been with the Group Annuity Division for five or six years. The original thought was that the sales force of John Hancock could be used directly to help. But it was impossible for them to do so because of the not-for-profit status of the Association. I was on a salary basis but I was paid by Hancock until I changed over to the Retirement Association as field director in January 1946" *(Christopher W. Stanwood Interview, March 31, 1988)*. These personnel additions were augmented by Samuel H. Ourbacker as field representative and another secretary. The John Hancock Company during the first critical months of 1945 also designated five officials to work closely with NHWRA: Winthrop Lewis, Philip Anderson, Jack Cunningham, Franklyne Allen, and Mary Diotauti.

The Retirement Association was governed initially by a small board of trustees, largely the same dedicated individuals who had been the incorporators. The decision in January 1945, to increase the number of board members to 60, the maximum permitted by law, was based more on the tradition of the social welfare community than on that of the commercial corporate community. For the latter, the board is the active governing body, exercising close oversight in discharging its responsibilities. For the former, a board position is often honorary, with management oversight being exercised by a smaller group. The smaller group in the case of the Retirement Association was the executive committee. There was never any question that the executive committee was the active management group: it met six times a year, the board as a whole met only once a year. After the second meeting of the board on May 1, 1945, the Retirement Association had a total of 56 trustees.

At the pre-meeting luncheon, Robert E. Dineen, New York State superintendent of insurance, commended NHWRA for its progress and for adopting the principle of reinsurance of its benefits rather than establishing a self-administered association. John Hancock President Paul Clark confirmed his company's desire to cooperate and contribute to the plan's success. Mr. Clark and his administrative assistant Robert Helsey remained for the actual board meeting.

New board members included such nationally known people as H. J. Heinz, II, Marshall Field, III, and Winthrop W. Aldrich. Officers and trustees with significant involvement in Community Chests and Councils comprised another group; twelve Community Chest professional or volunteer leaders took an active part in starting NHWRA. Community Chests and Councils made further loans. It advanced $7,500 on May 1, 1945, and another $5,000 in June. These sums were followed by a final $2,500 loan in late August. When combined with the previous loan at the beginning of 1945 of $10,000, this made a total of $25,000 provided by the CCC, all of it without interest. These loans were repaid to the CCC on October 30, 1947.

In early 1945, the Retirement Association considered the question of its tax status under the Internal Revenue Code. Section 200 of the New York State Insurance Law, under which the Retirement Association operated, had designated the Retirement Association as a not-for-profit corporation. However, income tax exemption is a federal matter, which has to be determined by the Internal Revenue Service (IRS). The Retirement Association board was familiar with the tax exemptions granted TIAA and the Church Life Insurance Corporation. Under the Internal Revenue Code Section 101(6), the former was tax-exempt as an educational organization, the latter as a religious organization.

The Retirement Association also sought exemption under Section 101(6) as a charitable organization because the services were available solely to charitable organizations, and it should thus be considered a charitable organization.

The IRS considered the exemption application, and in June 1945, declared the Retirement Association tax-exempt under Section 101(8) as an organization not operated for profit and devoted to the promotion of social welfare. It had rejected two other possibilities: 101(6) and 101(16), the exemption for voluntary employee benefit associations.

The Retirement Association was therefore exempt from paying federal income tax, but donations to it could not be deducted in determining the donor's income tax. The trustees considered this a significant disadvantage because they were still considering the possibility of foundation grants to strengthen the young corporation. Despite their disappointment, the trustees did not appeal the IRS ruling at that time.

The continuing dialogue and negotiations with the IRS, however, played an important role in the company's history. In 1950, the Retirement Association reopened the question of tax exemption with the Internal Revenue Service, seeking deductibility from income tax for a donor's contribution. Once again, the IRS ruled the Retirement Association to be tax-exempt, but again granted that exemption under Section 101(8) rather than 101(6). In the IRS Code of 1954, Section 101(6) was renumbered 501(c)(3), and Section 101(8) was renumbered 501(c)(4).

Although the Retirement Association was ruled to be tax-exempt because it was classified under Section 101(8) of the

Internal Revenue Code, it was not exempt from the FICA (Federal Insurance Contribution Act) tax for Social Security. Unlike the employees of most of its contributing members, employees of the Retirement Association were covered under the Social Security Law for the time worked with the Retirement Association.

Under Section 200 of the Insurance Law of New York State, the Retirement Association was required to set forth in the By-Laws the detailed terms of the retirement provisions—Plan A. This plan was being offered to the social agencies by the employees of the Retirement Association, who were crisscrossing the country in their effort to obtain the 5,000 participants necessary to begin actual operations.

"Homer Wickenden and I would go off on trips and we would handle about two meetings a day—one in the morning, one in the afternoon—and then travel at night to the next location. We went to Pittsburgh, Cincinnati, Columbus, Cleveland, Indianapolis, Detroit, and so on. At each stop we would tell them that this is a new program for your employees... and that we must have at least 5,000 people who wish to participate in order to get started. And we would say that the program was reinsured by the John Hancock.... I don't suppose it could have been done without that. And I might say that starting with the chairman of the board of the Hancock, whom I knew fairly well, and the president and their actuaries, they were all involved and helped to develop it" *(Christopher W. Stanwood Interview, March 31, 1988)*.

Plan A was a defined contribution plan. It required a contribution by each participant of 5 percent of his compensation. The employer was required to contribute an equal amount, and these combined contributions provided the future service annuity benefit. That benefit was based upon the premium rates of the Retirement Association, which were based on the rates of the John Hancock and the age of the participant at the time the rates were applied. As with any defined contribution plan, an exact estimate of the retirement benefit could not be given in advance of retirement.

Plan A also provided a past service benefit. This annual benefit was 0.7 percent of a participant's October 1, 1945, annual compensation multiplied by the participant's years of service after age 35 and prior to October 1, 1945.

The method chosen to fund this past service benefit was unique. It involved a pooling of contributions throughout the Plan A membership during a to-be-determined past service purchase period. Originally that period was estimated to be 19 years. The funding period actually ended in December 1956, taking only 11 years and 3 months. Each Plan A agency member paid a past service contribution of 2 percent of the compensation of all of its employees. This was in addition to the basic 5 percent contribution previously mentioned.

The past service contribution was required whether or not the contributing agency had employees eligible for past service. Because of this pooling method, it was necessary to limit the time in which Plan A was made available. Thus, no new Plan A agency enrollments would be accepted after October 1947. Plan A also provided an insurance benefit which was designed to provide, together with the death benefit based on the employees' and the employers' future service contributions, a total death benefit of approximately 10 months of salary. That insurance death benefit was paid for by a deduction from the employer's future service contribution.

Plan B became available on November 1, 1947, since Plan A was closed. Plan B was identical to Plan A except that past service benefits through the pooling device were not available. From 1945 until June 1951, the pension plans offered by the Retirement Association were Plans A, B, and C. Plan C—developed for the American Hospital Association—was established July 1, 1946.

The first trustees did not expect delays in organizing the new retirement system. The By-Laws stated that the "effective date" for the beginning of the business would be decided upon by the board "after 5,000 eligible employees of contributory members have made application to become participants."[7] This figure was considered to be a prudent minimum for sustained operations, and it was believed the number could quickly be achieved. Early estimates proved too optimistic, however. By mid-April 1945, it became clear that the expected May 1 target date would not be reached. Enrollment proceeded more slowly than anticipated, and the trustees set a new deadline of June 1.

Grace Blanchard, widow of the Association's founding spirit, has a more personal memory. "Ralph said that we needed 5,000 members in order to get started, and we watched the mail every day. He had set a figure of 5,000 and drove us nearly crazy until we could get to 5,001" *(Grace Blanchard Interview, April 13, 1988)*.

April saw strenuous sales efforts, which included meetings with health and welfare agencies, printing and distribution of sales kits, and preparation of employee booklets. Meetings were held in Boston, Massachusetts; Buffalo, New York; Dayton, Ohio; Hartford, Connecticut; New York City; and Washington, D.C. Representatives from more than 290 agencies employing in excess of 3,000 workers came and heard the NHWRA proposal. Sales kits and related forms went to 25 other cities, and 20,000 booklets for individual workers were shipped upon request to 97 Community Chests.

Christopher Stanwood recalls: "We had prepared literature which was given to the agency trustees and also to their related organizations so that they in turn could pass it along to their agencies and organizations, and eventually the employees would get the information....I did a tremendous amount of traveling all over the country. I spent six weeks, for example, in California opening up the entire west coast. Los Angeles was the big place. There were about 80 agencies and I met with the boards of every single one of them. Of course, I couldn't sell the employees at that point, but I sold the boards" *(Christopher W. Stanwood Interview, March 31, 1988)*.

The need to make decisions at multiple levels within the respective agencies caused delays. Unlike the ordinary life insurance transaction between salesman and policyholder, NHWRA protection involved adoption of the plan by the trustees of each specific agency and enrollment of every participant. Health and welfare workers did not qualify for NHWRA on an individual basis, but only as employees of a recognized not-for-profit agency.

The Retirement Association soon faced the question of licensing in states other than New York. This was a question which was to arise repeatedly between 1945 and 1978 and was not completely resolved until the organization, operating as an insurance company, became licensed in all states in 1986.

As Dan McGill, insurance expert, company consultant, and former trustee, explained: "While using Section 200 was a way for them to get started, very few people had heard of such an entity. And when they were small and unobtrusive no one cared or raised any questions. But as the company grew and prospered—especially under Bill Flynn—the need to be licensed to do business in the various states had to be resolved.

"In the beginning other companies didn't want that business, but when they saw the market developing, here was a rather formidable competitor that did not fit within typical life insurance regulation so changes were made" *(Dan M. McGill Interview, April 13, 1988)*.

The Retirement Association in its early years made the same argument that other insurers doing business by mail did. It asserted that it was a New York State corporation writing New York contracts in New York. The Retirement Association leaders believed the complexities of dealing with the laws of each state would present a task beyond their capabilities at that time since other states did not have legislation similar to Section 200. Furthermore, the Retirement Association was attempting to foster uniformity in its operations.

The Retirement Association in 1945 sought a ruling in Massachusetts on whether it could enter into contracts with health and welfare organizations there. Initially, the general counsel of the Massachusetts Insurance Department ruled that it would not be legal for a Massachusetts agency to become a member of the Retirement Association. The Retirement Association did not believe that this was the correct interpretation.

Ralph Blanchard was able to obtain an appointment with Lieutenant Governor Robert Bradford of Massachusetts, then president of the board of directors of the Boston Community Council. Through the good offices of the lieutenant governor, the attorney general of Massachusetts agreed to review the opinion of the general counsel of the Insurance Department. Subsequently, an attorney general's opinion was issued which held that a Massachusetts social welfare agency could become a member of the Retirement Association.

The original opinion of the Insurance Department was reversed, but precious months had been lost, causing a further postponement of the date to effect operation of the Retirement Association's protection plan.

The American Hospital Association (AHA) was the cause of more delay. A week after NHWRA's first board meeting, the hospital organization's pension committee met to discuss its own pension plan for hospital workers. Homer Wickenden attended the meeting to urge the group to join NHWRA, but AHA believed that many hospitals could not afford to join. It requested a 2 percent lower payroll cost with no death benefit other than the employee's own contribution plus interest. This was in contrast to the other NHWRA plans, which included employer contributions as a death benefit. There were other differences as well.

The AHA's pension committee wished to sponsor a separate Section 200 corporation "in conjunction with National Health & Welfare Retirement Association."[8] Through most of 1945, the committee moved in this direction, bringing in Aetna Life as a consultant, while continuing to confer with NHWRA. These complications prevented the enlisting of hospital workers, slowing the total enrollment process. Ralph Blanchard and his associates preferred to continue negotiations with the hospital group rather than to proceed on an independent course of action which would have presented hospital employees with competing and confusing choices.

The first 45 agency members joined the new retirement system by June 21, 1945, and an additional 89 applications from agency members were accepted that day, subject to the approval of John Hancock, the reinsurer. The initial group was located within twelve communities of six states: Alabama, Connecticut, Indiana, Massachusetts, New York, and Ohio. The largest contingent comprised 18 agency members from Boston. Birmingham came next with 11. Neighborhood houses predominated. There were local children's aid organizations, nursing associations, Girl Scout Councils, Community Chests and Community Funds as well as an art center, a museum, and a legal aid bureau.

Milton Glover and Gerard Swope boosted summer enrollment efforts by mailing a booklet to thousands of social work employees. Narratives about three imaginary workers "Mary Smith," "Henry Kelley," and "David Stein" provided examples of income and savings possible under the NHWRA plan. Welfare workers who came under the plan would retain earned benefits if they changed jobs or even quit their jobs. They could protect their dependents, as well, through a death benefit.[9]

At the end of May 1945, only 1,284 participant workers were enrolled. August brought the total to 3,136, but it was not until October 1, 1945, that the 5,000 minimum goal was officially reached. When NHWRA began operations on October 1, 1945, more than 400 health and welfare agencies and 5,000 individual employees were committed to being on the books. Further efforts maintained the momentum, and many agencies enrolled in the following months. Robert W. Moore, Jr., who was employed as field director with a salary contributed by the John Hancock, and Homer Wickenden sent a second message to the community services constituency which promised "an income for life for every social, health and welfare worker."[10]

When NHWRA began operations, the morale of hospital employees was low. Low wages and no pensions contributed to a high rate of employee turnover, and a shortage of non-professional health workers seemed imminent. Homer Wickenden represented NHWRA at the 23rd annual meeting of the New England Hospital Assembly, where 2,000 members convened to discuss the pressing matter. He discussed hospital rates and suggested they might have to increase to provide some kind of retirement plan for employees.[11]

The American Hospital Association had spent most of the previous year studying the pension part of the employment and staffing problem. Although they considered creating another Section 200 not-for-profit corporation to provide this kind of coverage, they eventually abandoned this idea and agreed to combine forces with NHWRA.

In February 1946, the changes in the By-Laws requested by the hospital organization were approved, and four AHA pension committee members filled the remaining board vacancies at NHWRA. George Bugbee, already a member of both groups, would be joined as an NHWRA trustee by John H. Hayes, president-elect of the hospital organization; Peter S. Husch, a St. Louis attorney; James M. Hamilton, a Yale University professor; and Raymond P. Sloan, the editor of *Modern Hospital.*

Plan C for hospital workers was established July 1, 1946. It involved lower employee contributions of 3 percent of compensation and 5 percent employer contributions and did not provide an insured death benefit, but met the needs of this particular group. The plan was well received when formally announced about October 1, 1946, and sped the growth of NHWRA.

The Retirement Association proved flexible in the matter of small agencies seeking membership when less than the required 75 percent of their eligible employees agreed to enter the plan. In most cases they approved admission. They refused, however, a Los Angeles Community Welfare Federation request for waiver of the NHWRA requirement that plan participation be a condition of employment in all member agencies. The exercise of underwriting discretion did not hamper the general strengthening of the early financial situation.

In the space of a few months, premium income poured in. Most of the money went to the John Hancock for reinsurance, but NHWRA covered its own operating expenses and paid the first death claim.

Chapter Three

STRENGTHENING THE BASE

"We met continually on this thing [pensions for not-for-profit workers] in the early 1940's, but it wasn't until the war was over that the first positive steps were made.... Then Ralph Blanchard, who was still the active head of Community Chests and Councils, began to give a tremendous amount of his time to it in the following years" *(C. Virgil Martin Interview, April 5, 1988).*

The most urgent requirements for NHWRA in the early period were to develop financial strength and to extend the number of people under coverage. These two goals were clearly related, and the main energy and impetus for accomplishing them came from Gerard Swope, Milton Glover, and Ralph Blanchard. The first two acted within their respective roles as chairman and president, but the third, who was simply a member of the board and the executive committee, exercised by far the greatest influence.

There was an urgent need to cover existing costs and to increase overall income in a short time. To achieve the latter, NHWRA needed to enlist as many new member agencies as possible to maintain its original momentum.

Two more organizations extended financial help at this juncture. In 1945 and 1946, the John Hancock Mutual Life made more than $30,000 available to help meet various expenses. The American Hospital Association provided the first edition of the Plan C information booklets issued by NHWRA and helped subsidize early development of that program.

To increase membership, promotional efforts included magazine articles and conference talks. One trade publication carried a story that described the need for a retirement program for hospital employees which "could be easily fitted in

Henry Bruère
Chairman, 1947–1955

with Social Security payments when and if the federal laws were changed to include workers in hospitals," and noted that the final program was developed with the cooperation of NHWRA.[1] The Wisconsin Hospital Association met in Milwaukee's Schroeder Hotel to hear Trustee George Bugbee and Corporate Secretary Homer Wickenden speak about NHWRA.[2]

Mary Stander, Homer Wickenden's secretary, remembers those days. "They would travel all over the country, and I recall that Mr. Wickenden would call from a particular city to find out how many dollars came in. When I could say to him, 'We got $50,000 today,' it was just like a miracle" *(Mary D. Stander Interview, May 10, 1988)*.

These activities brought results. Agency members and individual participants increased. In 1947, John H. Hayes, a Retirement Association trustee and the American Hospital Association president, announced enrollment of about 3,000 employees from fifty hospitals.[3] The increased business forced another move of the main office to larger quarters. Homer Wickenden and the staff moved to 15 Maiden Lane, where they occupied the entire 18th floor.

In June 1947, Gerard Swope announced the application of almost 1,600 social work agencies whose more than 14,000 employees enrolled during the first 20 months of company operations. These workers and their employers paid $3.7 million for protection; 96 percent of these monies was paid by NHWRA to the John Hancock as reinsurer. Actual payment of annuity benefits still lay ahead, but 40 death claims had been honored amounting to $72,500.

When Gerard Swope resigned as board chairman on June 11, 1947, he accepted the title "honorary chairman for life." Mr. Swope had made an outstanding two-year contribution to NHWRA. His business experience and national prestige had produced tangible results during the crucial early months of the company. His personal interest in NHWRA gave confidence to everyone connected with it and made their goals seem realistic and achievable.

The trustees elected Bowery Savings Bank President Henry Bruère as his successor. Mr. Bruère had been elected to the board two years before, and he too brought extensive business experience and community influence to the chairmanship. Prior to assuming the presidency of the bank, he had been a vice president of Metropolitan Life Insurance Company. Mr. Bruère, born in Missouri on January 15, 1882, earned a degree at the University of Chicago and did graduate work at Columbia, Harvard, and New York universities. While a student in Chicago, he became interested in Hull House, one of the first social settlements in North America, which was opened by Jane Addams in 1889. When in Boston for further studies, he helped local boys' clubs and later did welfare work for the International Harvester Company (now known as Navistar).

After a few years with the New York City Bureau of Municipal Research, Mr. Bruère advanced to the post of chamberlain and was charged with reorganization studies for the mayor. He served as economic adviser to President Franklin D. Roosevelt during the banking crisis of 1933 and earned high marks from the White House for his contribution to the national welfare.[4] He also engaged in other governmental tasks, including work with the New York Advisory Committee for the Reconstruction Finance Corporation and the United States Savings Bond Commission.

Mr. Bruère faced the immediate problem which involved possible expansion of NHWRA activities. Should NHWRA accept applications from religious, research, and educational organizations? John Hancock Vice President Clarence W. Wyatt warned that such an expansion would create some resentment on the part of life insurance brokers and agents. The trustees thought it over, took Mr. Wyatt's advice, and voted not to move in this direction, which would have involved seeking an enabling amendment to the NHWRA charter from the New York State superintendent of insurance.

NHWRA completed two years of operations on October 1, 1947, prompting President Glover to call his progress report a "Second Birthday" greeting. During that period, 1,700 health and welfare organizations had signed up and 18,000 employees had joined. The cumulative employer-employee contributions exceeded $5 million; the John Hancock's first dividend to NHWRA was $123,000; and the guaranteed death benefit protection exceeded $20 million.

President Glover made the figures more personal by mentioning representative families who had received death benefits including survivors of a Traveler's Aid secretary, a family caseworker, a hospital maintenance man, several visiting nurses, a cook in a children's home, and the janitor of a social settlement. He went on to note the popularity of two distinctive NHWRA features: the portability of its pensions as workers moved from one agency to another and the permanence of these benefits regardless of length of employment before retirement. Mr. Glover believed NHWRA's protection plans would wear like iron. The importance of these features and the foresight of that plan design are still acknowledged today.

Isadore Feferman, employed by the Retirement Association in 1947 and now a vice president, spoke of these early features: "I think of the foresight of these founding fathers. In our pension plan we had early vesting, and in 1945 such vesting was unheard of. The predominant pension plans written at that time called for vesting after twenty or even thirty years of service. But in 1945 we realized that this was like a family arrangement; that you couldn't have restrictive vesting and the mobility that the social welfare field requires for advancement. A professional in the field is going from Agency A to Agency B. He's carrying his retirement money with him, and he doesn't lose the contributions of his employer. So that's the vesting element and the portability. It was unheard of then, and to this day very few companies offer full and immediate vesting" *(Isadore Feferman Interview, March 1, 1988)*.

For years, CCC and NHWRA believed that health and welfare workers would eventually win Social Security benefits. They went beyond waiting for this circumstance, however, and took action to hasten the process. The Retirement Association approved a June 3, 1948, resolution to Congress urging adoption of Bill HR 6777, introduced by Representative Daniel A. Reed, providing for inclusion of not-for-profit organizations under Old Age and Survivors Insurance on a voluntary basis.

While Milton Glover and the other executive committee members attended to major policy matters, they also maintained an interest in individual cases. For example, one employee of the Philadelphia Welfare Federation handled the telephone switchboard of her agency and so could not attend the first enrollment meeting sponsored by her Community Chest. As a result, she did not file her application to be a participant at that time but did so as soon as the opportunity was presented to her at a later date. The Welfare Federation requested that she be permitted to receive credit for her past service under Plan A; the request was approved.

In the summer of 1949, NHWRA began paying retired hospital workers as Plan C participants under the program which had become effective three years earlier. Three employees of Robert Packer Hospital of Sayre, Pennsylvania, were among the first to qualify. Trustee John H. Hayes, in his dual capacity with the American Hospital Association and NHWRA, wrote about it in a journal article that appeared that summer. The accompanying photograph showed hospital administrator Howard Bishop presenting the checks to the recipients. [5]

Christopher W. Stanwood, as a company field consultant, went to St. Mary's Hospital, Rochester, New York, on October 17, 1949. He presented a check to Dominick Mancuso, a member of that institution's housekeeping department since 1942. The hospital bulletin advised other employees "to take another look at the picture of Mr. Mancuso" receiving his check and invited them to come to the personnel office for further particulars. [6]

In June 1950, the NHWRA home office moved once again to more adequate space at 10 East 40th Street in order to accommodate the increase in staff. Isadore Feferman recalls: "In 1950, we moved from Maiden Lane to 40th Street. In the early 1950's there was no such thing as air conditioning. At 10:15 in the morning and at 3:30 in the afternoon, everybody would stop work...and open up the windows. It was called an air break. Everybody would walk around for 15 minutes and let the fresh air in" *(Isadore Feferman Interview, March 1, 1988)*.

At the fifth annual meeting on November 2, 1950, Henry Bruère presented impressive figures to demonstrate the five years of growth of the Retirement Association. In that period the number of participants had increased from 5,000 to 25,000, and the accumulated contributions had risen to $21 million. He praised the John Hancock and announced that the original five-year contract with the reinsurer had been renewed on an annual basis.

Congress had expanded the Social Security Act in 1939 to include bank employees, and in 1946, maritime workers. A 1950 amendment made the program available on an elective basis to "religious, charitable, humane, and institutions not organized or operated for profit."[7] Mr. Bruère discussed this long-awaited development in the context of NHWRA's desire to combine its plans with the Social Security program to achieve a combined pension objective of 50 percent of average salary.

On November 2, 1950, Ralph H. Blanchard became a vice president of the Retirement Association. The other vice presidents at the time were Mrs. Charles S. Brown, William J. Flather, Jr., and John O. Stubbs.

Shortly thereafter, NHWRA sent an eight-page newsletter entitled *Bulletin* to all contributing member organizations. The publication supplied details of the Social Security amendments which would become law on January 1, 1951. The *Bulletin* mentioned proposed changes in Plan A and Plan B contribution levels and stressed the importance of combined Social Security and NHWRA protection for health and welfare workers.

These changes were introduced to the members in a supplementary *Bulletin* dated May 1951. Plan A and Plan B member organizations could continue as in the past with 5 percent of salary contributions from both employer and employee. Plan D and Plan E would be available July 1, 1951, for members in the early plans that agreed to accept a 30 percent benefit reduction for a 3.5 percent of salary contribution figure. Agencies were urged, however, to maintain their existing rates and, thereby, continue to provide better pension and death benefits.

In September 1951, Henry Bruère noted that careful preparation for the coming of Social Security for health and welfare workers had paid off. Instead of the feared cancellation of policies, only 4 percent of all member agencies left the plan. Furthermore, fewer than 17 percent of the member agencies with Plans A or B opted for the lower-contribution Plans D and E. During the Retirement Association's first six years, 357 death claims were paid, amounting to approximately $700,000.

At that time, three administrative officers became staff vice presidents: Paul E. Mais, comptroller; Samuel H. Ourbacker, field director; and Homer Wickenden, secretary.

On September 21, 1951, Ralph H. Blanchard succeeded Milton H. Glover as president. Mr. Glover, who had given outstanding service as chairman of the organizing committee and president of the Retirement Association since its inception, became vice chairman of the board. During Mr. Glover's tenure of office, the Retirement Association had been established on a firm basis.

PART TWO

GUIDING THE EXPANSION
(1951–1965)

Ralph H. Blanchard
President, 1951–1965

INTRODUCTION TO PART TWO

During the first six years of the Retirement Association's life, the foundation for programs and activities was cautiously established. By trial and error, and with much determined application, the number and range of clients and contracts were expanded.

In the period from 1951 to 1965, this growth continued and strengthened under the able, and extremely devoted leadership of President Ralph H. Blanchard. At first he was president only part-time because of the demands of his responsibilities as head of Community Chests and Councils. Later, however, in the last five years of his work with the Retirement Association, he gave all of his attention and energy on a full-time basis to the organization that was, indeed, so much his creation.

Ralph Blanchard manifested great imagination and energy in this task and closely watched over the general operations and the new directions that the company took. In 1950, NHWRA had approximately 2,300 member agencies under coverage, and the total number of insured participants was 25,000. In 1965, there were over 3,200 member agencies with a total of almost 55,000 participants.

The types of policies that were being fashioned then were as important as these increasing numbers. Several initiatives for not-for-profit agencies and their workers were taken during the tenure of President Blanchard and his board of trustees. Because of the new coverages offered by better plans and policies, NHWRA was becoming increasingly attractive to more agencies.

As these developments took place, the methods and direction of the management and staff were constantly challenged to keep pace with the growth in business. The administrative and technical requirements that stemmed from the demands of success greatly tested the capacities of eager, but unseasoned, personnel. Management was aware of this and focused on improving all aspects of the company's service and personnel needs.

The years from 1951 to 1965 were pivotal in making retirement insurance for not-for-profit workers more accessible and relevant to growing numbers of participants. Areas that needed improvement became evident, while the expansion of coverages remained an overriding goal.

The Blanchard period saw the Retirement Association become more sensitive to the needs of its membership, more aggressive in its approach to retirement insurance, and thus more competitive. The groundwork was being laid for the phenomenal expansion of recent years; expansion that would eventually require an earnest undertaking to transform the company into a still more professional operation.

Chapter Four
STYLE AND SUBSTANCE

"When Ralph Blanchard became full-time president...he saw certain areas of weakness...particularly in outside contacts, in which he felt that he had particular strengths. His task was really to take charge...of accounts with customers, with the Insurance Department, areas where it seemed we were weak in being able to communicate with the outside world" *(Daniel J. Robins Interview, March 15, 1988)*.

Throughout his career, Ralph H. Blanchard was concerned with basic, humanitarian values. Perhaps as a result of this, his leadership was imaginative and flavored with an original and colorful individuality. He had a unique style and his open personality was appealing to many people. He was capable of combining the attitudes of both banker and social worker, while retaining his sense of humor.

One aspect of Mr. Blanchard's business personality was to remain in the background and let others occupy prominent positions. For example, while he was always the driving force behind the Retirement Association, he assumed the presidency only when Milton Glover could no longer spare the time for it.

Speaking of Mr. Blanchard's almost legendary courtesy and modesty, Dan Robins has said: "He had a way, a sort of self-denigration which I never believed for a minute. He would say, 'Please explain this to an unschooled social worker.' It was a technique. He was as sharp as can be" *(Daniel J. Robins Interview, March 15, 1988)*. President Blanchard faced the persistent problem of certain agency membership applications from health and welfare organizations. The question was how to deal with those that had not enrolled at least 75 percent of their employees as specified in the By-Laws. He resolved to make these decisions on a case-by-case basis.

Mr. Blanchard was also concerned with the Retirement Association's decision to establish certain reserve accounts. During this period, NHWRA remitted almost all of its premium income to the John Hancock Mutual Life under their reinsurance agreement, retaining a small percentage to cover operational costs.

During Ralph Blanchard's first full year as president, which began in September 1951, the Retirement Association took the first steps to change its benefit plans. After more than five years of rapid growth, NHWRA had reached a temporary plateau. Although extension of Social Security coverage to welfare workers resulted in a relatively modest diversion of premium income, the complexities of the pension market place caught up with the Retirement Association. In addition to a rigidity in the original plans, no administrative accommodation had been made for the special needs of member agencies of large size whose participation had made possible the acceptance of so many small agencies. Between 1950 and 1952, the number of member organizations remained virtually constant, while individual participants actually declined.

The Retirement Association considered new directions and maintained a certain momentum through an active public relations effort that benefited from outside help. Helping to further this purpose, the American Hospital Association urged wider participation in its pension program underwritten by the National Health & Welfare Retirement Association. An industry newspaper publicized the program and reported the reinsurance arrangement with the John Hancock.[1]

Ralph Blanchard's input made the NHWRA news bulletin *Benefits* distinctly his own. Previous issues had combined "Retirement Quizzes," testimonials, and verse with messages from the board chairman, president, and other company officers.

Issue number 4 of *Benefits*, dated August 1952, appeared in two versions: one for Plans A and B; the other for Plans D and E. Plan C was dealt with in another issue number 4, which was dated September 1952. Mr. Blanchard retained the question and answer section and endorsement letter quotations. He included a list of suggested booklets and pamphlets for leisure reading but kept all other space for his unsigned announcements and the signed "Presidential Progress Report."

Since the beginning, the Retirement Association had paid nearly 450 death claims totalling $890,000. Fifteen hundred pensioners were receiving regular annuity checks. NHWRA had received $6.6 million in contributions for the previous fiscal period from social workers and their employers and planned a $750,000 dividend to increase future service annuity benefits for Plans A and B and $225,000 for participants of Plans D and E. Ralph Blanchard expressed great satisfaction with the growing sense of security enjoyed by 24,000 participants in these plans.[2]

Chairman Bruère believed the primary purpose of the Retirement Association was to help the employer provide retirement income and death benefits for his employees without an unexpected charge against his budget.[3] Mr. Blanchard thought in broader, more social terms, and spoke of workers and widows.[4] He called upon all concerned, from trustees to participants, to "spread the gospel" of a sound retirement program for them.[5]

Throughout his career, the ebullient executive paid tribute to others, thanked those with whom he worked, and let them know he looked forward to their future association. Ralph Blanchard numbered among his closest friends the executives of the largest Community Chests, and their respect was reflected in their desire to be associated with the Retirement Association.

Helmut Frick, who has been with the company for thirty years as a sales consultant, described this strength of the president quite succinctly: "Ralph was a social worker and...he could get people to talk to him. He had wonderful connections and he was able to use them to benefit the Retirement Association. He knew everyone in that movement to approach and write letters to, and which doors to knock on" *(Helmut Frick Interview, March 10, 1988)*.

In 1953, the participants in the member agencies numbered over 18,000 women and nearly 6,400 men, a total in excess of 24,400 names on the company books. The 74 to 26 percent gender mix was not surprising, for in social work females traditionally outnumbered males by a substantial margin. Of the total, almost 1,820 had retired on pension, while over 3,100 were no longer working for a member agency but owned a paid-up annuity deferred to retirement date.[6] The 24,400 persons did not represent all who joined the plan between October 1, 1945, and June 30, 1953. Approximately another 22,000 had been enrolled during the first eight years, but they had terminated their employment and did not retain a paid-up annuity.

From the outset, it was clear that the transferability of pension benefits when an employee moved from one job to another was a powerful selling point. During these years, the importance of transferability was properly described over and over again by NHWRA representatives to prospective clients.

This transferability of benefits depended upon two factors. One was early vesting of pension benefit accruals, making it possible for an employee moving from one employer to another to retain his pension credits with the first employer, in contrast to conventional industry pension plans which usually required a much longer period of service before benefits vested. The other factor came into play only if the employee moved from the first employer with an NHWRA plan to a second employer who also had an NHWRA plan. Then, the retention of a pension benefit through liberal vesting meant its retention in the same retirement system where the individual would accrue further benefits with NHWRA under the second employer's plan. In that case, both sets of pension benefits would be paid by NHWRA in a single check. The important aspect, however, was the early vesting encouraged by NHWRA. It did not really make that much difference whether the two pensions were combined in a single check or whether they were paid from two organizations in two checks.

One weakness of this concept of transferability was that the plans were contributory. Employees and employers shared the cost in some proportion, but the employer paid only if the employee joined and paid his portion of the contributions. Later, NHWRA developed and strongly recommended plans that were non-contributory, with all eligible employees covered, and the employer paying the entire cost.

In the early contributory NHWRA plans, the vesting was conditioned on the terminating employee's leaving his own contributions in the plan. If, instead, the employee took out his own contributions in cash (as he was entitled to do), then the employer benefit was canceled. Plan C employers received a credit for the canceled benefits based upon their own agency contributions if the employee was in good health at the time of withdrawal from the plan. In Plans A, B, D, and E, forfeiture of the employer-financed benefits of a terminating employee was reflected in a pro rata increase in the benefits of all remaining participants.

Unfortunately, a bird in the hand created a real incentive for a terminating employee to withdraw his own contributions. This was not a wise choice because the individual lost not only the benefit based on his own contributions but also the benefit based on the employer's contributions. The net effect of this situation largely neutralized the transferability of benefits under this system.

Young workers inevitably experienced greater job mobility than seasoned veterans. Some rose from entry-level positions, earned additional responsibilities, and went elsewhere in search of better opportunities; others ceased working far from retirement age. Men or women with decades of working life still ahead frequently found old-age finances less compelling than current concerns, particularly since Social Security would now provide something for their retirement.

The statistics for 1945 to 1953 show that 79.3 percent of the employees who discontinued withdrew their contributions and ended up with no benefits; 2.2 percent died and received a death benefit; 1.6 percent took a lump sum because the benefit was small; and 5.4 percent retired with full benefits. Only 11.5 percent of those who terminated opted for a vested deferred paid-up benefit by deciding not to withdraw their own employee contributions.

The eighth fiscal year milestone in 1953 also provided the opportunity to measure the Retirement Association's relationship with John Hancock Mutual Life. Henry Bruère described it as one "scrupulously observed," and had previously acknowledged the reinsurance arrangement to be "a source of strength."[7]

The companies were bound together by two reinsurance agreements—one that covered Plans A and B and the other that covered Plan C. Each document confirmed the John Hancock's responsibility for paying all retirement annuities underwritten by NHWRA.

The contracts entered into by NHWRA were all participating contracts. This meant that if the experience (for mortality, interest, and expense) was more favorable than assumed, NHWRA would increase benefits or make dividend payments to the member organizations, as appropriate. This was the traditional type of group annuity contract in those years. The John Hancock reinsurance group annuity contract with NHWRA was also a participating contract.

NHWRA had jurisdiction over the disposition of dividends payable to it by the John Hancock. Some were left on deposit with the John Hancock for investment; others were retained as NHWRA funds to provide a more secure base for current or future expense reserves. Under a mutual retirement system or a mutual life insurance company, the participants and the contract holders were the owners and ultimate beneficiaries of the favorable financial experience.

Most affiliated agencies remained enthusiastic regarding the quality of NHWRA pension plans, either managed directly or through the American Hospital Association. Occasionally, however, an agency presented a unique problem. In one such case due to under-enrollment for past service, a hospital in Pennsylvania had not paid premiums on the wages of all its eligible employees but wished to continue its affiliation. The executive committee appointed Ralph Blanchard and Hobart McPherson to work out an agreement with the medical facility that satisfied both parties. NHWRA accepted a sum for back payments due for the past service pool and continued the membership of the hospital.

There was an increase in membership for both hospitals and social work agencies during Mr. Blanchard's first two years as president. Employer and employee contributions for the year ending June 30, 1953, surged to almost a half-million dollars beyond the premium income figure for the previous year and set a new Retirement Association record of more than $7 million.[8] Nevertheless, NHWRA was experiencing swings in the overall number of members and had to alter its response to each.

As business increased, the trustees involved more board members in company activities. Fifteen trustees out of sixty did most of the board work. The executive committee met five times a year, the entire board but once. NHWRA's growth in size and complexity of operations placed a larger burden on the men and women of the smaller group. As a result, the board added three additional members to the executive committee before the annual meeting in October 1954.[9]

The Retirement Association was fortunate to have attracted to its board some of the most prominent people from the social work and business communities. They chose to become trustees of NHWRA out of recognition of its mission to provide security for those who devote their lives to serving others. Among them were the noted writer Margaret C. Banning, Joseph P. Anderson of the National Association of Social Workers, Lester Granger of the National Urban League, and Marion B. Folsom, who headed the U.S. Department of Health, Education and Welfare and also had a distinguished career at Eastman Kodak.

In the early years, the board was composed of people representing social service organizations and hospitals, unions, the legal profession, and the business and banking communities. The need for a large number of trustees from the insurance field was not so great then because the specialists required for plan administration were provided by the John Hancock as reinsurer. In later years, a greater number of insurance experts joined the board, a change which was reflected in the increased numbers of insurance professionals in the home office and field operation.

Mr. William MacDonald, a trustee since 1979 who has served as chairman of the executive committee and was formerly CEO of Ohio Bell, has said: "I have been so impressed with the quality of the board of directors all along. I don't know any company I've ever been associated with that has brought together the talent that they've been able to, and I think that it's partly because of its reputation" *(William E. MacDonald Interview, April 21, 1988)*.

Chapter Five

QUICKENING THE PACE

"During the 1950's, the pension industry as a whole developed at an enormous rate, so that by the mid- and late-1950's there began to be a demand for a little more sophistication in terms of product. In 1957, we made the first move in that direction.... Rather than having just two simple money purchase plans, we, working with the John Hancock, developed a whole new product line, and it was a very flexible kind of instrument. It was known internally as Article III.... We went out [to the public] with our tiny marketing force and with a great deal of correspondence. We wanted to find out if we could market this and whether we could handle it, and it involved upgrading our staff" *(Frank P. Montgomery Interview, March 18, 1988)*.

At the tenth anniversary of NHWRA in 1955, Ralph Blanchard pointed to the significant progress that had been made. He considered the Retirement Association's first decade "a promising beginning."[1] At the same time, he stated the need for providing greater usefulness and overall value to the health and welfare community.

Mr. Bruère's annual report listed impressive totals for the decade: more than $58 million in premium contributions, 47,000 employees protected by the Retirement Association's plans, and almost 3,000 retired workers receiving benefits worth more than $1.7 million. Ralph Blanchard summarized the figures for 1955, which showed an 11 percent premium increase over 1954; 2,340 member organizations; and approximately $56 million of death benefit protection in force.

President Blanchard noted the social inventiveness that had characterized American life in the first half of the twentieth century. He linked the vastly improved economic conditions since the depression years to, among other things, changed public attitudes toward employees' benefits and adequate retirement. Society not only accepted better financial protection for labor, but also expected continued improvement in retirement security. The Retirement Association had to increase its relatively slow growth since 1952 to meet these opportunities and protect its own viability.

Gains for the three years prior to the fiscal year ending June 1955 had left much to be desired for NHWRA. The actual member agency count, for example, remained almost constant. The participant roster rose only 7 percent. The number of annuitants served went from 1,500 to 1,750. Something had to be done.

Dan Robins spoke of this time in the company's history: "In the early 1950's, after Social Security was adopted for the not-for-profit field, there was some loss of business, and there were complaints about lack of flexibility of the pension plans being offered by the Retirement Association. You go into a fruit store and you say, 'I want Delicious apples.' 'Well, we don't have Delicious; we have McIntosh.' 'But I don't like McIntosh.' That's human nature. There was no choice.

"The pension industry was somewhat in its infancy, and there were pension advisors who would say, 'Why can't I have a defined benefit plan? I realize the advantages of your defined contribution plan, but I like defined benefit plans. Why can't I have one?' 'Well, we don't offer it.' And then we give the reasons why our plan is better, but somebody is still going to say, 'I don't want that defined contribution plan'" *(Daniel J. Robins Interview, March 29, 1988)*.

Dan Robins also observed that "the history of the Retirement Association is, in significant part, the history of its product changes" *(Daniel J. Robins Interview, March 29, 1988)*. An important part of the activity of the Retirement Association's management has been the constant updating and improvement of the product. A product designed in 1945 could not fit the needs of the membership of the Retirement Association as the years passed. Also, new products devised by the insurance and banking industries made it essential to adjust the company's products to the times.

The principal products of the early years were Plans A and B. Plan C was developed in conjunction with the American Hospital Association and differed in minor respects from Plans A and B. Plans D and E were substantially Plans A and B with lower contribution rates, adjusted to the 1951 rate of Social Security taxation.

In 1951, therefore, the Retirement Association was operating with five plans, all of which were money purchase plans. Four of them had an insurance component, the exception being Plan C. All five were funded by deferred annuity purchases, were contributory, had fixed ratios of contributions between employer and employee, and provided full and immediate vesting.

To compete with these plans were the myriad possibilities offered by other pension providers. Funding could be achieved through banks by the use of a trust fund; insurance companies countered with the deposit administration fund. The defined benefit plan was the most prevalent type of plan offered. Non-contributory plans were growing in numbers to exceed those of contributory plans. Most pension institutions provided plans with some degree of deferred vesting.

The Retirement Association was not advocating that small health and welfare organizations adopt a non-contributory defined benefit deposit administration plan, but there were voices in the Retirement Association's management and on the board saying the menu should be larger and the members should have some choice.

The early 1950's was a time of increased competition in the pension industry. To quote Frank Montgomery: "This was an early version of what you could call the consumer movement. People started asking questions. For the first time in the life of this organization, competition appeared. In each local community the board of the United Way, which was called the Community Chest then, or the board of the hospital or social welfare agency would have a local banker on it, or attorneys, or business people with some sophistication, and they would say, 'Are you sure we should be sending our money to New York?'" *(Frank P. Montgomery Interview, March 18, 1988).*

Wilmer A. Jenkins, a consultant to the Retirement
Association in the mid-1950's, also served as a trustee.

The banks and actuarial firms were taking the pension industry away from the insurance companies. The old deferred annuity type of plan was following the route of the horse-drawn milk wagon. Board members of the Retirement Association believed that a way to compete had to be found. It was not that size was necessary for a bottom line on an annual statement. It was a feeling that for the good of all, the Retirement Association had to maintain a positive rate of growth and could not remain stagnant and certainly should not be allowed to fall back. Management retained the services of Wilmer A. Jenkins to review the products, procedures, and administration of the Retirement Association.

Mr. Jenkins, at that time executive vice president of TIAA, was a nationally-renowned actuary. Dan Robins describes Wilmer Jenkins and his role: "Wilmer was an all-business guy. He was very serious and very meticulous. He spent time here. He studied the company. He interviewed people...at the top level. Jenkins recommended that we adopt an individual policy approach. Neither the Insurance Department nor the John Hancock was willing to allow us to do that then. I think that it is interesting to note that Jenkins also recommended a gradual moving away from reinsurance....The staff accepted the concept that eventually we'd have to move away from reinsurance, but we weren't ready. Jenkins had said, 'Move'" *(Daniel J. Robins Interview, March 29, 1988)*.

Mr. Jenkins presented his report in 1954. From a benefit structure standpoint, Mr. Jenkins proposed adopting the TIAA method of funding pension plans. That method is for the insurer to provide a plan document to the employer which sets up certain standards for eligibility and contributions. The insurer then issues an individual deferred annuity policy to each participant. That policy is fully portable even if the participant leaves his original profession.

Mr. Blanchard asked Vice President Paul E. Mais to chair a staff committee to analyze the Jenkins report and to recommend to the board a proper course of action. The Mais committee reported to the executive committee in 1955. In the interim, Chairman Bruère reported that a study was in progress with a goal of producing plans with more flexibility in eligibility and participation requirements, contribution rates and ratios, vesting, death benefits, and amount of retirement benefits.

In June 1955, Mr. Mais recommended a benefit program based on individual deferred annuity contracts, deposit administration contracts, and expanded life insurance coverage. No member would be required to change to the new plan, and Plans A, B, C, D, and E would continue to operate. The proposed new program would feature a right for employers and employees to elect contribution rates, retirement ages, forms of benefits, etc. The recommendations approved in principle in November 1955 became known as the long-range plan. Staff and counsel were directed to take the steps necessary to develop the proposed program for final consideration and action by the board of trustees.

Although the new program had been approved in principle, it needed time to develop. For one thing, approval by the New York State Insurance Department was necessary, and the department carefully reviewed what attorneys George S. Van Schaick and Frederick E. Donaldson believed were essential questions of law. They believed that answers to these questions were needed even in advance of formal submission of the proposed program.

Furthermore, reinsurance of a new program would require discussion with the John Hancock. Early in this process, it became evident that the reinsurer was unwilling to reinsure pension benefits on an individual policy basis. This was, in part, a matter of philosophy concerning pension planning.

In the development of a substitute approach, an opportunity for even more flexibility emerged. The John Hancock was willing to reinsure a more flexible defined contribution program and, in addition, for the first time in Retirement Association history, a defined benefit program.

There were several reasons why the Retirement Association had designed its original pension plans as "defined contribution" or "money purchase" plans. The principal reason was that the employer can easily budget the amount of pension payments to be made in a year. When an employer is on a tight budget, this is a marked advantage. Furthermore, although not absolutely predictable, the cost of deferred annuity defined benefit plans tends to rise with the passing of years. Also, TIAA's influence, through Dr. Rainard Robbins, may have influenced the Retirement Association's choice. TIAA offered, almost exclusively, money purchase plans, which operated quite effectively in the academic world.

But money purchase deferred annuity plans have a particular limitation. It is difficult to give an employee an accurate estimate of his retirement benefit. The employee's benefit depends upon his age at entry into the plan and the interest accumulation rates, as well as the annuity purchase rates of the insurer, from year to year, during his participation. Furthermore, in a money purchase plan, a significant portion of the total contributions is used to provide benefits for the younger employees versus the older. This may result in a large proportion of the employer dollars going to the short-term employees rather than to the long-term employees, who are usually the chief concern of the employer.

In a defined benefit plan, the benefit is fixed at the beginning of participation but subject to future amendment. A benefit estimate, assuming participation to retirement, is a simple calculation. More employer dollars go to the older employees. The major disadvantage is budgetary because of the annual variability.

Regional Vice President Larry Gerring, who started with the company in 1958 and has been in the field selling the products, remembers: "The defined contribution plans that we had were producing benefits that were not always adequate because it was a period of relatively high inflation and relatively low investment yield. Fortunately, we were able, at that time, to improve our plan options. We offered a defined benefit plan, which works out much better in that kind of interest, inflation environment" *(Lawrence H. Gerring Interview, April 22, 1988).*

Under the leadership of Paul Mais and Trustee Frederick E. Donaldson and with the active cooperation of the John Hancock experts, a series of amendments was prepared for submission to the board and to the Insurance Department. The amendments to the By-Laws adopted by the board of trustees effective July 1, 1956, were approved by the New York State Insurance Department in May 1957, two years after Mr. Mais' report. The Retirement Association was presenting to the Insurance Department novel and important questions which needed detailed consideration by that official body.

The New York State Insurance Department gave informal approval to most of the NHWRA program, but it could not approve the proposed deposit administration plan, noting that Section 200 of the Insurance Law did not permit it. Complete page proofs containing the many revisions and the entirely new Article III of the By-Laws were sent to the Insurance Department officials on June 21, 1957, and the new long-range plan became a reality on July 1, 1957.

Vice President Jack Harrigan, who worked in the field for 28 years with the company, speaks with a salesman's perspective of this product change that had occurred just before his arrival. [Article III] "permitted some specification, decision making on the part of the client which they did not have under the prior plan. It was an introduction of some flexibility. It was the proper step to take" *(John H. Harrigan Interview, May 12, 1988)*.

In the new program primarily set forth in Article III of the By-Laws, a contributing member would elect specific plan provisions on an extensive application form. For example, the By-Laws might indicate that the minimum age for eligibility could be between 25 and 35. The member's application would state that the minimum age for its plan would be 25.

When Articles III and IV were finally approved and became operative on July 1, 1957, the Retirement Association had accomplished the following:

— Both defined contribution and defined benefit plans could be offered.

— Rates of contribution were made flexible.

— Benefits could be related directly to anticipated Social Security benefits.

— Larger life insurance (or supplemental death benefits) could be offered.

— Pension benefits could be postponed beyond age 65.

— Employee contributions could be continued for 5 years after a person left his employer, even if the participant left the social welfare field entirely.

— Employer surrender credits could be applied to reduce future plan costs rather than being plowed back to increase existing benefits previously purchased.

The Article III program also established the community-wide plans. Several of the Community Chest organizations formally adopted programs for affiliated agencies in their areas under the more flexible options now offered. In these plans, the leading employer, usually the Community Chest, would adopt a pension plan for itself and those of its agencies that wished to be affiliated with it. This made it possible to centralize the administration for a city-wide group. It also made it possible for smaller agencies to group together with larger agencies to obtain a defined benefit plan. The cost of the plan was spread among all the agencies in the affiliated group, not on an agency-by-agency basis. These community-wide plans helped many of the affiliated agencies that might otherwise have been doubtful about making the financial commitment. The affiliated agencies were bonded more closely to the Community Chest agency that supported them.

At that time, Retirement Association officers were enthusiastic about community-wide plans, and the field personnel were successful in selling them. Larry Gerring remembers that "we were setting up defined benefit plans with the United Way as the contract holder and including those agencies that wanted

Senior Vice President and General Counsel Daniel J.
Robins joined the Retirement Association as an
executive assistant in June 1952.

to be included as affiliates. This made our job easier. At that time, community-wide defined benefit plans were really the way to go" *(Lawrence H. Gerring Interview, April 22, 1988)*.

As these plans developed, however, it became evident that this idea was no longer useful as a sales vehicle. In the late 1970's, NHWRA adopted a policy to encourage the disaffiliation and breakup of these community-wide plans. After the breakup, each affiliated agency had its own plan and was paying its own cost rather than an average cost for the group.

What had been accomplished by this long-range plan? A more marketable pension product had been developed and additional death benefit protection was made available. A first step had been made toward taking the terms of the plans out of the By-Laws. What had not been accomplished was that the deposit administration method of funding had not been put into place due to the restrictions of the Insurance Law.

Overall, the adoption of the long-range plan marked a significant and necessary advance for the Retirement Association. In retrospect, substituting more flexible deferred annuity plans for the rigid early plans may not seem like a great accomplishment, but it was a step forward in product development and pointed the way toward the more significant changes that were to come in later years.

In developing the new products, final checks had been made of the Retirement Association's administrative procedures for the new contracts, and administrative work had been done in four areas to prepare required descriptive material.

Daniel J. Robins, who came to NHWRA in June 1952 from the Federal Trade Commission, began work as an executive assistant and handled contract forms. Mr. Robins, a New York University graduate with a law degree from Columbia University, did particularly effective work and earned promotion to associate counsel in 1956. Coincident with this noteworthy administrative advance, Leland S. Brown, although a volunteer, was appointed vice president.

In 1956, the Retirement Association also promoted Mr. Mais to administrative vice president, and he assumed the duties of chief administrative officer, heretofore discharged by Homer Wickenden. After Mr. Wickenden reached the retirement age of 65 at the end of 1955, he became the secretary of the organization on a part-time basis.

Planned succession brought Milton H. Glover to the chairmanship when Henry Bruère retired from that position in 1955. Hobart McPherson, who died on October 1, 1955, and his successor, Vice President Leland S. Brown, deserve a closer look. From the founding, Mr. McPherson was closely identified with the affairs of the Retirement Association. During the entire ten years he served, he displayed at all times professional and personal qualities which elicited the respect, admiration, and affection of his associates.

Leland S. Brown was one of Mr. McPherson's associates at the First National City Bank of New York and had already been enlisted for service at the Retirement Association. "My answer always for how I came to the organization was that my boss volunteered my services.... Hobart McPherson had been treasurer for a few years, and he wished to get ready to retire and had me appointed as assistant treasurer. Ten months later he died, so I suddenly found myself as treasurer of this outfit in 1955" *(Leland S. Brown Interview, April 6, 1988)*.

Leland Brown was born May 21, 1908, in River Forest, Illinois, and grew up in Long Beach, California. After graduating from Northwestern University with a degree in economics in 1930, he secured his first job at National City Bank, where he spent his entire career—with three years off as a naval officer in Washington, D.C., during World War II. Richard Brockway, later president of the company and good friend of Leland Brown, describes his colleague this way: "He has a very personable and very attractive personality, and he has, too, the ethic of service. He's the kind of man who would not accept an assignment on this board, for example, or any other, unless he was going to work at it and be at all the meetings. He was a very active member of the board" *(Richard C. Brockway Interview, March 25, 1988)*.

The succession from Henry Bruère to Milton Glover as chairman of the board represented more than a simple change in positions. Due to other commitments, Mr. Glover had relinquished the presidency after six years in 1951, and Ralph Blanchard became president at NHWRA in addition to his regular job at the Community Chest. He persuaded Mr. Glover then to stand by as vice chairman while Henry Bruère continued as chairman of the board.

Mr. Bruère served as chairman of the board from 1947 to 1955 and during this time won further professional recognition when he became the chairman of the Bowery Savings Bank. Henry Bruère's rich baritone voice made him an excellent public speaker. He loved the theater, belonged to the Players Club, and liked to stage employee holiday shows in the bank to entertain the customers.[2] Mr. Bruère had earned the admiration of his fellow board members for his consistent leadership. He was designated an honorary chairman for life in 1955 along with Gerard Swope, who had held that title on a year-to-year basis since 1947.

Milton Glover, who was the first person in the company to serve in the capacities of both president and chairman, was happy to become active again in 1955. He reignited the successful working arrangement he had enjoyed with Ralph Blanchard during the corporation's first six years.

December 1956 marked the end of the past service purchase period for Plans A and D, nearly eight years ahead of schedule. This was, in part, the result of a larger than estimated agency membership in the early years, together with rising wage and salary levels on which to base the 2 percent allocation. The other factors included deaths and election of cash withdrawals by terminating employees.

Despite the delays in bringing the new products into effect, NHWRA enjoyed its best year thus far in volume of business in 1957. Premium contribution income rose to more than $9.5 million, which included approximately $2.6 million from hospitals and other health institutions. Later, in his annual report dated

October 24, 1957, Ralph Blanchard said that the fiscal year end-ing June 1957 "marked the close of one era and the opening of a new one."[3]

The three-year figures from June 1955 to June 1957 were impressive, clearly exceeding those from June 1952 to June 1954. The number of agency members rose 9 percent; the par-ticipant count climbed 15 percent. Assets grew by more than $524,000; insurance in force rose more than $12 million; and the number of annuitants increased by one third.

NHWRA benefited from the growing popularity of private pension plans. These plans were increasing in appeal because a larger number of older people faced retirement in an economic environment that was eroding savings. This made it increas-ingly difficult for senior citizens to maintain their standard of living in a world where everything was becoming more expensive.

NHWRA's new plans were also more attractive in their own right. The promise of greater flexibility kept member agencies on the rolls and helped enlist others. Past performance helped as well. The low-cost NHWRA service was becoming relatively more efficient, and this strengthened many small, modestly funded social agencies which otherwise could not have afforded retirement protection for their workers. It assisted in providing security without depleting or jeopardizing the lim-ited assets of these members. Moreover, it did this in a manner which Milton H. Glover declared kept "the social and ethical obligations of the employer foremost."[4]

A physical move had been contemplated for several years as the 10 East 40th Street space proved increasingly inadequate for the expanding company. Temporary relief had come through leasing an adjacent 800 square feet of floor space for a two-year period ending April 30, 1957. Within 18 months the trustees approved a lease at a new building at 800 Second Avenue near the United Nations headquarters, and the com-pany moved May 1, 1957. It was NHWRA's fifth address in 12 years.

Chapter Six

LOOKING AHEAD

"Now that the legal aspects of this program have been worked out by the trustees and approved by the Insurance Department, we have the green light. We now have the responsibility to see that every not-for-profit health or welfare organization in our various communities is enrolled. This should be a most rewarding and satisfying undertaking for all of us" *(Ralph H. Blanchard, from the 12th* Annual Report *of the National Health & Welfare Retirement Association, October 31, 1957)*.

When the New York State Insurance Department sanctioned the Article III plans, the more flexible provisions served a positive and broadening function for NHWRA. Chairman Milton Glover predicted that there would be "many thousands more" participants in the future.[1]

President Blanchard used the occasion of the 12th annual meeting in October 1957, to define the enhanced capacity of NHWRA for its trustees and the social agency representatives. Many who attended were past, present, and future leaders of the company. Former Chairmen Gerard Swope and Henry Bruère sat with Chairman Milton H. Glover and President Ralph H. Blanchard. Also in attendance were two future board chairmen: Vice President and Treasurer Leland S. Brown and C. Virgil Martin. Together, these six men held top trustee positions for the 29 years between 1945 and 1974.

Gerard Swope died on November 20, 1957, at the age of 85. Although he had served but two years as board chairman, his contribution during the corporation's critical first years was judged to be of inestimable value.[2] As much as any other single person, the General Electric executive and civic leader had assured NHWRA's safe passage through business infancy and, thereby, earned for himself a unique place in its history.

The Retirement Association's executives continued to mold corporate policy while maintaining close personal interest in the practical details. Sometimes these involved individual participants whose cases benefited from more direct treatment. Two examples in 1957, brought to their attention by administrative officers, illustrate their concern.

A social welfare agency employee quit work. Being over 55 years, he elected to withdraw his own contributions to the Retirement Association. As his annuity would amount to less than $40 per year, he was entitled to a lump-sum settlement that would include his employer contributions. However, he died a week later, before he could choose the annuity or lump sum. The Retirement Association paid his estate the lump sum that he would have received as an early retiree.

An employee elected early retirement from the National Travelers' Aid Society of New York at age 61. An NHWRA office error credited her with longer past service than that to which she was actually entitled. She received written confirmation of an annual $863 annuity when she should have been advised of $641 per year. The Retirement Association, nevertheless, authorized the greater amount since the larger figure had been stated to her on several occasions, and she relied on that figure.

On February 17, 1958, Henry Bruère, who is remembered for his dynamic role in the development of the company, died at age 76. This was just a few months after the death of Gerard Swope. Both served approximately 12 years as either active or honorary chairmen of the board.

The Retirement Association trustees continued to serve without compensation and did not receive any fees for services rendered. The practice was modeled after the voluntary boards of the not-for-profit agencies served by NHWRA. However, beginning July 1, 1950, they had been permitted a modest $150 per meeting travel allowance. Now, eight years later, the figure was raised to $300. It seemed little enough for what Ralph Blanchard termed "the devoted service of our volunteer leaders."[3]

The results of the fiscal year ending June 30, 1958, were considered "an unqualified success."[4] Membership growth figures revealed a consistent ten-to-one ratio between agencies joining the Retirement Association and those discontinuing.

Over the five-year period, the Retirement Association had a net increase in its membership from 2,280 to 2,532. Participant totals were even more impressive, rising 34 percent from the 24,400 enrollment of individual workers in 1953 to a new high of 32,611 in 1958. However, attrition had persisted, and large numbers of insured health and welfare workers had surrendered their policies for cash prior to retirement.

Building upon the July 1, 1957, reinsurance agreement with the John Hancock Mutual Life, which also covered Article III plans, the Retirement Association announced a liberalization in rate basis stemming from an increase in the interest assumption. It was passed on to the NHWRA plans which, in most cases, provided higher annuity benefits.

Members were informed that this increase (together with the 1/4 percent augmentation of both 1950 and 1955) would yield a 30 percent greater annuity benefit at retirement for a 45-year-old worker than the amount available under original rates. Higher rates, lower costs, and greater flexibility had begun to pay off. At the 13th annual meeting on October 30, 1958, Mr. Blanchard noted that 130 member organizations changed to improved plans; 174 members began to explore possible plan revision; and 29 new members initiated their membership under the new Article III program.[5]

The president announced further help for committees of agency members considering changes in the pension coverage for their employees. He called attention to a new booklet written by the home office staff entitled *Designing Improved Retirement Plans,* which described the Article III program. The booklet discussed "adequate benefits" through a comparison of fixed contribution and fixed benefit programs. Both death and retirement coverage were evaluated in light of agency costs and worker budgets. The booklet presented general concepts and related each to Retirement Association experience, stressing NHWRA's willingness to discuss possible modifications to meet special situations. A planning sheet was included for local committee use.

Wilbur J. Cohen, a professor of public welfare administration at the University of Michigan and a former Social Security official, extolled the booklet that "...has taken a complex problem and made it understandable to hospital trustees, administrators and employees.... (It) can be read with profit...where a retirement plan now exists and where it does not now exist but should."[6]

Ralph Blanchard, furthermore, discussed the need of the health and welfare community professional worker for maximum employee mobility among social agencies, stressing NHWRA's advocacy of liberal vesting and pension portability.

Administrative Vice President Paul E. Mais went to Indiana University in the summer of 1959 to address the 17th Annual Institute on Hospital Accounting and Finance. Based on that experience and the success of the Retirement Association's previous booklet, *Designing Improved Retirement Plans,* NHWRA issued a new publication entitled *Pension Planning for Hospitals.*

The announcements at the annual meeting of the members held in October 1959, contained much to applaud. For the first time, over $1 million was paid in pensions, and insurance in force exceeded $85 million.[7]

During the course of the meeting, Milton Glover spoke of the future of the national economy and the insurance industry and stressed the dangers of inflation:

> Our nation has experienced varying degrees of inflation from time to time, and we must consider this threat in relation to the program of financial security we offer.
>
> Inflation has an especially undesirable effect on the fixed incomes that are the support of our retired people.
>
> Certain optional provisions are available within our present programs... but these provisions in themselves cannot be regarded as a panacea for the problems brought on by inflation.[8]

Mr. Glover mentioned efforts "to find a more fundamental solution to the difficulties that inflation inflicts on retirement incomes." Consideration of greater investments of pension assets in common stocks would not, he pointed out, "perfectly counteract possible effects of inflation."[9] The chairman promised to explore with the New York State Insurance Department the expansion of the not-for-profit corporation's powers to permit still greater variety in the plans offered its members.

On February 4, 1960, United Community Funds and Councils of America (UCFCA, formerly Community Chests and Councils) honored Ralph Blanchard for 17 years of exceptional service as executive director. Ralph Blanchard's official retirement from UCFCA was to begin in July, but the testimonial committee headed by Mr. Blanchard's long-time friend and fellow NHWRA trustee Virgil Martin decided to recognize him at the UCFCA Biennial National Conference held that year in St. Louis.

Six hundred attended the "This Is Your Night" program in the Chase Hotel. Mr. Martin presided. Mr. Blanchard's wife, Grace, and his two married daughters, Susan Bliss and Sally Erickson, took part. United Community Funds and Councils ignored the customary present of a watch and surprised the Blanchards with a trip around the world.

Described as a "passport to relaxation," the "wondertour" would actually be taken in three separate parts when the tireless worker found time to schedule an occasional absence from his increased duties at NHWRA.[10] The approaching end of Mr. Blanchard's first career and the beginning of a new phase of his second work responsibility was signaled by the St. Louis dinner, linking his connection with the past and future of NHWRA.

In June 1960, Ralph Blanchard agreed to continue as president beginning in November and to devote as much time as the responsibility of that office required. For the first time in its history, the Retirement Association had a full-time president. When President Blanchard began his full-time role with the

Retirement Association, he concentrated on future plans, negotiations with the New York State Insurance Department and the John Hancock, and the promotion of further relationships with UCFCA.

Throughout his career he displayed a talent for transforming his ideas and concepts into realities. He was able to achieve this through a sense of purpose energized by discipline and persistent hard work. Mr. Blanchard took his office habits home with him, and each night before retiring balanced his personal accounts in a little diary. In this careful fashion, he maintained continuity of thought and direction in his daily life.

Chapter Seven
SEEKING NEEDED TOOLS

"I remember Ralph Blanchard had appointed a long-range planning committee about 1960,...and the people on it were very active and interested trustees. The Retirement Association hadn't really cut a big swath. The committee wanted to see whether the organization needed to continue to exist. That was really the first question we addressed. It was felt that because there was now competition and there were commercial organizations which could cover the field, should we bother to continue with this thing or would the field be taken care of? It was a serious question. But the serious answer was that it needed to continue.... The focus arising out of that 1960 long-range planning committee was that we had to enlarge the organization and get it some executive strength of its own" *(Leland S. Brown Interview, April 6, 1988)*.

The committee on long-range objectives was formed in March 1960. NHWRA was facing inflationary pressures that called for new types of coverages, and the company also had to deal with increased competition among financial institutions for pension business. The group's task was to make a long-range study of the Retirement Association's objectives and the means for accomplishing them.

Ralph Blanchard was chairman of the committee, and Trustees Leland S. Brown, George Bugbee, J. Douglas Colman, and Frederick I. Daniels were selected to work with Frederick E. Donaldson, Esq., and Administrative Vice President Paul E. Mais. George E. Johnson, who became a trustee of the Retirement Association in 1961, was retained to advise the committee.

Mr. Johnson, then working as a pension consultant with such clients as Metropolitan Life and New York Life, was one of the most fascinating personalities ever to play a leading role with

George E. Johnson, who served as a pension consultant
to the Retirement Association, became a trustee in 1961
and was appointed acting president in 1965.

NHWRA. A Nebraskan by birth, his voice still reflected the flat tones of the American Midwest. Legally blind from his earliest years, he, nevertheless, completed college and law school at the University of Nebraska with highest honors. At the time he was retained by the Retirement Association, Mr. Johnson was in his mid-fifties with a lifetime of accomplishments already behind him.

He had served as vice president and general counsel of TIAA and had played a leading role in the development of the variable annuity. He had founded first the Variable Annuity Life Insurance Company (VALIC) and, subsequently, the Equity Annuity Life Insurance Company (EALIC) and had served as president of each.

Mr. Johnson's fertile mind constantly produced new ideas and new approaches to insurance problems. When one of his ideas seemed to have promise, he would pursue it relentlessly to completion. He was one of the premier idea men of the insurance industry.

Richard Brockway, third president of the company, worked with George Johnson for several years. He recalls: "George Johnson was, in many respects, a kind of genius. He was a very determined and highly technical man. He was also a lone operator. He thought that major insurance companies were huge bureaucracies, slow moving, without any kind of imagination or initiative. He wanted a more aggressive posture for the Retirement Association in terms of getting out and selling the plans and he was the board expert" *(Richard C. Brockway Interview, March 25, 1988)*.

One of Mr. Blanchard's priorities for 1961 was deposit administration. When the president conferred with New York State Insurance Department Superintendent Thomas Thatcher in December 1960, the latter explained that the Retirement Association could not write deposit administration contracts without converting to a life insurance company, and that it could not take this step without appropriate legislation. This was due to the fact that NHWRA was governed by Section 200, which was more restrictive than the code section covering life insurance companies.

The committee on long-range objectives had investigated other possibilities, which Counsel Frederick E. Donaldson reviewed in February 1961. NHWRA might consider the following in one form or another:

— Reorganize as a mutual life insurance company

— Reorganize as a not-for-profit stock life insurance company

— Organize a new life insurance company to be affiliated with the Retirement Association

— Secure legislation to permit reorganization of any retirement system

— Secure legislation pertaining only to the Retirement Association.

President Blanchard pressed for continued discussions with the New York State Insurance Department by both Mr. Donaldson and Special Counsel Raymond Harris. Mr. Harris had recently retired as deputy superintendent and general counsel of the New York State Insurance Department. The committee on long-range objectives and the administrative policy committee were to review all steps taken and make every effort to present a specific proposal no later than June 1961.

NHWRA had paid more than $500,000 in supplemental death benefits by the end of the business year, June 30, 1961. Moreover, it planned to offer this coverage at lower rates in the future. The John Hancock, as reinsurer, announced new rates effective July 1, 1961. The results would considerably reduce member costs for this protection. The Retirement Association, however, needed New York State Insurance Department approval for this action. Despite the fact that these new rates had not yet been approved, social agencies continued to join in significant numbers. Forty additional Girl Scout Councils, for example, voted to join the national Girl Scout retirement plan underwritten by NHWRA.

In June 1961, the committee on long-range objectives presented the first of a series of reports. This one addressed three issues: a separate account common stock fund, reduction of operating costs, and additional benefit coverage. Major medical protection, disability income coverage, and a full line of life policies were listed as products in demand by their member agencies.

NHWRA's lack of authority to write deposit administration contracts was a considerable handicap. It was essential to write deposit administration contracts and to have a separate account common stock investment facility in order to compete in the market.

Dan McGill recalls the competitive pressures when "...the employers were so upset by this [inability to get better investing of their money], they would terminate the old arrangement and say, 'Well, we'll just let our old money sit there, and we'll put our new money with some other company or bank or investment counselor.' So the companies, in self-defense, had to develop more flexible contracts, ... what goes under the generic name of deposit administration group annuity, which is one big, unallocated fund that accommodates any sort of benefits that you want and the assumptions you want" *(Dan M. McGill Interview, April 13, 1988)*.

Deposit administration plans permit placing contributions in an unallocated account. This is done instead of allocating them to a specific individual's annuity until retirement payout, as is the system under the deferred group annuity plan. Deposit administration plans make it easier for employers to vary rates of contributions to conform to budget situations, avoid excessive outlays in early years, provide more easily benefits based upon final salaries, and reduce administrative details and expenses. By taking into account anticipated employee turnover, and by using less conservative assumptions as to mortality, disability, retirement, and interest than those used by the insurer in guaranteeing benefit payments, current pension costs to the employer can usually be reduced.

The committee on long-range objectives also noted the need to obtain more flexibility than was allowed by the Section 200 provision of the New York State Insurance Law. That provision required the Retirement Association to spell out each contract and policy detail in its By-Laws. Cost cutting came to focus on the matter of tax status, and possible foundation grant funding to start the new programs was mentioned.

NHWRA was compared to the Church Pension Fund, the YMCA and the YWCA Retirement Funds, and TIAA. These organizations secured liberal financial help in their early years in the form of grants from tax-exempt foundations. This financial help enabled them to offer new programs on a low cost basis right from the start. The Carnegie Corporation, for example, gave TIAA large grants for initial capital, as did the Ford Foundation for later initiatives. Although the Retirement Association already had 501(c)(4) tax status, which exempted it from the payment of federal income taxes, the committee had studied the desirability of NHWRA's becoming an Internal Revenue Service 501(c)(3) organization to make it eligible for foundation funding, something which had been denied at the time of the company's founding.

Leland Brown speaks about that active time for the Retirement Association: "Having decided that the Retirement Association should continue, we looked into what was needed to make it a real organization instead of what it was then, an administrative conduit to the John Hancock which handled the insurance business and the real underwriting. The intention was to get it so it would be able to stand on its own feet, disengage itself from Hancock eventually, and improve the operating staff so they could branch out from simply administrative responsibilities" *(Leland S. Brown Interview, April 6, 1988).*

The John Hancock was charging NHWRA for payment of the federal taxes the John Hancock had to pay on profits it made on the business of reinsuring the Retirement Association. Perhaps other possible reinsurers should be considered for other types of coverage that might be offered in the future. The committee also questioned whether NHWRA should continue under Section 200 of the New York State Insurance Law or should be converted to a life insurance company.

The work of the committee on long-range objectives represented a landmark in the history of NHWRA. The committee considered the company's prestige and reputation based upon sound and progressive policies and recommended some steps that the Retirement Association could take:

— Offer an adequate line of life insurance policies

— Seek New York State legislative approval to write deposit administration contracts

— Consider greater funding flexibility, including common stock equity funding and the writing of variable annuities

— Study the possibility of changing the corporation's legal status

— Make a determined effort to secure 50l(c)(3) federal tax status

— Seek foundation grants to finance incorporation of a life insurance company and/or to finance the rapid development in the disability income and major medical fields

— Develop procedures to do business more effectively in other states.

As a short-range objective, the committee urged NHWRA to proceed as rapidly as possible to offer major medical and disability income coverage through the vehicle of a specially created trust, if necessary. Committee members conceded the difficulty of achieving these objectives and recognized the possibility of failure, but they knew the Retirement Association had more to gain than to lose in attempting them.

The Article III plans, which had been proclaimed a long-range program, became operative in 1957. These rapidly became the principal plans offered by the Retirement Association, supplanting the original plans. The results that had not been achieved by the Article III plans were among the items considered by the new committee on long-range objectives in March 1960. The action taken on the recommendations in its June 1961 report led to significant changes in the product in the early and mid-1960's.

One of these recommendations was to continue the efforts to obtain immediate legislative authority that would permit the Retirement Association to underwrite pension plans on the deposit administration basis. At the end of 1961, the Insurance Department agreed to support such an amendment in the legislature. General Counsel Frederick E. Donaldson worked with Special Counsel Raymond Harris to achieve this result.

Obtaining legislative approval was only the first step in making deposit administration plans available. Administrative Vice President Paul Mais led the management effort to implement this type of plan. Contracts had to be developed and approved by the New York State Insurance Department. Administrative procedures had to be developed, administrative forms written, and underwriting rules had to be instituted.

The John Hancock agreed to reinsure the Retirement Association's deposit administration plans. They also arranged to assist the Retirement Association in getting these contracts off the ground. For a period of time, experts in various fields at the John Hancock—underwriters, actuaries, and salesmen—conducted training sessions at 800 Second Avenue for their counterparts at the Retirement Association.

The terms of the deposit administration plans with respect to eligibility, participation, and benefits were not very different from those of the earlier Article III defined benefit plans. However, the deposit administration plan provided greater flexibility in the level of deposits required of the employer in order to maintain a fund sufficient to provide benefits when they became due.

Unfortunately, the first expansion into this field was not a great success. In the three years between the offering of the plan and the development of the Flexi-Fund Program allowing the use of a common stock separate account, only 17 deposit administration plans were written. But, the deposit administration plans developed in the early 1960's gave the staff the experience it needed to work with this kind of plan and to deal better with later plans, such as the Cost of Living Plan.

In October 1961, the committee on long-range objectives presented a supplementary report with recommendations. It refined earlier proposals and urged management to approve all actions to date with respect to major medical and disability income. It also sought authorization to seek enabling legislation at the 1962 session of the New York State Legislature.

In December 1961, the New York State Insurance Department announced that it would permit the Retirement Association to write major medical insurance without incorporating the contract provisions in its By-Laws as had been required before. Later, additional legislative action allowed the establishment of separate accounts invested in whole or in part in common stocks.

The committee on long-range objectives had studied alternatives to the reinsurance agreement with the John Hancock. At this time, however, the Retirement Association recognized the reinsurer's great contribution to the very existence of NHWRA and acknowledged it publicly. Credit was given to the John Hancock when the Retirement Association announced a reduced rate basis for deferred annuities to be effective July 1, 1962. This was the sixth time since 1945 that the interest rate assumption in the premium rates had been increased.

At the 17th annual meeting in 1962, Mr. Blanchard stressed the necessity of NHWRA's making "available at all times well-rounded, up-to-date programs." He also affirmed the close relationship between NHWRA and "the vast network of privately financed and operated health and welfare organizations in this country" because NHWRA pension and insurance plans helped the health and welfare agencies to enlist and retain better personnel, instead of settling for labor that might be unable to compete effectively in the business world.[1] Only 2,800 of America's more than 100,000 private health and welfare organizations held NHWRA membership, and the 40,000 worker participants constituted but a tiny fraction of the more than one million employees of these agencies.[2] The Retirement Association had barely scratched the surface of the job that needed to be done.

In November 1962, Milton Glover stepped down after 17 years of leadership as president, vice chairman, and chairman of NHWRA. He predicted that future company growth would depend not only upon its own efforts, but also on "...the readiness of social welfare organizations to finance retirement and other insurance plans as a matter of permanent policy."[3]

He looked back, too, and acknowledged the contribution made by the board, thanking the trustees for their devotion and capability, and praising the outstanding leaders who gave "wise and effective counsel to the Retirement Association without thought of remuneration."[4] Mr. Glover's words also expressed his own commitment. In recognition of his devotion, he was given the same honor tendered his predecessors, Gerard Swope and Henry Bruère, when they relinquished power. He became honorary chairman.

Chapter Eight

MAJOR DEVELOPMENTS
IN THE MID-1960s

"The 1960s presented increased opportunities for growth for the Retirement Association. Both the public and private sectors began to emphasize in a much more significant way, social, medical, and educational programs. This emphasis benefited not-for-profit organizations which were positioned to deliver the kinds of services which were needed. There was a real expansion in many of the social welfare organizations, particularly in the number of their employees delivering their services, and we were able to expand our retirement plan services, in turn, to them" *(Helmut Frick Interview, March 10, 1988)*.

In 1962, NHWRA paid more than $1.4 million to retired workers and almost $700,000 in death benefits to survivors of deceased employees. The added agencies and enrolled employees represented more than just numerical growth. The impetus was clearly in the direction of further expansion, and the committee on long-range objectives had urged prompt action in the areas of accident and health insurance. The time had come for NHWRA to offer major medical and disability income protection to its people.

Ralph Blanchard now implemented the plans with the help of the new board chairman, Leland S. Brown, who assumed that office at the annual meeting on November 2, 1962. Mr. Brown had already demonstrated leadership capacity as vice president and treasurer. He was the fourth chairman of the Retirement Association.

Leland Brown's promotion made it necessary to find a new treasurer. Trustee Joseph P. Anderson, executive secretary of the National Association of Social Workers, and James A. Brennan, a First National City Bank associate of Mr. Brown's,

Leland S. Brown
Chairman, 1962–1972

had been assistant treasurers for a number of years. Mr. Brennan's services had been offered by his boss as Mr. Brown's had been by his superior, Hobart M. McPherson, in 1954.

With Leland Brown's elevation to the chairmanship, however, Mr. Brennan's close business connection to Mr. Brown made his appointment as treasurer inappropriate. Joseph Anderson's other commitments precluded his taking the job, so Frederick I. Daniels filled the crucial post of treasurer. Mr. Daniels, executive director of the Brooklyn Bureau of Social Service and Children's Aid Society, had become an NHWRA trustee in 1953 and later served on the committee on long-range objectives. At the same time in 1962, the Retirement Association promoted Isadore Feferman to assistant field director in recognition of his six years of good service as administrative supervisor.

January 1963 marked the beginning of major medical coverage for NHWRA participants. Reinsured by Health Services, Inc., a wholly-owned subsidiary of the National Blue Cross Association, protection was offered only to employers covered by an NHWRA retirement plan. It covered those people who also carried a basic plan of hospitalization and medical-surgical benefits in force with a not-for-profit carrier acceptable to Health Services, Inc. Within these eligibility limitations, however, the protection provisions were quite liberal.

Workers qualified for coverage if they met four conditions: were employed for at least three months; were regular employees working a minimum of 20 hours per week; were eligible for their agency's retirement plan; and had not waived retirement plan participation. There were no minimum or maximum age conditions. Employees over 65, past normal retirement date, and past the retirement plan maximum eligibility age could be included.

Benefits were built around essentially standard provisions of a $100 deductible, $5,000 reimbursement of covered expenses for each worker per benefit period, and a $10,000 lifetime maximum. Expenses for treatment of nervous or mental disorders outside of a hospital would be reimbursed at the rate of 50 percent of covered expenses up to the maximum amount specified.

While providing health coverage and preparing to offer disability income protection in the near future, the Retirement Association continued to emphasize its original purpose. "The main objective of the organization is to provide adequate pension plans for personnel of not-for-profit hospital, health and welfare agencies at low cost to both employer and employee."[1]

Staff employees of NHWRA also had pension coverage underwritten by NHWRA. The retirement in 1963 of Samuel H. Ourbacker, at age 72, caused the trustees to take a closer look at arrangements for the company's employees, particularly those who worked beyond age 65. Ralph Blanchard had appointed a special committee earlier to study the matter, and its report was completed in April 1963.

Mr. Ourbacker, a former field director and vice president, became senior field consultant on a part-time basis in 1955, when he reached the age of 65. Ralph Blanchard restored him to full-time status five years later, but now the time had come for the veteran officer to retire.[2] Mary D. Stander, the office manager, also retired in 1963. She had been with NHWRA since June 1944 when she came as secretary to Homer Wickenden. President Blanchard praised them both as people "who have rendered able and devoted service over many years."[3]

The Retirement Association's 18th year of operation was ending. New highs had been reached in virtually every area of activity. The number of contributing members had risen to nearly 3,000; participating workers reached almost 33,400; and annual contributions increased 8 percent over the preceding year, totaling $16.5 million. The new major medical insurance coverage was off to a good start: over 100 agencies with more than 700 employees signed up for this important coverage.

The Retirement Association needed a larger staff and more space to handle the increasing business. As a temporary measure, it leased an additional 9,400 square feet located on the third floor at 800 Second Avenue. This provided breathing room for four years, during which time a special committee would study the question of space and recommend a long-term solution.[4]

The annual report for the year ending June 30, 1964, summarized the Retirement Association's progress in bringing about the changes recommended by the committee on long-range objectives. The New York State Legislature had approved legislation permitting Section 200 organizations to write deposit administration pension plans. The Retirement Association had inaugurated a major medical program and planned to offer long-term disability income coverage, and the New York State Insurance Department had given permission for NHWRA to remove plan details from the By-Laws.

In 1964, the Retirement Association began to carry out the remaining recommendations of the committee on long-range objectives. Some of the objectives involved negotiations with John Hancock Mutual Life, and these were matters that had to be handled with discretion. NHWRA had derived great benefit from the prestige and the enormous resources of the New England company whose original reinsurance had made the existence of the Retirement Association possible.

More recently, they had provided ongoing assistance through the cooperative attitude of company officers and staff members. Furthermore, John Hancock had cooperated with the committee on long-range objectives and responded readily to the probing of that group as it examined every aspect of the joint enterprise.

The original arrangement between the two companies gave NHWRA the responsibility for sales, policy service, and legal functions. The premium payments came first to NHWRA and then were sent on to the John Hancock. The ongoing annuity or installment death benefit payments were sent by the John Hancock directly to the workers or their beneficiaries. The John Hancock also invested the funds that supported the benefit reserves. These funds had exceeded $133 million by the end of the fiscal year in 1963.

The two organizations shared the administrative burden. The Retirement Association maintained all contact with member agencies. The John Hancock was also involved in the administrative work associated with new contracts, collection of premiums, and terminations of coverage. Isadore Feferman describes the administrative work in the early days of the relationship: "...What we were really doing was acting like a conduit for almost everything that went up to the John Hancock. If, for example, somebody enrolled in a plan, they'd send us an application card in two parts. It was our responsibility to tear it off, retain one, and send one to the Hancock. And you could say that about almost everything we did—whether it was a financial report or whatever. It would be sent in triplicate or quadruplicate. And one copy would always go to the Hancock. So we were always, in the years of reinsurance, maintaining a double set of records. We were really middlemen in the day-to-day operation. They had to have a copy of everything we had" *(Isadore Feferman Interview, March 1, 1988)*.

Roxie Sookikian, who began work for the company in 1947 and held a variety of jobs over her nearly forty-year-long career, remembers the early situation graphically: "The files were a bit disorganized. But they were files and I typed proposals. That was before we had Xerox machines. They all had to be done individually. It was before we had form pages set up. Every single proposal we gave to an agency was done on a manual typewriter. No word processor" *(Araxe Sookikian Interview, March 16, 1988)*.

The total costs of operation came from a combination of expenses incurred by the two companies. In 1961, for example, the John Hancock charged 2.6 percent of premiums for its administration of the reinsurance contracts, while NHWRA, for the same year, allocated 3.3 percent of premiums to cover its expenses.

The committee on long-range objectives pointed out that while a number of life insurance companies had started with reinsurance, there were no companies with reserves of $100 million continuing to reinsure the bulk of their business. For example, well-known religious and educational pension plans, such as those of the Young Men's Christian Association (YMCA) and the Teachers Insurance & Annuity Association (TIAA) were almost universally self-operating.

86

The need for better investment performance motivated the first change in this area. The John Hancock's past record had been acceptable, but the Retirement Association believed it would do better with an investment policy geared to its own needs rather than to factors outside of its control. Furthermore, the reinsurance agreements contained no provision to transfer funds back to the Retirement Association upon termination of these contracts.

The time had come for NHWRA to manage its own money, and the first step in this direction was to form a finance committee to supervise the investment of surplus dividend and interest funds then on deposit with the John Hancock. These funds, amounting to approximately $5 million over and above the reserves held by the John Hancock, were to be withdrawn and managed by the Retirement Association.

The finance committee established in April 1964 was composed of eight trustees, including the board chairman, president, and treasurer. Leland Brown describes this initiative: "The first thing that I recall [concerning disengagement from the John Hancock] is that around the mid-1960's, having accumulated about $5 million of surplus which the organization had control of and could withdraw from the John Hancock, we decided that we ought to start our own investment operation. We got Howard Sheperd, my former boss, who had been chairman of Citibank, to be the chairman of the first finance committee. The finance committee then hired professional advisors. The one we got was Morgan Guaranty Trust to begin with. So that was really the first operation on its own..." *(Leland S. Brown Interview, April 6, 1988)*.

Ralph Blanchard believed that effective management required implementing present policy at the same time future plans were being formulated. The Retirement Association commissioned a study of the "basic structure and general operating procedures," which was undertaken by the O'Toole Division of the accounting firm of Peat, Marwick, Mitchell & Company.[5] Their report in October 1964 recommended that greater authority and responsibility be vested in the office of president. Since Mr. Blanchard had already announced his intended retirement in June 1965, the change advocated would be of primary concern to his successors.

The report of the committee on long-range objectives in 1961 recommended expansion of investment authorization to include common stocks. The Retirement Association believed the use of common stocks could reduce costs, increase benefits, and serve as the asset base for variable annuities.

The variable annuity is a device intended as a partial protection against inflation and was, in those days, funded by a portfolio principally made up of common stocks. The theory is, that over an extended period as the consumer price index rises, the market value of common stocks will also rise. The amount of annuity paid to the annuitant varies with the value of the underlying stock investments.

In 1961, the only variable annuity authorized by state law was that being written for TIAA policyholders through its companion company College Retirement Equities Fund (CREF). CREF had gone into business in 1952 following special legislation obtained from the New York State Legislature. In those days of a slow but steady rise in the consumer price index and the stock market, it appeared that the CREF variable annuity was doing the job for which it was intended.

The states were reluctant to authorize increased use of common stocks. Now, when every state has an insurance law provision permitting the establishment of a separate account that can be wholly invested in common stock, it may be difficult to understand the vitriolic arguments raised against such a provision—not only by regulators, but also by some major insurers. Once the legislature had broken the ice and permitted the insurance companies to establish separate accounts, Raymond Harris and Frederick Donaldson went back to the legislature to get the benefits of these accounts extended to Section 200 retirement systems. They were successful in establishing this in principle in 1964.

The annual report for the year ending June 30, 1964, noted that NHWRA was planning to establish a wholly-owned life insurance company as a subsidiary as permitted under the new law. It announced the appointment of the Morgan Guaranty Trust Company of New York as the investment advisor and custodian of securities for the Retirement Association. The Retirement Association also planned to offer separate account plans.[6]

Dan Robins, active as staff counsel then, recalls the appointment of George Johnson to work on establishing a separate accounts program: "They brought in George for two reasons. First, he was a knowledgeable lawyer. Second, he was a person convinced, almost obsessed, by the variable annuity. He had been at TIAA when it was established there. George was dedicated to the idea of the variable annuity, and when George is dedicated to something, he makes his dedication known" *(Daniel J. Robins Interview, March 29, 1988)*.

Shortly thereafter, the Retirement Association specifically sought approval from the New York State Insurance Department for a separate account and throughout 1965 worked with the department to achieve this result. It took two years to obtain approval and another year to make plans funded through the newly established separate account available to member agencies. All this delay was for reasons that will become apparent.

Section 227 of the Insurance Law provided that the separate account contract had to be a group contract and that the group had to consist of at least 25 people. Most of the NHWRA member agencies that would wish to take advantage of the new equity-funded plan had fewer than 25 people. This quandary was discussed at length between the Retirement Association officers and the general counsel of the New York State Insurance Department.

The New York State group annuity statute prescribed several types of groups which could enter into group annuity contracts. The most common type was a group consisting of the employees of one employer. Also permitted was a group consisting of the employees of an association of employers having business interests in common.

Accordingly, NHWRA proposed to establish the National Flexi-Fund Association. Any health or welfare organization wishing to obtain an equity-funded contract (now called a Flexi-Fund contract or Flexi-Fund Plan) had to join the National Flexi-Fund Association in addition to being a member agency of the Retirement Association. The group annuity contract was between the Retirement Association and the National Flexi-Fund Association. The Retirement Association members with Flexi-Fund Plans signed a participating agreement. It provided that the business between the Retirement Association and its Flexi-Fund members would be conducted as though the National Flexi-Fund Association did not exist.

This was a cumbersome contractual arrangement, legalistic in nature. Nevertheless, for its time it served the purpose of satisfying the formal requirements of the Insurance Law. The Flexi-Fund Association continued to exist until 1975, when it was possible and desirable to terminate it. Thereafter, Flexi-Fund Plans were written directly between the Retirement Association and the members. However, by that time Flexi-Fund Plans were dwindling, and they were ultimately replaced by the National Retirement Plans introduced by NHWRA in the early 1970's.

There were two Flexi-Fund contracts. One was a defined benefit plan operated as a deposit administration fund. The employer could elect the percentages of his contributions to be allocated to the separate account and the general account. At an employee's retirement, his retirement annuity would be determined according to a benefit formula, e.g., a percentage of final average salary times years of participation. Sufficient funds would be withdrawn from the employer's deposit administration fund to provide the retirement annuity, which was then fixed for life.

The other contract was a defined contribution contract with an individual allocation made to each employee. It, therefore, resembled a deferred annuity plan. Employee contributions were not placed in the separate account, but the employee might have an interest in the separate account as a result of employer contributions placed in that account. At retirement, a benefit was provided on a money purchase basis. That part of the annuity provided by the general account was a fixed annuity. That portion of the annuity provided by the separate account could be a variable annuity or a fixed annuity, at the option of the employee.

Jack Harrigan explained the salesman's viewpoint on Flexi-Fund: "...the clients that we were serving were in dire need of building up better benefits because historically,...back in the 1940's and 1950's, their salaries were so low it was pathetic ...and their pensions were so small in comparison to the increase in prices and the economic situation. There was a horrendous need to build up. I think that's what George Johnson saw. Now this Flexi-Fund product began to let us offer these better benefits, particularly for the individuals getting right at retirement age" *(John H. Harrigan Interview, May 12, 1988)*.

An important feature of Flexi-Fund was that it was not reinsured. In 1961, the committee on long-range objectives had recommended moving away from 100 percent reinsurance. Although committees had been formed to meet with the John Hancock, in fact, the establishment of Flexi-Fund was the first major break away from the John Hancock, aside from the creation of the finance committee to manage the investments. Flexi-Fund grew rapidly, and as it became a larger and larger part of the organization's business, the proportion of the business reinsured at the John Hancock declined.

The Flexi-Fund Plans became the dominant Retirement Association plans of the late 1960's, as the Article III plans had been in the late 1950's and early 1960's. They remained the dominant plans until the advent of the National Retirement Program introduced in the early 1970's.

The time taken in establishing Flexi-Fund was caused, in part, by the necessity of obtaining approvals. However, two other bridges had to be crossed before Flexi-Fund could become operative.

Frank Montgomery comments: "Flexi-Fund was a forerunner of today's products. We had to go and convince the New York Insurance Department that we were capable of doing this. And here's the key: the Hancock wouldn't be involved in this. None of the money would go to the Hancock. We would do the investment and all the technical work. And then the other key: this immediately says, how are you going to do this? You're going to do this with pencil and paper? Never. You have to have a computer" *(Frank P. Montgomery Interview, March 18, 1988)*.

It was clear to everyone concerned that Flexi-Fund required a more sophisticated investment facility on the part of the Retirement Association. Even though the Retirement Association had outside investment advisors for both the general account and the separate account, the ultimate responsibility in the law rested with the company's board of trustees and its finance committee.

Flexi-Fund also presented complicated administrative problems, as Frank Montgomery noted. The program could not be operated manually; therefore, in the late 1960's the Retirement Association was forced to come to grips with the challenge of computerization.

Chapter Nine

BEGINNING THE TRANSITION

"With its splendid body of volunteer officers and trustees added to its staff officers and personnel, the Association approaches the critical period of its growth immediately ahead with every expectation of continued success in meeting its challenge" *(Ralph H. Blanchard, from the 20th* Annual Report *of the National Health & Welfare Retirement Association, October 1, 1965)*.

With these encouraging words, Ralph Blanchard concluded the "Report of the President" for 1965, a highlight of the 20th *Annual Report.*

The report explained the purpose and work of the committee on long-range objectives and discussed recent initiatives that had been undertaken based upon the recommendations of that group. Among these were the move away from complete reinsurance, deposit administration plans, the Flexi-Fund, the creation of the life insurance company, and the decision to install data processing equipment.[1]

In 1965, the Retirement Association continued to address the outstanding problems and needs noted by the committee. The directives had been set, but the new goals could not be achieved without surmounting further obstacles. Satisfying regulatory agency requirements was one, undertaking crucial reinsurance consultations another. Many administrative and operational details had to be worked out before NHWRA could provide "better and better" retirement and insurance plans at lower cost.[2]

The Retirement Association had established a personnel and salary administration program in 1964. In 1965, it engaged its first full-time, professional personnel manager and retained a consulting firm, Sibson & Company, to conduct a personnel study and develop a suitable salary scale for clerical workers covered by provisions of the wage and hour laws.

The first Sibson & Company report, submitted in June 1965, recommended pay ranges for all non-executive positions and did it so persuasively that President Ralph Blanchard proposed an additional study to cover executive employees.

Salaries were always a problem in the early decades of the Retirement Association. Dan Robins recalls that "salaries were low and they moved slowly. The income of the company was limited,... and we were working within a framework of expenses that had to be kept low" *(Daniel J. Robins Interview, March 29, 1988)*.

Sarah Belle remembers dealing with Mr. Blanchard on the subject: "I was offered the job of manager in the benefits department, which had been an officer's position, and I remember Mr. Blanchard called me in to tell me that I was accepted for the position and told me what my salary would be. And he looked at me and he said, 'Now, Sarah, isn't that a substantial raise?' I said, 'Mr. Blanchard, substantial is a relative term.' As a result, I got a couple of hundred dollars more a year. We didn't make much money then, and if I had gotten only $2 more out of it, it would have been worth it" *(Sarah W. Belle Interview, March 3, 1988)*.

The members of the executive committee had a spirit of cooperation fostered by frequent meetings and a shared enthusiasm for the mission of the company. Nevertheless, agreement sometimes came only after vigorous debate. Early discussions over computers provide a case in point. The John Hancock installed its first computer in 1959 to obtain a more accurate reserve calculation program. By the end of 1962, the reinsurer had added improvements and carried information for each individual certificate in force on individual valuation punch cards. The Retirement Association, on the other hand, had continued to use manually posted cards for this kind of participant data.

In February 1965, NHWRA prepared to enter the electronic data processing world, and a three-member staff committee was appointed to study the subject. Vice President Frank Montgomery, Vice President and Actuary George Cherlin, and Comptroller Michael Reape recommended that the Retirement Association begin with an IBM 1440.

President Blanchard preferred immediate rental of this equipment, but Virgil Martin demurred. Both recognized the need for office modernization, but they differed with respect to funding the improvements and the scope of the task.

Messrs. Blanchard and Martin were old friends dating back to 1943, when the Community Chests and Councils study committee first considered formation of the National Health & Welfare Retirement Association. Virgil Martin was Ralph Blanchard's associate in those days although he did not actually serve with that pioneering group. He had been elected a trustee of NHWRA in 1953. At the time of these discussions, Mr. Martin was chairman of a Chicago department store, Carson Pirie Scott & Company.

Mr. Martin believed that the Retirement Association was "embarking on a long-term program which should not be contemplated as a one year extra, but which should be put in proper context by extending it over the length of time which the staff felt would be required to set up a satisfactory EDP (electronic data processing) operation."[3] To him, this meant avoiding a short-range approach in electronic equipment selection just as in methods of funding. He rightly suspected the proposed computer would cost much more than the 12-month budgetary increase that had been provided.

Virgil Martin recalls: "The Retirement Association had a lot of problems getting electronic data processing started because they were inexperienced. It was one thing my business years at Carson's had taught me. They were one of the first in the country to go into EDP. So I'd been through this thing before, and I knew what all the pitfalls were..." *(C. Virgil Martin Interview, April 5, 1988).* The Retirement Association decided to rent the IBM 1440 Series Card System with disk drives, but to do it within the context of a broad program which would expand over a period of five or more years.

During this period of transition, the finance committee was able to gain investment experience in the control of company assets. The committee's efforts had resulted in productive but prudent investment of more than $6 million of company assets at the close of the fiscal year ending June 30, 1965. This money represented accumulated dividends that had previously been left on deposit with the John Hancock Mutual Life and was entirely separate from $160 million or more of contractual reserves held by the reinsurer to back up NHWRA retirement and insurance contracts with health and welfare agencies. The finance committee put 20 percent of the $6.4 million in United States Government Bonds and divided most of the rest among 20 industrial and miscellaneous bond issues.[4]

President Ralph Blanchard wished to retire on June 30, 1965, but agreed to remain until his successor was chosen. Because the company founder might not always be available, George E. Johnson was designated to perform the duties of the president in Mr. Blanchard's absence. When President Blanchard became ill in the spring of 1965, George Johnson replaced him as acting president before the anticipated date of July 1. Technically, Mr. Blanchard still held the presidential title, but Mr. Johnson now carried most of the responsibility.

Dan Robins recollects this period: "George Johnson was acting president. He was here full-time. It lasted a little less than a year, but that was a very important year. It was the year that we were developing the actual terms of the Flexi-Fund Program" *(Daniel J. Robins Interview, April 12, 1988)*.

George E. Johnson's elevation to the acting presidency of NHWRA was accompanied by the advancement of other company officers: Paul E. Mais became a senior vice president; Field Director Christopher Stanwood became a vice president; and Daniel Robins moved up from secretary and associate counsel to secretary and attorney. The Retirement Association continued to follow a policy of promotion from within whenever possible.

Richard C. Brockway became the third president of NHWRA in November 1965, with the understanding he would take office no later than February 15, 1966. Leland Brown speaks of this selection: "They really sought a full-time executive who would be with us for a time, and for that there was a search committee. One of the very important members of the board was J. Douglas Colman, who was president of Blue Cross of New York. He was the most active member of the search committee. It was through his searches that we found Brockway, Colman having known Brockway through the Blue Cross organization (Brockway being president of the Blue Cross of Massachusetts). Brockway had been on the governor's cabinet in New York. He was about 57 years old, . . . with some experience in the field, but of a specialized type. He was really hired for his executive capacity" *(Leland S. Brown Interview, April 6, 1988)*.

Honorary President Blanchard and George Johnson assisted the incoming president on a part-time basis in 1966. Mr. Blanchard was responsible for developing working relationships with national social welfare groups and individual national agencies, as well as continuing and extending the close relationships with the United Fund and Community Chests and Councils movement. In addition, he was to analyze and make recommendations on the composition of the board of trustees, the method of selecting board candidates, and the nominating committee procedures.

President Brockway and Chairman Brown got off to a good start and quickly made an effective leadership team. On a personal level, they soon discovered that they shared a common interest in sailing.

PART THREE

TIME OF TRANSITION
(1966–1971)

Richard C. Brockway
President, 1966–1971

INTRODUCTION TO PART THREE

From 1966 to 1971, the period of the presidency of Richard C. Brockway, NHWRA underwent the lasting changes and expansions that brought on its transition to a larger and more competitive organization. The market place had dramatically altered since 1945, when the big insurance companies had no interest in offering coverage to the health and welfare workers.

NHWRA had flourished while it was the only organization that filled this gap. But now there was more money and more people were involved in the health and welfare field. The commercial firms were also seeking to expand their insurance business in that direction. Clearly, the Retirement Association would have to streamline further its operations and diversify its products to stay in the forefront of meeting the needs of its unique clientele.

Mr. Brockway and the trustees created a subsidiary life insurance company, the Health & Welfare Life Insurance Association, Inc. (HWLIA). The additional coverage that could then be offered was considered competitively essential at the time. However, the preliminary work necessary to bring such a project to completion was formidable and required much time and determined effort.

The efforts finally bore fruit, and the new organization progressed with some success after a few years. However, the creation of the subsidiary life insurance company was only an effective temporary response to a rapidly changing environment to which NHWRA had to adapt. In later years, HWLIA was expanded and made permanent when the parent company itself ultimately became a mutual life insurance company.

One of the accomplishments of President Brockway was to oversee organizational reforms that made the governing boards of the company more manageable, more capable of making quick decisions, and more cognizant of the ongoing operations. In conjunction with this, the president's council was created to utilize the services, contacts, and interests of retired trustees and others concerned with the success of the organization. This body began the practice of meeting with member agencies in various regions of the country, reflecting the nationwide character of NHWRA.

Also, during Mr. Brockway's tenure, the company grappled with the important need to reassess and reform its relationship with its original reinsurer, the John Hancock Mutual Life Insurance Company. The original arrangements with that company had been essential for the early success of NHWRA, but as the Retirement Association grew stronger and more self-sufficient, it sought to gain greater independence in financial and operating matters. These arduous negotiations lasted over a number of years before solutions could be achieved that were satisfactory to NHWRA.

Throughout the period from 1966 to 1971, NHWRA was in the continuous process of modernizing itself to face a volatile and competitive future. It is symbolic of this that one of the most indispensable, aggravating, and yet ultimately rewarding challenges that faced NHWRA, as well as all major American corporations, was putting electronic data processing into place.

No thriving insurance company could hope any longer to survive without sophisticated computers to aid in the awesome reporting, accounting, and statistical work of effecting coverage for growing numbers of agencies and people. Under President Brockway, NHWRA set out to resolve the problems that were besetting all organizations that were facing this complete transformation of their communications methods.

The challenges to management were many, and not all of the desired solutions were implemented during the presidency of Richard Brockway. With the precedents of perseverance and determination established then, however, the company over the years has continued to develop and modernize its computer capability.

Chapter Ten
STARTING A SUBSIDIARY

"Dick Brockway was always a dedicated and selfless president of this company, and I have benefited from his considerable talents of management and organization. For example, his restructuring of the board was a crucial factor in our continued growth over the years. Dick is a gentleman and more than that, a friend. How many executives can say that about their predecessor after seventeen years? From the moment that I arrived to head the company, he was eager to be of help and guide me in whatever way he could. It may seem a small thing, but I remember how graciously he switched to a smaller office so that I could have his. I wonder if I'd be as considerate in the same circumstances" *(William J. Flynn Interview, April 19, 1988)*.

Richard Crane Brockway was born on February 18, 1908, in Rochester, New York, the son of a jewelry salesman. He was educated in the public schools of that city and graduated from the Wharton School of the University of Pennsylvania in 1931. Mr. Brockway went to Washington, D.C., in 1935 to take a job in the personnel division of the Works Progress Administration. In 1936, he went to New York City to work with another section of that agency and a year later began a 20-year career with the New York State Department of Labor in the Brooklyn office. Mr. Brockway was director of the employment service during the Albany administrations of Herbert H. Lehman and Thomas E. Dewey. He held the post of executive director of the employment division under Governor W. Averell Harriman.

Mr. Brockway later served as executive director of the Massachusetts Hospital Service, Inc., the Blue Cross organization in the Boston area. For six years, he headed that organization, which counted 3 million members, assets of $73 million, and an annual income of $120 million.

When Richard Brockway came in January 1966, NHWRA was beginning to develop confidence after two decades of substantial progress. Only 12 of the more than 1,000 existing American life insurance companies had more group annuity annual premium income than the $20.8 million paid into NHWRA.[1] In the 20 years since its founding, member organizations had gone from 400 to more than 3,200; employee certificate holders rose from 5,000 to almost 54,600; and pensioners from zero to nearly 7,800. Pension dollars paid in a single year increased to almost $2.1 million, and NHWRA's assets plus the John Hancock reserves for the payment of future pension benefits exceeded $168 million.[2]

Originally, the Retirement Association had faced little competition for the health and welfare worker's pension dollar. Now, two decades later, this could no longer be said. Other commercial contenders had appeared, and they exerted increasing market pressure on NHWRA.

The service that was being provided by the home office was such that certain improvements were clearly needed in the light of this growing market competition. Operations were sometimes slow, and occasional procedural breakdowns confirmed that the company would benefit from some organizational changes in order to deal more efficiently with the rapidly growing volume of business. The delays were partly internal and stemmed partly from confusions inherent in the double work necessitated by the John Hancock aspect of administration. Another source of difficulty was the occasional administrative lapse in the offices of the members.

The disadvantages of the complicated relationship with the John Hancock had become more apparent over the years and sometimes added to NHWRA's operational problems. When the Retirement Association began paying death claims directly in January 1966, instead of leaving this task to the John Hancock, it took less than six weeks to cut in half the average time involved. Mr. Brockway indicated that NHWRA would itself handle cash withdrawal requests in early March 1966 and, before long, would also take over full administration of the major medical program.

The installation and use of electronic data processing (EDP) equipment was clearly crucial to genuine improvement. Dividend calculations and the development of a monthly billing schedule were already partly handled electronically, but more people were needed in the EDP department to speed up the application of this new technique.

Richard Brockway had direct experience with large-scale office operations with Blue Cross, but he turned to George E. Johnson when it came to dealing with the New York State Insurance Department regarding the schedule for beginning the Life Insurance Association subsidiary and the separate account common stock program known as Flexi-Fund.

By April 1965, the New York State Insurance Department's approval process for NHWRA's separate account was proceeding well. The proposed life insurance subsidiary would be a limited-purpose company formed under Section 191(2) of the Insurance Law, in which the minimum capital and surplus requirement was $300,000.

However, the application for the subsidiary had been caught in the timing of a pending change in chartering requirements. Furthermore, Superintendent Henry Root Stern, Jr., was concerned about the large number of new life insurance companies being formed at that time, possibly in anticipation of the stiffened requirements.

The New York State Legislature was considering a bill that would increase the capital and surplus requirement for a new life insurance company to a minimum of $1.5 million. With a backlog of 31 companies in the process of organization, Mr. Stern grew concerned and wanted to move with caution. George Johnson, who chaired the Retirement Association's insurance committee, predicted that NHWRA's new subsidiary would not be permitted to begin operations until the following year.

In June 1965, the Retirement Association provided a stock investment of $400,000 to fund a subsidiary life company to be known as the Health & Welfare Life Insurance Association, Inc. NHWRA would manage the life company for an annual service fee.

105

On May 12, 1966, George Johnson and Richard Brockway wrote letters to Mr. Stern. Both letters concentrated on what they promised would be an "arm's length" method of operation between the two companies. All transactions between their organizations would be conducted on this basis.

These letters were intentionally coordinated and were written in response to a request for assurance from the New York State Insurance Department that the two associations would establish and maintain a certain degree of autonomy. President Brockway stated that NHWRA would not do anything, directly or indirectly, on behalf of HWLIA which was prohibited to the Life Association by any statute, regulation, or administrative ruling of the New York State Insurance Department. Mr. Johnson promised in his letter to maintain a similar position for the Life Insurance Association.

Mr. Johnson also affirmed that there would be no subsidization by either party. The expense allocation for services rendered or received would be in accordance with regulations and properly documented. Reinsurance treaties and servicing agreements would be fully disclosed and effective only after approval by the authorities. Mr. Johnson stated that the Life Insurance Association would maintain its own bank accounts, receive premium income and pay expenses directly, and keep separate books and records.

Until HWLIA found it feasible, for more efficient business operations, to acquire its own staff, both companies would clearly define services performed by shared staff. The costs would be accurately determined and separately charged. In addition, the Life Association would issue only participating policies and would limit its surplus in accordance with statutory restrictions.

The arguments sufficed, and the New York State Insurance Department issued a license for the Health & Welfare Life Insurance Association, Inc., on May 27, 1966. The new company issued the first policy on June 18, 1966, culminating an effort which had begun in 1964. The establishment of the new company made a broader spectrum of coverage possible and permitted greater internal flexibility.

From the standpoint of the salesman in the field, the working reality of selling the new life insurance was somewhat different. As Larry Gerring remarked: "I don't remember any aggressive effort to sell life insurance. I know we offered those policies for the first time in the 1960's, but I don't remember anybody's really selling them" *(Lawrence H. Gerring Interview, April 22, 1988)*.

Clem McCormack, later treasurer of HWLIA, confirms this from the home office perspective: "Any new life insurance requires aggressive promotion. It really does get down to sales. The field staff that we had at the time probably didn't amount to more than ten people to cover the United States, and they had all they could do to handle the pension business" *(Clement R. McCormack Interview, March 30, 1988)*.

To facilitate activity between the two, their boards executed a management agreement enabling each company to make full use of the other's resources. Richard Brockway and Leland Brown were president and chairman, respectively, of both organizations.

Viewing the founding of HWLIA in retrospect, George Johnson comments: "We did need this life company to do these ancillary things [steps toward gaining independence], and we did set up this company. But almost immediately from ...the time we did it, we began to have some reservations about how much we should proceed with it. The two companies working together seemed a little confusing, and gradually that evolved into the idea of making the whole thing a life insurance company" *(George E. Johnson Interview, May 13, 1988)*.

Now other matters required attention. One of the most important was employee compensation. Sibson & Company, the consultants who a year before had presented a study of lower-level jobs, completed a second report in early June 1966. Sibson focused upon holders of executive positions known as "exempt personnel" because these people were not under the legislative wage and hour restrictions.

Sibson & Company confirmed that NHWRA salaries were low and recommended immediate increases of up to 20 percent for those company officials who were just below the senior officer level and who reported directly to the president.

Mr. Brockway recalls: "We were evaluating our salary levels and we weren't very attractive. We weren't paying really competitive salaries, and it wasn't that we didn't have a good thing to offer. This was partly related to the board structure. One of the rules was: you must not pay anybody more than he'd get at one of our member agencies. You have a man sitting on the board who ran a family service agency and he'd say, 'There's no reason anybody working here should make more than my people do.' So this hampered you a great deal. You weren't out there in the market" *(Richard C. Brockway Interview, March 25, 1988)* .

In a reminder of the previous review, Sibson also noted a need to raise starting salaries for clerical people. For entry level positions, NHWRA paid $60 per week at that time in contrast to an average of $65 offered by a representative group of Manhattan companies, including General Reinsurance, TIAA, and Mutual of New York (MONY).

In June 1966, Dr. Cherlin was designated to take charge of operations during Mr. Brockway's summertime vacation absences. He had come to NHWRA in 1962 as an actuary with fifteen years service at Mutual Benefit Life Insurance Company, where he held the title assistant mathematician. He had earned three degrees from Rutgers University, where he also taught for four years. Born in 1925, in New Haven, Connecticut, Dr. Cherlin held volunteer community leadership positions with the Boy Scouts of America and other organizations. He was also a member of a number of professional groups including the Mathematical Association of America, New York Actuaries' Club, and the Society of Actuaries. During World War II, he had served in the United States Navy.

Since being hired by Ralph Blanchard in 1962 as NHWRA's first actuary, George Cherlin's title had remained the same, vice president and actuary. As NHWRA began to expand its operations independent of the John Hancock, it was evident that the need for in-house actuarial capability was greater than ever.

The number of annuitants had risen to almost 9,000, and these people had received more than $2.3 million during the previous twelve months. Death benefits paid passed the million dollar mark for the first time, and total assets were almost $8.5 million. The client base was growing, and reinsurance was becoming more constraining.

Therefore, in July 1966, the Retirement Association approved an amicable and mutually acceptable agreement negotiated with the John Hancock that gave the Retirement Association more freedom of independent action in handling its own affairs. Originally, NHWRA could not legally sell life insurance because it was a Section 200 retirement association. The transfer of reinsurance to HWLIA on this particular business represented a natural, early step in the reinsurance disengagement process.

This new arrangement did two things for the Retirement Association. It helped implement a major goal of the committee on long-range objectives in a manner that preserved a congenial relationship with the John Hancock. It also gave the Life Association more than $125 million of insurance in force and helped offset the operating costs of the new organization.

Shortly thereafter, the Retirement Association secured the New York State Insurance Department's approval to establish its separate account business. The Insurance Department would not authorize the new direction until the Retirement Association built a corporate structure to sustain the broader program. The most important single part of that was the recruitment of a full-time financial officer. Once NHWRA had found a qualified person for the job, the Empire State authorities granted separate account permission within 96 hours.

In August 1966, NHWRA hired its first full-time, salaried financial vice president/treasurer. His name was Clement R. McCormack. Mr. McCormack, who was born on March 31, 1916, had gained investment experience with the Boston firm of J. H. Goddard before being elected president of RIC (a holding company for group life insurance companies) and later, the Loyal American Life Insurance Company.

Executive Vice President Clement R. McCormack
joined NHWRA in August 1966 as the first full-time,
salaried financial vice president/treasurer.

As Mr. McCormack recalls his hiring: "I responded to an advertisement. Dick Brockway interviewed me and explained that the Retirement Association was beginning to disassociate itself from 100 percent reinsurance with John Hancock. It was going to open up a separate account, and the Insurance Department had said that as a prerequisite they had to have somebody on board who had investment experience and insurance experience. I had both of these things in my background and I believe that is why I was hired" *(Clement R. McCormack Interview, March 30, 1988)*.

The new corporate officer, Clem McCormack, had two functions for both companies. He served as treasurer of both NHWRA and HWLIA in connection with the customary handling of income and expense, record keeping, and financial statement preparation. He also oversaw the investment program of both organizations. Within the parent structure, he served as secretary of the finance committee and, in this capacity, coordinated the investment decisions of Morgan Guaranty to assure compliance with New York State Insurance Department requirements. With the more modest subsidiary assets, he performed the same function directly.

Another employee who became a key member of Mutual of America began his career with the Retirement Association a few months later. John Cerrato, Jr., a 25-year-old Fairleigh Dickinson University graduate, started in the treasurer's office in October 1966. Later Mr. Cerrato became the senior vice president in charge of administrative services.

Richard Brockway's November 1966 progress report on further reduction of reinsurance with the John Hancock discussed the need for the Retirement Association to invest the funds that had been left on deposit with the reinsurer. He considered two alternate methods of discontinuing reinsurance. The first was merely to cease purchase of further coverage, and the second involved total cancellation of existing reinsurance.

Under the first method, the John Hancock would continue to hold and manage a large asset total for the lifetime of the participants covered by the deferred annuities. Under the second method, the assets, risks, and any subsequent gains or losses would belong to the Retirement Association, which would make its own determination of divisible surplus and dividend declarations.

Setting a tentative date of January 1, 1968, the president recommended that the Retirement Association begin as soon as possible to move away from its policy of 100 percent reinsurance of the business.

As always, George Johnson was at the forefront in urging reduction and finally termination of the John Hancock's reinsurance role in the developing business of the Retirement Association. "The point was that you need a pilot to get out of the harbor of New York, but you don't need him all the way across the Atlantic. They needed the Hancock to get started, but when they reached the size they were at this time, they didn't need the Hancock anymore" *(George E. Johnson Interview, May 13, 1988)*.

Mr. Brockway's first annual report to the member agencies was in 1966. It appeared in a new format which included a number of colorful drawings of office life. President Brockway took pride in recounting the achievements of the 12-month period, including the welcome news that retirement claims were now being processed in a shorter time. He commended the staff for their response to the heavy demands for more and improved service despite rapid changes in program and procedures.[3]

At the end of 1966, NHWRA presented to the membership the long-awaited Flexible-Funding Program. Flexi-Fund would be available January 1, 1967, to Retirement Association members who wished to "participate in a wider diversification of investment," and "share in the economic growth of the nation's industrial and business establishment, and thus to some degree . . ." offset the effect of inflation on retirement plans.[4]

Readers were assured that "tested buying and selling methods" would be used "to offset the speculative nature of common stock investments." Employer contributions would be placed in this separate account, but employee money would

112

still continue to be in the general account, "invested in bonds, mortgages, and other fixed obligations since a definite, fixed return of employee contributions is always guaranteed."[5]

Larry Gerring comments on the arrival of Flexi-Fund Plans in the field: "At that point we started to get more competition. What the competition had was unallocated funds. It's a much better way to fund a defined benefit pension plan and, more importantly, they had equity investments—stock market investments. This was during a period of stock market boom, and we were unable to do that. Then along came Flexi-Fund, which was a very good concept and met the need. It was a really up-to-date way of funding pension plans and offered equity investments and was just what the market needed at that time" *(Lawrence H. Gerring Interview, April 22, 1988)*.

During all of 1967, Mr. Brockway publicized the value of NHWRA's new investment program. In the *Annual Report,* he termed it a "defense against inflation."[6] A few months later, he sent a new communication to member agencies called *The Significance of Flexi-Fund*. These efforts were augmented by an early autumn magazine article that Mr. Brockway wrote on the subject.[7]

The Retirement Association declined to recommend that a member agency either use or not use the new investment program, but it deemed it "advisable for each member to review and appraise the suitability of Flexible Funding to its needs."[8] At the time that the 1967 *Annual Report* was prepared, 84 agencies had signed up for the new option, with monthly contributions of over $97,200 of which 59 percent was being invested in common stocks.[9]

Unquestionably, it had been a productive second year for Richard Brockway. The Life Insurance Association had repaid NHWRA for advanced organizational expenses and was self-supporting. Flexi-Fund had become a reality. Reinsurance disengagement from John Hancock Mutual Life was under discussion. There were still many challenges ahead, however, and the third president soon experienced further testing.

Chapter Eleven

RESTRUCTURING THE BOARD

"I came to the conclusion that we either had to go out of the business or go into it and revamp it as a business, as an institution, with an executive committee, with a board that was active, with an executive who made the decisions and made recommendations to the board, and had a professional staff" *(Richard C. Brockway Interview, March 25, 1988)*.

Richard Brockway and the trustees knew that they urgently needed to expand the Retirement Association's capacity to serve a growing number of health and welfare clients and to do it far more effectively. This necessarily involved reforming aspects of the organizational structure established in 1945.

Richard Brockway remembers the situation this way: "The board...was honorific. The organization was put together on the pattern of the agencies we served. It was to be a mirror image, and you would depend on your associations, your friends. You were not in the competitive market. The leadership of this organization at that time, as the leadership of the voluntary agencies, looked to the boards for direction.

"The board had on it a large number of agency heads. But it was important to realize that we no longer had a market exclusive. The insurance companies and the banks were getting into it, and since they sat on the boards of the local agencies, they were having something to say about who got the business. For example, you're the Community Chest of Rochester, New York, and we're talking about a pension system. The local bank is going to say, 'Well, we can do a pension system for you. We can provide investment services'" *(Richard C. Brockway Interview, March 25, 1988)*.

With the move away from complete reinsurance, Chairman Brown estimated that the next fiscal year, beginning July 1, 1968, would bring the Retirement Association direct responsibility for the investment of about $21 million of reserves, the handling of approximately $10 million of non-reinsured contributions, and the payment of some $1.5 million of benefits.[1]

Leland Brown recalls that "as this chart for the future was laid out before the full board which met only annually, a number of the trustees said to me and to Martin and to others, 'Look, a board of this kind can't take on the responsibility for an active, running organization that's going to do its own investing and make its own decisions. So we've got to get a different kind of board.' That was when the decision was made... to come up with a revision of the organization" *(Leland S. Brown Interview, April 6, 1988)*.

C. Virgil Martin, a Chicago merchandising executive, chaired a committee to study questions of financial management and reorganization. The committee was comprised of Edmund J. Beazley, administrative assistant to the Episcopal Bishop of New York; Lyman S. Ford, executive director of United Community Funds and Councils, Inc.; Harold Hinderer, controller of the Daughters of Charity in St. Louis; Richard F. Huegli, managing director, United Community Services of Metropolitan Detroit; Holgar J. Johnson, president of the Council for Financial Aid to Education, New York; and Frank C. Sutton, M.D., director of the Miami Valley Hospital in Dayton, Ohio. Ralph H. Blanchard was committee secretary and Frederick E. Donaldson committee counsel. Richard Brockway and Leland Brown served as ex officio members.[2]

In November 1967, the Retirement Association reexamined the 60-member board created in January 1945 to determine whether the structure was still appropriate under current conditions. Should a board with statutory responsibilities for the proper functioning of so large a scheme meet only once a year? Would there be any advantage in a far greater delegation of authority to the executive committee? In December 1967, the group began to study the feasibility and desirability of a smaller, active board, ways to continue to provide broad community identification and interest, and ways to encourage a more active role for contributing members.[3]

The existing board then numbered 59 members. The approximate geographic distribution of the board members in 1967 was 60 percent from the Northeast, 20 percent from the Midwest, 8 percent from the South, and 12 percent from the West, including one person from Hawaii. Five trustees were charter members and had served 23 years: Mrs. Margaret Culkin Banning, the novelist from Duluth, Minnesota; Ralph H. Blanchard; Milton H. Glover; Sidney Hollander, former president of the Maryland Pharmaceutical Company, Baltimore, Maryland; and Ralph B. Mayo, partner, Arthur Young and Company, Denver, Colorado.

Some of the trustees who were elected later were also active for a long time, including the Philadelphia lawyer, Robert Dechert and former Health, Education and Welfare Department Secretary Marion B. Folsom. Some, however, were able to serve only a short time. Among these trustees were Stanley C. Allyn, former chairman of the National Cash Register Company, Dayton, Ohio; Cecil B. Feldman, executive director of Community Services, Harrisburg, Pennsylvania; Mrs. John Graham, a community planner in Seattle, Washington; and the Most Reverend John Wright, bishop of Pittsburgh, Pennsylvania. Each trustee made a contribution to NHWRA through his identification with it, even though membership on the board actually involved minimal service except for members of the executive committee who met five times a year. Various members of the committee expressed the need for a more businesslike approach which they believed could be provided by a smaller, more active board.

Virgil Martin presented the complementary idea of an additional, informal "president's council," with a nucleus of the then current board members who were not asked to continue as trustees. NHWRA officers would consult with council members concerning activities of the Retirement Association in their home communities. In this way, retired board members would keep in touch with the organization, and the active board could, in the meantime, be streamlined.

William Kaufman remembers his early days on the board and the president's council: "The way that I got really involved with this thing was that I began to make so many critical queries to Ralph Blanchard. Finally Ralph Blanchard asked, 'Will you come to New York and bring evidence of all this stuff?' And so I did. Kind of nervy on my part. Then Ralph asked me to serve on the board. So way back then I was on the board with Ralph Blanchard. We met about once a year, maybe, and he had a chance to tell us what was going on. But it wasn't much, and people said, 'The board has to get more involved in these things.' So [during Brockway's term] it was decided to do away with the large board and appoint a smaller board, and I was asked to serve on the smaller board.

"And then the question was: how are we going to have representation from this larger group?...We still need representation from all over the country, and so the president's council idea came into being.

"Years later Bill Flynn flew to Mobile to have lunch with me, and that's when he asked me to serve as the new chairman of the president's council after Terrance Webster, the first chairman, had died" *(William Kaufman Interview, April 28, 1988)*.

The committee's recommendations were accepted in February 1968, and the appropriate article of the By-Laws amended in April. The New York State Insurance Department confirmed the changes in May 1968. The board of trustees of the Retirement Association was reduced to twenty-four elected members consisting of three classes of eight trustees each, elected for three-year terms. The board of twenty-four would meet at least five times each year, and the 7-member executive committee would meet primarily in emergency situations rather than for regular, ongoing business matters. The Retirement Association would encourage contributing agency members to remain on an active participating basis.[4]

During the reorganization, management concentrated on asset investment. The finance committee, which was created in

October 1964, in anticipation of at least partial reinsurance discontinuance and the expected beginning of the Flexible-Funding Program, had gotten off to a slow start. It had met only twice in all of 1966. With Flexi-Fund money to invest, however, it met four times the following year and continued this more active schedule in 1968.

NHWRA placed contributions in either the general account or a separate account for Flexi-Fund investments, as directed by the member agency, pursuant to Section 227 of the New York State Insurance Law. Investment strategies to minimize the effects of inflation, which caused such hardship for annuitants, had received a boost when the law was modified to permit greater common stock investment for general account assets. The permitted amount of common stocks doubled from 10 to 20 percent.

In this climate of greater freedom, the finance committee, chaired by Thomas W. Keesee, Jr., an executive with Bessemer Securities, had much to do to increase the proportion of common stocks to a level that would be closer to the permissible amount. A monthly program of common stock purchases began then.

Clem McCormack served as staff investment officer. "The separate account really got going, as my recollection is, at the beginning of 1967. It was then known as Flexible Funding, which gave the employer or employee the ability to elect what portion of their monthly contribution would be invested in the separate account, which was all equities, or in the general account. We hired Morgan Guaranty Trust. I was secretary of the investment committee and sat in on all the meetings and was the liaison between Morgan Guaranty Trust and the Association. One of my particular responsibilities was to make sure that the investments met the regulations of the Insurance Department.

"There was plenty of room to move about, but there were certain types of investments that you could not invest in...speculative things. This was particularly true in the general account, which Morgan Guaranty also supervised. There were distinct limitations, percentages of the total assets that could be invested in any particular security. That was part of my responsibility" *(Clement R. McCormack Interview, March 30, 1988)*.

In June 1968, Mr. Brockway issued reports as president of both the parent organization and the subsidiary life company. The 23rd *Annual Report* showed the Retirement Association's assets (exclusive of the separate account) increased by 15.5 percent over the previous year, reaching an all time high of more than $11 million. However, the most dramatic growth during that year was in the number of member agencies enrolled in the Flexible-Funding Program. In July 1967, there were fewer than 70 participating agencies or affiliates; by July 1968, over 400 were taking advantage of the Flexi-Fund investment opportunity.

The HWLIA report emphasized its growth from the modest base of 12 months before. Assets almost doubled to $1.28 million; insurance in force climbed to $108.5 million from less than $45 million; policy reserves more than tripled.

In the summer of 1968, Richard Brockway sent a brochure, *A Matter of Some Importance*, to all NHWRA agency members. It informed them of NHWRA's decision to reorganize its board of trustees for more efficient service and described how the voluntary health and welfare field would soon be able to "show the way" for many people to a "satisfying full life in retirement."[5]

Of the people selected for the smaller board of 24 trustees, the majority had careers in professional social work. There were business leaders, bankers, lawyers, and people from organized labor and the media. One of the financial men, Jacques Chabrier, executive vice president of the Hartford National Bank, continued the relationship begun 23 years before by Milton H. Glover between that institution and the Retirement Association. The new board also included Wilmer A. Jenkins, formerly executive vice president and, at that time, trustee of TIAA-CREF.

Three nominees were new. A. Crawford Greene, Esq., succeeded his late father, A. Crawford Greene, Sr., Esq., who had been a charter trustee of the Retirement Association and had served with distinction for more than two decades. The son was a member of the same San Francisco law firm, McCutcheon, Doyle, Brown & Enersen. Francis X. McNamara, Jr., was the general manager of the United Way of Los Angeles, Inc. Lewis D. Cole was vice president of Mail Photo Service, Inc., in Louisville, Kentucky, and later became chairman of the board of NHWRA.

Lewis Cole recalls his selection to the board in 1968: "I was chairman of the board of United Way of Louisville just around that time. I'd been very active in community agencies. It was very natural that I became aware of the kinds of plans that came out of the Retirement Association and the kinds of service that they gave, and I suspect that I got on the board because they were very anxious to have representation throughout the country. I was asked by Dick Brockway" *(Lewis D. Cole Interview, April 29, 1988)*.

The annual meeting of the members on October 31, 1968, marked NHWRA's carefully planned change of executive organization. That morning at Carnegie International Center in New York City, members of the Retirement Association family honored 38 men and women with a special award for service as members of the outgoing, larger board of trustees.

The new, 24-member board's first meeting was held later that day. The trustees named the executive, finance, and insurance committees and appointed the first president's council. Among those appointed to the president's council were Mrs. Ann Chapin, controller of the Jewish Welfare Federation, Detroit, Michigan, and Dr. Ellen Winston, former United States commissioner of welfare, Raleigh, North Carolina.

Half of the council members were social work professionals, including United Way directors, hospital and other health field executives, and leaders of large, well-known agencies such as National Family Service and Girl Scouts of the USA. The rest reflected a wide spectrum of occupations, including banking, general business, accounting, law, and the clergy, the latter being represented by the Most Reverend Joseph L. Bernardin, general secretary of the United States Catholic Conference (who later became a cardinal), and the Most Reverend Joseph Brunini, auxiliary bishop of the Catholic Diocese of Natchez-Jackson, Mississippi. Ralph H. Blanchard and Milton H. Glover were counted among the first members of the president's council.

A Matter of Some Importance also included information about the newly created president's council. The 60 members of the council would meet at least once each year to communicate directly with NHWRA's chief executive about subjects of both his and their choosing. Regional meetings would be sponsored by local members of the council. Having the president's council would increase the number of health and welfare field representatives in direct contact with the president.[6]

Richard Brockway explained the council to membership agencies as being comprised of "representatives of major health and welfare organizations currently participating in the program of the Association as well as persons identified with organizations not yet affiliated with NHWRA."[7] The council had no legal status and was not mentioned in the By-Laws. It would, however, be in a position to influence NHWRA policies and practices because of its close identification with the world of social work.

Council members were selected by the president, who also chose the chairman of the new group. For that job, Richard Brockway named Terrance L. Webster, former executive director, United Fund of Hennepin County, Minneapolis, Minnesota. Mr. Webster, a trustee of NHWRA since 1965, had served three years as a member of the executive committee until his retirement as a trustee in 1968. He chaired the council until his death in 1972.

The council held its yearly meeting in conjunction with the board of trustees. In January 1969, both groups assembled at the Biltmore Hotel. Forty of 59 council members convened on

January 16, 1969. Terrance Webster presided at the first meeting of the president's council and attended the trustees meeting the following day as a non-voting guest.

In response to the president's council's request for improved communication between the Retirement Association and the field, NHWRA made organizational changes in the field service division designed to improve relations between members and the home office.

In the spring of 1969, board and president's council members met in Cincinnati for their first joint, regional gathering. At the conference, 28 representatives from agencies in that area met the trustees in what the president termed "a discussion of program objectives, new developments, and pension plan trends."[8]

The council initiatives for further direct meetings with member agencies resulted in other gatherings throughout the country. April in Atlanta, Georgia, for example, featured an NHWRA presentation at the United Community Funds and Councils of America Southeastern Regional Conference. Vice President/Field Director Stanwood and Vice President and Treasurer McCormack teamed with Senior Consultant B. Stanley Gill in a series of prepared talks which stimulated lively discussion of the Flexible Funding and separate account programs. Mr. Brockway reported on the presence of Retirement Association staff at 20 meetings sponsored by agency members that year as an example of the information exchange suggested by the president's council.[9]

In 1969, arrangements were also being made for the home office move to larger quarters. The planned relocation was to 360 Park Avenue South, between 25th and 26th streets, where four or more floors were to be leased. Cost and space details took time to negotiate, and the need for extensive renovations postponed the actual move to April 1970. This was NHWRA's fifth move and sixth Manhattan address in 25 years. The energetic and constantly expanding company had to seek larger facilities to handle the increased staff required by the greater size and complexity of its distinctive insurance programs.

Chapter Twelve
COMPUTER CHALLENGE

"I think that the big problem with the computer was that we aimed for too much too soon. We wanted the ultimate system, and when you're going into something brand new, you know, you go by steps. One of the big jobs we do, the most important, is to write a retirement check. In those days, back in the 1960's, we said, 'Oh, let's create a system, when a retirement comes up, you push a button, and the check is produced.' It can happen today; it is happening today. Maybe then we were a little naive. Our business compared to the other companies was quite small" *(Sarah W. Belle Interview, March 3, 1988)*.

Richard Brockway had accomplished many significant things in almost four years as president. Flexi-Fund was off and running; the new board had been formed; the president's council was in place and making contributions; administrative staff changes had brought new, qualified people to the company; and HWLIA was in business.

Pressing events, however, gave President Brockway no time to enjoy these achievements. In 1968, the Retirement Association had faced an unexpected challenge from John Hancock Mutual Life. That company had reacted to NHWRA's effort to move away from reinsurance with it by announcing that it would substantially reduce dividend payments to NHWRA if the latter followed through on its plan. The discontinuance of reinsurance of new business was scheduled to become effective July 1, 1969. However, under an amendment to the New York State Insurance Law, effective November 1, 1968, a company was required to have a surplus to policyholders of at least $2 million in order to write separate account contracts. Projections were made based on the assumptions that all new business would no longer be reinsured effective July 1, 1969; payment of dividends to members would remain at the current rate; and the John Hancock would adhere strictly to its policy on dividends after discontinuance.

The announcement by the John Hancock upset the Retirement Association's management. George E. Johnson was unhappy with the position taken by the John Hancock and felt that it was perhaps unjustified and inconsistent with the assurances previously given by its management in past years.

Robert Dechert, Esq., a founder of the prestigious law firm of Dechert, Price & Rhoads in Philadelphia, chaired the special committee established to study the issues. J. Douglas Colman, Wilmer A. Jenkins, George E. Johnson, and Eugene J. Patton served on the committee. In September 1969, Robert Dechert outlined three objectives for NHWRA: provisions for recapture of money held by the John Hancock, operational reforms, and clarification of the commitments and intentions of the John Hancock toward the Retirement Association.

He recommended that the John Hancock transfer to the Retirement Association the funds covering the risks that had been reinsured. That would permit the two organizations to enter into a more conventional type of agreement. In this new arrangement, the Retirement Association would maintain all records, perform most of the administrative functions, and have more control over the types of benefits offered and those discretionary decisions which are a part of the day-to-day operation of a pension system.

Operational objectives included avoidance of work duplication and greater disclosure of expense allocation by the John Hancock. NHWRA decided to secure from the John Hancock a written statement of intentions regarding payment of full dividends on non-Flexi-Fund 100 percent reinsured business and a binding promise from the John Hancock eventually to return to NHWRA all funds shown on the John Hancock financial reports relating to NHWRA.

At the same time, the Retirement Association faced a major challenge: the conversion of company record keeping to electronic data processing. Begun in 1965, the program soon fell behind schedule, exceeded estimated costs, and brought great frustration to management. Richard Brockway kept the clients abreast of the developments in this aggravating process. Frank Montgomery, who in 1969 was vice president of systems and data processing, kept management informed. Mr. Montgomery, who was born November 6, 1924, joined the Retirement Association in 1953 after service in the United States Air Force. He had studied mathematics at the University of Tampa, Iowa State, and the University of Chicago.

Mr. Montgomery is held in high regard by his colleagues from those past, intense days. George Johnson, a hard taskmaster, says of him: "Frank was a very good man. When I was in there [as acting president] he was...one solid guy I could rely on. I got more out of Frank than I did anybody else" *(George E. Johnson Interview, May 13, 1988)*.

Frank Montgomery describes his early career at the Retirement Association: "I came in as a trainee supervisor to run the calculation work for the company. During my first seven years with the organization, I served an apprenticeship; in fact, I learned everything that the company was doing, all the contracts, all the actuarial considerations, etc." *(Frank P. Montgomery Interview, March 18, 1988)*.

Frank Montgomery recalls the situation during the time he was assuming direction of the computer program: "I was asked to take charge of this in 1968. I had no knowledge whatever of computers. When Brockway asked me to do this, I was in a state of total shock because I knew the problem we were in. I knew it extremely well because I was trying to run the administration. It was almost impossible and getting more difficult all the time.

"In the meantime, we had started to sell Flexi-Fund, and it took off. Our clients said, 'This is just what we want.' People started buying it all over the place, switching their plans over. We were running a tape system to keep these records, and I can't tell you how limited it was. Furthermore, the Hancock reinsured business hadn't gone away. All of that had to be administered, and people were asking, 'Well, when are you

Executive Vice President Frank P. Montgomery
joined NHWRA in March 1953 as a trainee
supervisor to run the calculation work.

going to pay the claim?' And we have the claim up in Boston with the Hancock. We were still doing all that" *(Frank P. Montgomery Interview, March 18, 1988)*.

The Retirement Association's computer experience must be viewed both in the light of the conditions that existed at NHWRA at that time and in the perspective of the upheaval the computer caused in American business. The computer revolution surged through American enterprises with irresistible force. The life insurance industry proved particularly receptive to the sophisticated technology because of the enormous advances it offered to statistical and reportorial accuracy. John Naisbitt, a business consultant, noted: "Almost all of the people in these companies and industries spend their time processing information in one way or another...."[1] The Prudential Insurance Company of America helped lead the way in 1955 with home office installation of IBM Models 650 and 702. By 1967, the Prudential had 52 electronic computers.[2]

At NHWRA, the procedure developed far more slowly. For one thing, the step was irrevocable. The conversion cost money, and the modest Retirement Association resources were no match for the research and development budgets of the huge insurance firms. Added to this was the fact that operational savings proved illusory. Even the most experienced companies discovered an increase in current expenses as well as substantial development costs. Richard Brockway and his associates recognized that it was essential to computerize but discovered it was costly. It necessitated hiring more, rather than fewer, highly-trained employees, and company computer rental and associated costs rose from a 1966 figure of $66,500 to $83,200 the following year. At the same time, related personnel expenses jumped from $33,000 to over $122,000.

When setting the first target dates for the new system, NHWRA believed it possible to prepare Flexi-Fund annual account statements for employers and annual benefit statements to participants by December 1968. Non-Flexi-Fund billing management reports also seemed possible by that date.

The Retirement Association had replaced the first central processor in October 1967, with the more advanced IBM Model 360-30. This machine increased mechanical memory capacity from 32,000 to 128,000 characters and disk storage from 2 million to 40 million characters. However, this equipment was by no means completely operational. Although the NHWRA staff used the machines an average of 30 hours per week, only 65 percent of that time could be devoted to actual production. The remaining hours were used to test systems that needed further development.

By June 14, 1968, some of the goals set two and a half years before had been met. Efforts to construct a so-called total system for Flexi-Fund business continued to lag. The Retirement Association was working with a combination of computerized and manual methods and did not have enough staff capability to meet projected company requirements and development schedules for a Flexi-Fund system by December 1969.

Montgomery says: "Now our planning for the use of the computer was, from the earliest, ambitious. We said, 'What we are going to create is a total system.' It would do everything. It would keep all the records. . . . But for the first three years of that effort the progress was minimal. A primitive system was created to handle Flexi-Fund, and a number of simple things were put on the machine, but it wasn't enough" *(Frank P. Montgomery Interview, March 18, 1988)*.

And so the Retirement Association decided to contract for software from an outside service. President Brockway's special committee, composed of George Cherlin, Clement McCormack, and Frank Montgomery, had studied the situation for eight months. They could come to no other conclusion but to retain a professional consultant with experience in the field.

Frank Montgomery recalls: "There were unrealistic deadlines set. You'd take a stab in the dark; you'd do all your analyses and so on. The deadlines would wash away. There were essentially two painful problems. One was to maintain staff operations and staff morale under these conditions, and the other was to maintain our customer relationships" *(Frank P. Montgomery Interview, March 18, 1988)*.

Four bids were submitted for the contract which the Retirement Association finally awarded to the Programming Sciences Corporation. Cost estimates for the complete systems projects and EDP operation were then increased 9 percent from the February 1967 forecast of $1.7 million to a new total of $1.9 million. The outside experts came none too soon, for service to member agencies and participants had suffered, particularly in replying to inquiries and obtaining needed documentation for some claim processing.[3]

Dan Robins describes the feelings of general unease and dissatisfaction that were felt during this difficult period: "There was the complaint about slowness. There was a complaint about getting information. Now, part of that was that we had undertaken to do something and raised expectations that we weren't able to fulfill. We were going to give this kind of information on a running basis, and if the computer couldn't do it, if it produced the wrong information, the people who had their expectations raised thought in terms of, 'Well, you promised to do it and now you're not coming through.' I don't think that I ever felt demoralized, but it was a confused time. It was a difficult time" *(Daniel J. Robins Interview, March 29, 1988)*.

From the vantage point of the salesman in the field, it was just as disturbing. Larry Gerring remembers: "We thought we would get a computer program to handle the new business from Flexi-Fund, and the computer program didn't work, so there were a lot of administrative problems. It got so that you didn't want to answer the phone because you were pretty sure it was an irate customer. These were people with whom I had established a relationship. I was the representative, and I would try to calm them and soothe them and say, 'We're working on it.' I used to call New York several times a day to get various things for various customers. The people in New York were trying, but they were overwhelmed by the job itself. We got things straightened out" *(Lawrence H. Gerring Interview, April 22, 1988)*.

In November 1969, Frank Montgomery summarized the four-year struggle to automate the Retirement Association's record keeping. The three parts of the EDP program needing attention were: the Flexi-Fund project, including preparation of a master file of employer and employee records and the creation of computer programs to provide service for Flexi-Fund members on an automated basis; assembly of a less inclusive project of automating certain functions in connection with the presently reinsured coverages; and preparation of benefit statements for all policyholders and developing linkage of coverage applicable to all plans.

The task of simultaneously implementing these three EDP programs took a tremendous effort on the part of the staff of the Retirement Association, as well as its outside computer consulting firm, Programming Sciences Corporation. Several key individuals who played a major role in the three programs were Sarah Belle, Hae Soo Whang, and Teresita StaCruz, who all later became vice presidents.

New to the world of computers, Mrs. Belle, a seasoned veteran of Retirement Association service, provided the administrative expertise in the reinsured coverages. Another veteran, Mr. Whang, provided the expertise for the Flexi-Fund project. One of the consultants from Programming Sciences Corporation, Ms. StaCruz, joined the Retirement Association and quickly became a valuable asset to the computer operations.

By January 1970, the consultant, Programming Sciences Corporation, was having difficulty with the complexity of the task. Frank Montgomery expressed confidence that the new system and the others being developed would lead to a substantial improvement in the quality and quantity of service to the Retirement Association's members, but cost was of great concern.

In September 1970, Frank Montgomery described a computer trial run covering a typical community plan—one covering the 328 employees of the Atlanta, Georgia, Community Chest and its affiliates. The experiment revealed that relatively complete and accurate Flexi-Fund data had been attained, but that they had still found and corrected minor errors in the computer programs. The missing items of paid-up data were found and corrected.

As a result of special efforts made by 19 employees who worked 21 days straight, including weekends, the Flexi-Fund accounting system was put into operation on September 1, 1970. They machine-processed 58,000 transactions to produce the first bills for 1,500 member agencies and their 25,000 employees.

Although occupied with EDP problems during his presidency, Richard Brockway continued his active involvement in the health and welfare pension world. He made the most of the president's council and its efforts to involve member agencies in area seminars and praised the executives who contributed to the success of the conferences. Council meetings were scheduled for March 1970 in St. Louis and for May in Boston. The council also endorsed the Buffalo, New York, and Pittsburgh, Pennsylvania, agency meetings planned for June, as the Retirement Association attempted to extend its personal reach beyond the New York Metropolitan area.

Richard Brockway attended numerous president's council meetings, as well as others around the country, taking with him members of the New York staff. Due to the problems in service that had stemmed from computer and administrative difficulties, these meetings were often tense. Mr. Brockway looks back on them:

"Our president's council would sponsor meetings...or we'd have other meetings with the customers, and what we did was just stand up and take it and talk to them, let them know that we were alive and that we were concerned, that we were trying to do something about it.

"We also took issues to them that would stir things up,...whatever was the issue of the day. Should we invest with a social point of view?

"One of the things that I had going for me was that I had, through my government operation and through the Blue Cross, a network of people all over the country that I knew. I had been on the board of the Welfare Council here in New York for many years. I knew some of the names of the key people in the social work and health field so that I could appear to them as a professional manager.

"There was a loss of confidence and a desire and a need to be reassured that at least the company was going in the right direction and was trying to do the things that they wanted done. I think that I had something do to with reassuring them" *(Richard C. Brockway Interview, March 25, 1988).*

Clem McCormack was at Mr. Brockway's side at many of the meetings. He remembered one meeting in particular: "Most of the remarks were directed to Dick Brockway. One executive after another of a member agency would get up and cite some kind of a horror story, you know, somebody waiting six or seven months before they got the first retirement check and that sort of thing. We knew we had problems but we never realized the magnitude" *(Clement R. McCormack Interview, March 30, 1988).*

In the 1970 *Annual Report*, President Brockway acknowledged a reduction in HWLIA's insurance in force from the previous year. For the parent company, he noted an increase in assets and policy reserves and emphasized that better things lay ahead. He anticipated a marked reduction in developmental and extraordinary costs and expected improvement in promptness and the quality of policyholder service.[4]

In June 1970, NHWRA published a pamphlet entitled *Retirement, Death and Long Term Disability Plan Objectives* in response to many requests for such information from members and from other health and welfare agencies considering affiliation with the Retirement Association. The pamphlet urged voluntary social agencies to reject the idea that health and welfare workers should make an economic sacrifice in the pursuit of their careers and to insist that jobs offered in the field rival other occupations in both compensation and benefits. It stated: "The private health and welfare field is competing with education, government, science, and industry for the same kinds of people with the same skills and interest."[5]

A good benefit plan would enable an agency to attract qualified workers in the labor market. A "less-than-adequate plan" could cause high labor turnover and minimal worker qualifications as well as poor motivation and performance. A good retirement plan should "make clear to each employee that his worth is recognized and properly valued; that the benefits, means of financing and guarantees of his retirement plans are at least equal to those enjoyed by people with comparable training and skill in private business, government or education." It should "provide an income after retirement which will support the employee in a life of dignity, economic security, and independence."[6] The booklet further offered a checklist of seven items for the employer's consideration and advised that retirement plan costs should be viewed from both a budget and a program perspective.

The pace of NHWRA events, both within the home office and in the field, accelerated during the first half of 1971, culminating in a change in leadership. For some months, the Retirement Association had been seeking a successor to the president. Richard Brockway had taken part in the process from the start, along with Leland S. Brown, C. Virgil Martin, J. Douglas Colman, and Richard F. Huegli, among others. Mr. Brockway, who after four full years in office was approaching normal retirement age, looked forward to stepping down as president.

In May 1971, the chairman and president spoke enthusiastically about the qualifications of William J. Flynn, a vice president of The Equitable Life Assurance Society of the United States. He held a degree in economics from Fordham University, had served in the United States Air Force during the Korean conflict, and had done excellent work at the Equitable. The chairman's interest in attracting Mr. Flynn to the position of president was, in part, based upon the strong, unqualified recommendation he had received from Grant Keehn, former vice chairman of the Equitable.

Three weeks later, on June 11, 1971, Mr. Flynn was elected first a trustee and then the fourth president of NHWRA. The corporate By-Laws were amended that day to define the duties of the chairman, vice chairman, and president, spelling out the relationships among these positions. Now any of the three incumbents could be designated "chief executive officer."[7]

William J. Flynn was given responsibility for duties pertaining to the general supervision of the business of the Retirement Association and the administration of the retirement system as might be assigned to him by the CEO or by the board. The president would preside at meetings of the contributing members and be an ex officio member of all board committees. Richard Brockway became vice chairman and CEO. Both were pleased with this arrangement which facilitated a harmonious and gradual transfer of authority.

Mr. Flynn sent a message to the NHWRA constituency in which he made a full commitment to NHWRA's primary objective to provide for the pension needs in the voluntary health and welfare field; assigned the highest priority to the perfection of NHWRA's administrative procedures; and expressed a willingness to meet as many of the members as possible during the course of the next several months. William J. Flynn was ready to begin his new career with the National Health & Welfare Retirement Association.

PART FOUR

ACHIEVING BREADTH
AND MATURITY
(1971–1985)

William J. Flynn
President, 1971–1984
Chief Executive Officer, 1972–Present
Chairman, 1982–Present

INTRODUCTION TO PART FOUR

When William J. Flynn became president of the National Health & Welfare Retirement Association in 1971, he promptly established his personal style. He expressly stated where he wanted the company to go at each stage and how it would get there. He analyzed concepts and operations that could be strengthened and explained how he would implement changes.

Mr. Flynn was determined to enlarge the company for the overriding purpose of effecting more and better pension and insurance coverage for the not-for-profit worker. His vision of how to do this was clear, and his ability to find the most fruitful directions in which to lead was proven over and over again by NHWRA's achievements during the 13 years of his presidency.

He sought and created expanded coverage that was carefully designed for the challenging conditions of increased competition, more complex government regulation, and perilous inflation. He founded the National Retirement Program, which represented a needed return to standardization of plans. More accessible to all the clients, it was thorough, being comprised of three major programs of coverage that became immensely appealing in the not-for-profit market place. This was evidenced by major increases both in total assets and in the number of member agencies.

From the first days after his appointment, Mr. Flynn began to confront the need to improve substantially service capabilities. He completely reorganized the administrative operations and recast the entire sales effort to meet the requirements of a swiftly expanding, national company.

Mr. Flynn also saw early in his tenure that increased means of communication between the company and its customers were essential and should become a forceful selling point in NHWRA's entire program.

To further this end, he and his staff met continuously with clients and other interested people throughout the country. At these meetings, the successes as well as the problems of the Retirement Association were discussed frankly. By doing this, a spirit of cooperative openness was forged at a time of considerable confusion and need for both the insurer and the clients.

Mr. Flynn also initiated three publications: the *NHWRA Report* and *A Closer Look*, both pamphlets that spelled out specific policies and challenges in detail, and the *NHW Participant News*, which offered a personal link between the company and the individual employee. He also increased promotion and advertising, making the company better known to the public. It was gratifying to NHWRA that a poll sponsored in 1981 indicated that effective communications had become one of its most noted attributes.

The achievement of complete financial independence for the company and its freedom to offer new programs and insurance initiatives are among the most important accomplishments of this era. By successfully negotiating the termination of the reinsurance arrangements with the John Hancock, Mr. Flynn and the board of trustees launched the company on a future course of complete control and responsibility for all of its actions.

The conversion of NHWRA into a mutual life insurance company was also a landmark in the organization's history. From that time forward, the revamped organization was able to create a greater and more flexible variety of programs. Furthermore, it was able to compete more easily in the national market and sell these programs throughout the country without hindrance.

The result of these manifold changes and developments, and others that occurred between 1971 and 1985, can be clearly seen at work in Mutual of America's operations today.

Chapter Thirteen

A NEW PROFESSIONALISM

"I know that it took every ounce of everything I had ever learned, and especially everything that I had learned about people, in motivating people, and dealing with people. It took every ounce of it, and it took one other thing, and that was willingness to work around the clock, day after day, year in and year out to do what had to be done" *(William J. Flynn Interview, March 21, 1988)*.

William J. Flynn came to NHWRA with impressive credentials. The Equitable's president, J. Henry Smith, gave his young associate high marks for character, ambition, and integrity. He also indicated how sorry he was to lose a man of such promise.

Other business leaders were equally complimentary about Mr. Flynn. A Detroit executive and NHWRA trustee, Richard Huegli, noted the new president's public speaking ability. The vice president of National Tea Company emphasized his impressive combination of ability and firmness. A third corporate official, Ray Peterson, cited his great intellectual capacity. Several not-for-profit executives added similar sentiments. Richard Mills, president of the American Bar Retirement Association, asserted that Mr. Flynn was a superb choice. J. Douglas Colman, who headed the Associated Hospital Service of New York, mentioned his marketing experience and administrative sense.

But most important of all was the impact that William Flynn had on the trustees who were responsible for appointing the new president. Leland Brown, chairman of the board of NHWRA then, was a key figure in that effort: "Dick Brockway felt that it should be Bill Flynn. He asked me to interview him, which I did. And it was very interesting to me that I was attracted to him immediately. I felt that Brockway had made a good choice. So I went to see Grant Keehn [former vice chairman of the Equitable] and said, 'We are very interested and would like to know about Flynn.' He said, 'He's first class, but I want to know about your organization. Is it any good for Bill Flynn?' And I'd keep saying, 'Well now, tell me about Bill Flynn in this aspect and that aspect,' and he'd say, 'Oh, he's terrific, but is this organization good enough for Bill Flynn?' The Equitable didn't want to lose him at all" *(Leland S. Brown Interview, April 6, 1988)*.

William Flynn comments about this: "When I indicated to Equitable that I was coming here, that I had made up my mind, they put me through a whole set of interviews with the chairman, the chief executive, and others. They then offered me the job of chief of staff at Equitable. It was very difficult to turn it down,... but I felt that I had given my word and shaken hands on it, and I was not about to turn back" *(William J. Flynn Interview, March 21, 1988)*.

The new president of NHWRA was born on September 6, 1926, in New York City. The son of a stationery engineer employed by the *World Telegram-Sun* newspaper and his wife, Anne, Mr. Flynn graduated from Cathedral High School, Brooklyn, New York, and then went to Cathedral College of the Immaculate Conception, Huntington, Long Island.

Mr. Flynn was employed by the New York City Board of Education and also taught mathematics at Regis High School. He remembers being busy in those days: "I taught mathematics at Regis for a year. I did it to pay tuition at the Fordham Graduate School. Also, I worked with the Park Avenue Women's League. Basically, I taught their children how to handle themselves socially, including dancing. I coached basketball for the kids up in Yorkville, and I enjoyed doing it all. I got paid more money for teaching dancing than I did for all the rest" *(William J. Flynn Interview, March 21, 1988)*.

By 1951, he received a master's degree in economics from Fordham University. Two years later, Mr. Flynn began his insurance career at The Equitable Life Assurance Society of the United States. He still managed, however, to lecture part-time in economics at Fordham until 1956.

Mr. Flynn found areas of strength and weakness at NHWRA when he assumed the presidency in the spring of 1971. Company operations for the previous twelve months were impressive. Member organizations and insured participant workers had reached record levels. Annuity payments and death benefits hit new highs. Better still, income rose to $47.1 million while expenses were kept low enough to register a net gain of $439,000, in contrast to a $268,000 loss for fiscal 1970. Assets had increased by 81 percent, from $34.3 million to almost $61.9 million, but much of this growth came from a rise in the stock market.

Overall costs were lower because the expenses for computer systems development had decreased. Behind the balance sheet, however, stood a year of continuing frustration caused by electronic data processing problems. The new computer systems had not increased operating efficiency as much as anticipated, and the delivery of the Annual Participant Benefit statement was delayed.[1]

President Flynn spent his first months during the second half of 1971 getting acquainted with the company officers who reported to him, concentrating upon administrative problems, and preparing for the September 17, 1971, board meeting.

In September 1971, the Retirement Association studied the modification of the reinsurance agreement with the John Hancock based on the recommendations of a special committee consisting of Eldon Wallingford, executive secretary of the Insurance Federation of New York, Inc., Ray M. Peterson, retired vice president and actuary from the Equitable, and Wilmer A. Jenkins, retired executive vice president of TIAA. There were four alternative courses of action, each of which contemplated continued NHWRA payment of considerations to the John Hancock at a mutually agreed upon minimum level. All of these alternatives took into account the fact that the John Hancock would continue its reinsurance on benefits already accrued. The Hancock was not in a position to transfer to NHWRA any substantial part of the funds it had accumulated under the reinsurance contracts.

The four alternatives all involved, to varying degrees, a change in the way the actual investment returns, mortality experience, and expenses were reflected in the credits to NHWRA. In the existing arrangement, such credits for favorable experience came in the form of dividends declared by the John Hancock. To the extent that the experience was more favorable than the interest, mortality, and loading margins in the rates established, the John Hancock would set aside contingency reserves for adverse future experience, and the remaining favorable experience would flow into dividends. The contingency reserve itself would also be a source of future dividends.

Under the revised arrangements, the contract would be converted into a type of group annuity contract under which the release of favorable experience would occur sooner and more automatically, with less opportunity for the John Hancock to hold back contingency reserves.

The four alternatives were all acceptable to the John Hancock, and NHWRA could select one of the alternatives and proceed accordingly. The Retirement Association management decided it was too important a matter to decide without greater reflection and recommended further study.

William Flynn had already chosen the four aspects of the business that would be his top priorities in the months ahead: administration, communication with members, product study, and a thorough market review.

As he had indicated, improvement in administrative procedure came first. The Retirement Association's EDP system concept was one of the most comprehensive developed by any organization in the pension field and could lead to a dramatic increase in both the quantity and the quality of NHWRA service to its members. But much remained to be done and done quickly to actually utilize the new capacity. President Flynn assured the board that nothing would interfere with achieving this goal.

Mr. Flynn had learned quickly about discontent among the membership. He had met with members of the field sales force in the early days and heard their attitudes toward the problems at hand. Jack Harrigan recalls one episode: "We were not really geared to selling from the standpoint of computer operations. Administration was poor, and the problem was not resolved. I can remember a day right after Bill joined NHWRA. We were walking down a street in Indianapolis, and I don't recall the exact words, but, in essence, the conversation was: 'What is wrong?' I said, 'Bill, our computer system has got a lot of bad data in it. Until all of that comes out, we're in big trouble. We must take a look and begin correcting it'" *(John H. Harrigan Interview, May 12, 1988)*.

Many of the agencies felt frustrated with home office delays in answering questions about their plans. Mr. Flynn realized the need for a far greater exchange of views and promised extensive regional meetings for the coming year. Representatives from both large and small agencies would have the opportunity to meet top company officers and discuss their pension problems with them.

The problems of administration were broader and more basic than just the changeover to computers. Mr. Flynn speaks vividly about some of the challenges he first faced: "Whenever a complaint came in, I would investigate it thoroughly. One day, during an investigation, I was looking for the file room and I learned that there was no central file room. So I asked, 'Well, where are all the records kept?' A young lady, Karen Whitmore, said, 'Oh, that's in the files over there.' And here was this old file with papers falling out of it. I said, 'Help me.' We found a vacant room, and I got the fellows from the mail room, and we started to set up a file room. By that evening we started to organize things physically" *(William J. Flynn Interview, April 19, 1988)*.

Mr. Flynn continues on the subject of administration: "The most important decision that I ever made at this company was my first decision. That was to cease all activities for one year and get the administration right. And that's what we did. We went to work and called our sales people in and put them to work on nothing but administration. Nobody in the competing insurance world even knew about the problem we had. The company was simply not a factor. However, our clients knew about it, and our employees knew about it. It was clear that we had no future unless the problem was corrected" *(William J. Flynn Interview, April 19, 1988)*.

A thorough review of the Retirement Association benefit plan products was of equal importance and long overdue, and that was Mr. Flynn's third priority. In 26 years of service to the social work community, NHWRA had continually added new pension products to its portfolio of retirement programs. It had first offered plans A, B, C, D, and E. Then came the products identified with a portion of the company By-Laws, the so-called Article III plans. These were followed by the Flexi-Fund offerings.

Mr. Flynn believed it important to find the answers to such questions as: How do the various programs relate to each other? What is the relationship among benefit adequacy, the cost, and the total budget of a member agency? How can the economy of administration for a given plan be measured and improved?

On November 17, 1971, NHWRA leaders came together for a series of three meetings which involved the executive committee, the contributing members, and the entire board of trustees. Each session reflected a significant aspect of the health and welfare retirement enterprise.

An impasse had developed between the Retirement Association and St. Mary's Hospital in Racine, Wisconsin, which had discontinued its membership in 1970. The hospital had taken this step in order to enroll its employees in the Franciscan Sisters' retirement plan. In the process, it tried to recapture the reserves NHWRA held for Plan C paid-up annuities credited to hospital participants. Ordinarily, the Retirement Association did not permit split-funding arrangements by its members. However, Mr. Flynn made this case an exception. In what was to become his typical direct and personal response to problems, the president went to Wisconsin to discuss the situation directly. He later persuaded the hospital to pay at least half its future pension contributions to NHWRA with the balance going to the fund sponsored by the hospital's Mother House.

Stephanie Kopp, now an executive vice president of the company and someone who has worked with Mr. Flynn over the years, remembers this incident very well, for it was the first business she had with the new president. "He went out to visit one of our discontinued cases, St. Mary's Hospital in Racine, Wisconsin, and his motive was to find out why agencies were leaving the Retirement Association. Although the hospital had discontinued two or three years before, it still didn't have all its paperwork finalized. I wrote a memo on the situation. Mr. Flynn called me into his office and said that he wanted this case to be cleaned up. He showed a keen interest in wanting to know everything from A to Z. He really put me through the third degree as to what went wrong, why it went wrong, how it could be changed. And then Mr. Flynn invited the sister in charge to come to New York, and she agreed. When she was here, he asked me to go to St. Patrick's with her in the morning for Mass. It seems kind of quaint now. We don't give that kind of customer service anymore. A couple of months later, Mr. Flynn called me to his office and told me that he was looking for an assistant, and would I like to take on that assignment and work directly with him? He said that there were a number of projects that he was going to undertake as the new president, and I remember immediately accepting the job. 'OK,' he said. 'The effective date will be December 1'" *(Stephanie J. Kopp Interview, March 24, 1988)*.

At the November 19, 1971, meeting, Mr. Flynn secured board approval for the St. Mary's arrangement and an ensuing contract. He not only enabled the Retirement Association to retain these reserves but also garnered additional business. He arranged that dividends and surrender credits accruing under the Retirement Association's portion of the plan would be plowed back into the plan. At retirement, annuities could be provided through the Retirement Association or could be transferred to the Franciscan Sisters' retirement fund for use in providing benefits from that fund.

Dan M. McGill, who has served both as a director
and a consultant, chaired the Long Range Planning
Committee established in 1983.

The 26th annual meeting of the contributing members on November 19, 1971, was particularly noteworthy because of the attendance and participation by agency representatives. In contrast to the experience of all but the first few years of NHWRA history, a large number of representatives came to the gathering at the Prince George Hotel in New York. The increased size of the group reflected the interest in the change of company leadership. However, those present came not only to meet the new president but also to confront him with their dissatisfaction. William Flynn acknowledged difficulties but stated his firm conviction that the Retirement Association, with its new data processing system, was well along the way to solving many of the current service problems.

That same day, Richard Brockway, vice chairman and CEO, made a surprise announcement. Since the transition to President Flynn had proceeded with greater speed than Mr. Brockway had anticipated, he asked to be relieved of all active responsibility as of January 31, 1972. Mr. Flynn responded by declaring that the company would still need the benefit of Mr. Brockway's continuing advice and support when he finished working actively and was retired.

This anticipated change in leadership came at a time of other important and symbolic NHWRA personnel changes. Dan M. McGill, chairman of the Insurance Department of the Wharton School, joined the board to fill the vacancy created by the death of Edmund J. Beazley. Dr. McGill, one of the nation's acknowledged experts on insurance, became a member of the insurance committee where he served with distinction. He chaired the committee during most of his tenure on the board.

After two consecutive terms as trustee, he was appointed consultant to the board on insurance matters, a relationship that continues to the present. He has always been one of the most expert and influential voices in the company's decision making process on questions of insurance and general policy.

Dan McGill recalls when he first joined the board: "I became involved through association with Bill Flynn. He was the principal person I had dealt with when he was at the Equitable. I think that we developed a healthy respect for each other even though we were on different sides of the table then. When he became president of the National Health & Welfare Retirement Association, I frankly admitted I had never heard of it. We had lunch together, and he told me about the organization, its origins, and that it had to be turned around. And one of his first jobs was to get a strong board, and he wanted to know if I would be willing to go on his board. He made it clear that there would be no compensation; it would be pro bono service, and I said I'd be happy to do it" *(Dan M. McGill Interview, April 13, 1988)*.

The addition of Dr. McGill to the board was seen as the beginning of one of the great achievements of William Flynn's executive direction, which was to generate a professionalism and expertise in all of the company's operations.

Leland Brown remarks upon this: "Dan McGill was one of the first people that Bill Flynn brought in. He was a very fine, high-grade man who knew the insurance field technically and professionally. It was of very great interest to so many of us that Bill Flynn had someone like that he could turn to. I remember Bill's telling me that when he first got into the insurance business, one of the things that he had to do was study Dan McGill's books on insurance" *(Leland S. Brown Interview, April 6, 1988)*.

Indeed, these were the early signs of a slowly changing attitude toward the work and the responsibilities that came with belonging to a dedicated and successful insurance company. Many of the people who were involved with the Retirement Association, both before and after the arrival of Mr. Flynn, remark upon the spirit of professional commitment and pride that began to develop. For example, John Cerrato recalls: "There was a need for more professionalism. When Bill Flynn came aboard, the company changed from a not-for-profit type of agency. We turned into a full-fledged insurance company. The mentality changed tremendously. It's a fact that Bill Flynn brought this with him. I think this was the real major change in the organization" *(John Cerrato, Jr., Interview, May 7, 1988)*.

In December 1971, Stephanie Kopp was appointed Mr. Flynn's executive assistant. Ms. Kopp had served as a Peace Corps teacher in East Africa before entering the business world and began work at the Retirement Association in February 1968. She had started as a correspondent in the Flexi-Fund department but, after a few months, she was transferred to the member service unit. As part of a reorganization in November 1969, she joined the company's administrative training program and the following summer was promoted to administrative assistant to Helmut Frick, then general manager of insurance services.

At the same time, the Retirement Association appointed Frank Montgomery vice president in charge of administration. The upward mobility of Frank Montgomery and Stephanie Kopp at the National Health & Welfare Retirement Association was not uncommon. Helmut Frick was promoted to senior field vice president, and Lawrence Gerring, another employee with long service who had begun as a field consultant, became the regional vice president in the Seattle office. They, and numerous other men and women, were recognized for their efforts and talent and rose to positions of responsibility and authority.

Another major contribution was made by Linda DeHooge, who had been Mr. Flynn's secretary at the Equitable and who was invited to come to the Retirement Association with him. He gave her new and important responsibilities that led to her appointment later as vice president and executive assistant to the chairman. She has served Mr. Flynn with devotion and dedication over many years.

Linda DeHooge describes her first impression of the Retirement Association: "On the day of the board meeting at which Mr. Flynn was being appointed president, Mr. Brockway's secretary called me at the Equitable and asked if I would like to come down to the office at 360 Park Avenue South.

"Having worked in a modern skyscraper in the attractive midtown area, the older and much smaller NHWRA offices in a less developed downtown location were much less appealing.

151

But the people to whom I was introduced were receptive and friendly. Besides, I had long before learned to trust Mr. Flynn's instincts.

"Almost from day one, the first two items on the top of Mr. Flynn's 'Things to Do List' (which he still keeps) were to change the name of the company and relocate. It took years to accomplish those things but he did them" *(Linda DeHooge Interview, March 3, 1988)*.

The board of trustees held a reception and dinner for Richard Brockway on January 20, 1972, at the St. Regis Hotel. They invited Retirement Association officers, Mr. and Mrs. Ralph Blanchard, several other former trustees, and the guest of honor's family. William Flynn served as master of ceremonies, and Leland Brown gave the main address. The evening provided a fitting climax to a conscientious and admirable career.

Richard Brockway's final official appearance as CEO came the following day when he reported for a special committee of three trustees composed of himself, Thomas W. Keesee, Jr., and C. Virgil Martin. They had been appointed to study the subject of NHWRA votes on corporate proxies of companies in which the Retirement Association held shares.

Certain social issues had been raised at many of the 1971 annual meetings of the corporations in which NHWRA had invested. Mr. Brockway believed that resolutions on such controversial topics (for the time) as ceasing operations in certain countries; placing consumers, minorities and women on governing boards; and protecting the environment, would be broached again in 1972. Mr. Brockway recommended that the Retirement Association adopt a policy of voting with management on such issues; NHWRA could write a letter to the management of any particular corporation when it seemed necessary to express a company opinion on a resolution. Management concurred. This was before the social responsibility issue had become so pervasive and sensitive. Mr. Brockway continued to serve as vice chairman when William J. Flynn became chief executive officer effective February 1, 1972.

In February 1972, William Flynn held the 4th annual meeting of the president's council of NHWRA. He joined with Terrance L. Webster, council chairman, and the other members of that group, to explore pension products that were devised to meet the needs of health and welfare workers. Mr. Flynn, as an experienced insurance executive, also convinced the council to help him achieve two of his high-priority, first-year goals: product study and market analysis. He intended to establish a greater uniformity of the benefit plans, thereby easing the home office administrative snarl. The council also proved to be gratifyingly responsive to product review.

Mr. Flynn then embarked upon a series of regional conferences in 23 cities attended by more than 600 representatives from some 400 agencies.[2] After this, he convened the very first general meeting of employees for the entire home office staff. The March 10, 1972, meeting gave the president an opportunity to describe the regional meetings and explain what needed to be done in the months ahead. Reorganization plans were discussed at that meeting.

One week later, President Flynn made the most of this momentum by announcing his plan to improve the company's communications capability. The plan involved a complete reorganization of Retirement Association field and administrative services. There would be a shift from a functional to a regional, member-oriented basis in order to improve control and follow-up. Seven geographical regions were established, each with a separate team of representatives headed by a regional manager. Their assignment was to provide all field and administrative services required by the agencies and participants in that territory. The regions were to be backed up by the support services department.[3]

Mr. Flynn did more than devise a new program and set it in motion. He helped assure its success by forming a support services department headed by Vice President Isadore Feferman and then Assistant Vice President Sarah W. Belle, who had attained this rank in 1966 after experience as a senior actuarial assistant and then as manager of the benefits department.

Ralph Harris Blanchard died on May 6, 1972. The NHWRA founder had suffered a stroke five weeks before while preparing for a meeting at the home office where he had been composing a record of the organization's early years. After two weeks in the hospital, Mr. Blanchard returned to his Bronxville home. Richard Brockway and William Flynn paid him a visit there two days before he died.

Two weeks later, Leland S. Brown and the trustees of the National Health & Welfare Retirement Association honored him with a resolution stating:

> Ralph H. Blanchard has truly been called the father of the Retirement Association, but more than that, to those of us on the Board of Trustees; to his lifelong associates in the United Fund field; and to the staff of the Retirement Association, he was a warm and dear friend.
>
> It was Mr. Blanchard's insistence upon improving the financial position of social workers that led to the organization of the Retirement Association, and to its successful beginning. Yet in his modesty, he always gave credit to others, and downgraded his own indispensable role.
>
> He retired as President in 1965, but to the end of his life, he maintained his interest in, and performed duties for the Retirement Association, never obtrusive, but always available to serve his successors.
>
> Ralph Blanchard was too close to all of us and too important to our Association for a resolution to capture more than a small part of what he meant to us individually.

Mr. Flynn proposed that a committee be formed to consider an appropriate Blanchard Memorial. C. Virgil Martin chaired the group consisting of: William Aramony; Richard C. Brockway; Leland S. Brown; Dan M. McGill; and Frank C. Sutton, M.D.

The summer of 1972 was a season of personnel change. Christopher W. Stanwood, vice president and field director, took early retirement. He had been affiliated with NHWRA since 1944. George Cherlin, vice president and actuary, resigned in August, having served well in that capacity for a decade.

A few weeks later, Leland S. Brown also announced his resignation as chairman of the board. He told his colleagues that the time had come for him to relinquish the chairmanship, and he would do so officially in November. Virgil Martin would succeed him at that time, but Mr. Brown would remain on the board. Messrs. Brown, Brockway, and Martin had discussed the matter for some time and were in complete agreement. Three factors were pertinent: the chairman's own tenure, the availability of another seasoned trustee to assume the role, and the new president's splendid first year.[4]

Mr. Brown believed that a decade as chairman should suffice. Since 1962, he had worked in this capacity with three presidents: Ralph Blanchard, Richard Brockway, and William Flynn. Furthermore, Mr. Brown reasoned that his retirement from the chairmanship represented a vote of confidence in Mr. Flynn. Now a new person would take charge, C. Virgil Martin. A trustee since 1953 and a member of the finance committee, Mr. Martin had just retired as chairman of Chicago's Carson Pirie Scott & Company and had the time for this extensive volunteer commitment.

The NHWRA family gathered for the annual board meeting and the president's council meeting at the Biltmore Hotel in New York City on November 17, 1972. During the traditional moment of silence to honor trustees who had died during the year, everyone present remembered Sidney Hollander, an original board member, and Terrance L. Webster, a former trustee and the first chairman of the president's council.

William Kaufman, executive director of the United Fund of Mobile County, Inc., declined renomination for another board term but accepted the chairmanship of the president's council. Milton H. Glover retired from the board after 27 years. He had been honorary chairman since 1962. Lewis D. Cole paid tribute to Leland Brown's services and noted that all of the trustees were indebted to Mr. Brown for the devoted and dedicated leadership that he had given the Retirement Association during his ten years as chairman.

C. Virgil Martin
Chairman, 1972–1974

Thomas C. Edwards, president of TIAA-CREF, and Robert J. Myers, professor of actuarial science at Temple University and former chief actuary of the Social Security Administration, became trustees. William J. Flynn announced three executive appointments: William H. Hackett as director of research and competition, who later became vice president and corporate secretary; Robert W. Allmang as first director of internal audit; and Donald S. Grubbs as vice president and chief actuary for the company.

In November 1972, the Retirement Association established the Ralph H. Blanchard Memorial Endowment Fund at the University of Pennsylvania. The principal sum would be funded over the coming decade; the income of the endowment fund would be used by the Pension Research Council of the Wharton School to conduct research consistent with Mr. Blanchard's life-long concern for the retirement needs of persons employed in social welfare activities.

Chapter Fourteen
CREATING INNOVATIVE PROGRAMS

"There was an executive in one of our United Ways who was dying of cancer. I called Bill Flynn and said, 'You know, this guy is only 45, 47 maybe, and he's definitely not going to make it. It's really important that we get some coverage for his family.' There was no coverage; you get the insurance, but that's no way to support a family. He's got kids. So out of that Flynn went right to work. He put together a program and got the board's approval just a week before this man passed away.

"Now the program is in place all across the country. It covers that kind of early death so that you have some income for the family. It was incredible. No company, no commercial company would have responded that way. And this is a business that undergirds the health and human care system of the country. It's important that Mutual of America continue that sensitivity and responsiveness" *(William Aramony Interview, May 9, 1988)*.

In 1973 and 1974, William Flynn directed the development of a variety of new programs and products to be presented by NHWRA to the clients. He also saw to the institution of operating improvements that were designed to increase the efficiency of the company's service. In the process of doing all this, he brought greater coordination to the conduct of business. This was partly achieved by streamlining and quickening both decision making and implementation of those decisions.

Mr. Flynn had acquired from his group life insurance and pension experience an understanding of the relationship between people and their needs and a sense of what could be accomplished practically. He possessed essential elements of leadership: vision, perseverance, and a sense of timing, and he was able to combine them to lead the company into a period of unparalleled growth.

Mr. Flynn's farsightedness was evident when he secured trustee approval for the establishment of a program concerning corporate gifts. This was a decision of some consequence for the future. It involved the question of whether it is appropriate for one not-for-profit organization to make a gift to another not-for-profit organization. Some would argue that such a practice is an improper diversion of funds from the purpose for which they were contributed.

Mr. Flynn proposed, however, that since the Retirement Association owed its very existence and continued growth to the not-for-profit sector, it had a moral obligation to use some part of its resources to support worthy causes sponsored or espoused by its member agencies. Moreover, it would be good business to show the not-for-profit field that NHWRA has a corporate conscience.

The corporate gifts committee, created in January 1973, was composed of Leland Brown, chairman; Richard Brockway; William Flynn; Richard Huegli; Virgil Martin; Dan McGill; Harold Hinderer; Thomas Keesee; and Daniel Robins, secretary. In April of that year, the group recommended that the Retirement Association contribute to the United Fund of Greater New York, and management approved. In addition to the Ralph H. Blanchard Memorial Endowment at the University of Pennsylvania, the trustees also considered other future company gifts. The corporate gifts committee was also charged with a study of the United Fund's new policy of seeking financial support from not-for-profit employers.

When William J. Flynn assumed the presidency, a major concern was to improve the accuracy of the NHWRA records. In addition, he coped with the problem of inadequate communication between the home office and the member agencies by organizing a series of regional meetings across the country. Soon it became apparent, however, that other, more extensive methods were needed. A newsletter was one of these, and in March 1973, the Retirement Association published the first issue of the *NHWRA Report*.

Through this publication, Mr. Flynn could communicate with each client. The first issue included the following message from the president:

> NHWRA Report will serve us—you and the Association—in this modern age of pension planning. Through these pages we hope to keep you posted on the newest techniques of employee benefit plan design and funding. We also hope to keep you informed of activities here at the Association, and in the general interest of your fellow members, we would very much like to publish regular items about yourselves, your agencies, and your pension plans.[1]

The publication contained pictures of the February 9 president's council meeting in New York, as well as excerpts from addresses given by President William Flynn, Vice President and Chief Actuary Donald S. Grubbs, Council Chairman William Kaufman, and Board Chairman C. Virgil Martin.

The first *NHWRA Report* also emphasized efforts being made to formulate a new national pension plan system that would include an NHWRA Cost of Living Retirement Plan. Pension plans had become more complex. To be viable and responsive to participant needs, they were often amended for the sake of modernity, but this patchwork approach tended to create complexity and raise administrative costs, absorbing funds that could be used to increase benefits. Pernicious inflation was causing trouble for those people on pensions who rarely, if ever, had enjoyed the cost-of-living increases that were now becoming commonplace in the work force.

In response to this inflationary pressure, which grew worse in the early 1970's, NHWRA introduced a non-contributory plan that provided for increases in pension benefits for all retired participants of up to 4 percent a year, as a reflection of changes in the Consumer Price Index from year to year.

This Cost of Living Supplement was an optional feature of the Cost of Living Plan. The plan was a defined benefit plan based on final average earnings and years of credited service.

The fact that the plan was non-contributory, i.e., paid for entirely by the employer, meant that all eligible employees were covered. Likewise, vesting was made more effective because terminating employees no longer had the opportunity and temptation to defeat the vesting by withdrawing their own contributions and losing accrued pension credits.

An innovative, optional feature permitted an employer to include credited service with a prior NHWRA plan with an offset for the accrued benefit under the prior plan. This critically important provision meant that the final average salary applied to all service including that with a prior employer as well as service with the current employer. Under this arrangement, an employee was not penalized for moving from one employer to another in the calculation of final average salary benefits. The absence of this type of provision in corporate sponsored plans is a fundamental weakness in the private pension system.

Dan McGill speaks of this innovative work: "It was very fortunate that a person of Bill Flynn's experience and background was brought in at that time because he not only adapted these new products to what was going on in the business but also added a few features. The contracts that were developed for the social welfare field were cutting edge and had features that were really more attractive to the participants than were available in the corporate market. Among other things, he developed contracts that were to have a built-in cost-of-living arrangement. Well, the corporate community felt it couldn't afford it, but some of these social welfare agencies bought it. He was really offering the most progressive contracts.

"Bill is surprisingly social-minded. He's very marketing oriented, but he's also very social-minded. These were contracts and arrangements, benefit structures that I'd have to say in the best of all possible worlds, were exactly what was needed" *(Dan M. McGill Interview, April 13, 1988)*.

The case of York Hospital of York, Pennsylvania, presented a situation requiring a decision in the spring of 1973. The hospital had negotiated a new plan with another firm to provide actuarial, administrative, and consulting services. It requested

Retirement Association approval for this unusual arrangement but wished at the same time to have NHWRA retain the investment function and provide annuities at retirement for their workers. The Retirement Association granted this request.

The 27th *Annual Report* for 1972 contained a map showing the NHWRA regional organization created for administrative purposes during that fiscal year. The United States was divided into seven regions: Western, Southern, Greater New York, North Central, East Central, New England, and Middle Atlantic. Each area was headed by a regional manager, and some of these managers were appointed officers of the company in 1973.

While the regionalization was operative with respect to the performance of many functions, it was not yet regional in physical location because most field members still remained in New York. By mid-1973, however, the time had come to open branch offices in other cities to regionalize in both function and location.

The Retirement Association decided to open the first field office in Philadelphia in June 1973. Experience gained from this experiment would be helpful later in establishing additional regional offices in other cities. Although company field representatives would staff these offices, policyholder services would still be centralized in New York. Mr. Flynn designated Helmut Frick to run the Philadelphia office. Mr. Frick already headed the Middle Atlantic regional area comprised of Pennsylvania, Maryland, Delaware, Virginia, Washington, D.C., and southern New Jersey.

Helmut Frick recalls his appointment to the job: "When Bill Flynn took over, I was in charge of all administration. I was not in the field. Bill asked, 'How do you like your job?' I said, 'Bill, I hate it. I don't like to be pushing paper around. I would love to be in the field. I like people and I know the product in and out.' He said, 'You're in charge of the first office.' That was the Philadelphia office. I could run the office pretty much from New York. I never moved to Philly. The region was very large. We called it the Middle Atlantic region. It went all the way

The staff of the first regional office in
Philadelphia with the New York support
staff, about 1973 (Left to right, front row:
Cynthia Wood, Charles Jennerjahn,
Marion Gray. Back row: Thomas Gilliam,
May Baranowski, Raymond Kraft, Nessa
O'Toole, Helmut Frick)

down to Virginia. We had the whole state of Pennsylvania, then Washington, D.C., Maryland, and Delaware. It was a huge office" *(Helmut Frick Interview, March 10, 1988)*.

While regionalization promised to solve, or at least ease, several operational problems, it would clearly aggravate the long-standing problem of "doing business" in states from which it had not received a certificate of authority as a life insurance company within their jurisdiction. In the early years it was very rare for the Retirement Association to be contacted by state insurance departments. That may have been because the Retirement Association was small, operated in a limited market, and had a unique basis of organization under the New York Insurance Statutes. It may also have been because insurance departments did not have then the same interest in regulating out-of-state companies that they were later to demonstrate beginning in the mid-1960's, particularly companies that did not readily fit a given state's regulatory structure. When a state insurance department did take an interest in the Retirement Association's activities, generally as a result of an inquiry to it by a local insurance agent, the insurance commissioner was usually satisfied by a response that the Retirement Association was doing business only by mail and was not "present" in any state but New York; or that the Retirement Association was not an insurance company and, therefore, should not be regulated as an out-of-state insurer.

Impelled by several developments in the mid-1960's, the National Association of Insurance Commissioners (NAIC), in 1966, set up a subcommittee to develop a model law on "unauthorized insurers," i.e., insurers which, though legitimately licensed in one state, operated in other states without a certificate of authority from those states. The principal targets were unauthorized accident and health insurers. The thrust of the model bill was to list certain activities that constituted "doing an insurance business" within a state and then to state that doing an insurance business could subject the company to regulation by the insurance department and to taxation by that state. The sweep of the proposed legislation would have included entities other than the Retirement Association. The very large and highly visible TIAA-CREF was also very concerned about this development since TIAA-CREF was at that time licensed in only a few states.

The NAIC moved deliberately on this important question. The subcommittee, under the chairmanship of James Faulstich, then commissioner of insurance for the state of Oregon, first met at the June 1966 NAIC meeting in Richmond, Virginia. Action was postponed from meeting to meeting, although a text of a model bill had been proposed. One of the sticking points was a provision proposed by TIAA and opposed by much of the insurance industry, particularly by insurance agent organizations, that would have exempted TIAA-CREF from the provisions of the model bill. The model bill was finally adopted at the Los Angeles meeting of NAIC in December 1968. Some states had jumped the gun on the NAIC and had enacted unauthorized insurer statutes between 1966 and 1968 based on the developing NAIC model. Some enacted these laws only to regulate unauthorized insurers; other states also subjected them to taxation. Following the adoption of the model bill by the NAIC, the states quickly enacted unauthorized insurer legislation. By the end of 1970, a sizable majority of the states had enacted such legislation substantially in the form of the NAIC model.

In September 1971, the Retirement Association adopted a policy on "doing business." Basically, the policy institutionalized what management had been doing for years. The Retirement Association would continue to sell and service plans in all states. If contacted by an insurance department, the Retirement Association would first assert its exemption from regulation on the grounds that it was not an insurance company. If that was not successful, the Retirement Association would press for legislative relief. In any event, the Retirement Association would accept such regulation as a state might impose so that it would not have to abandon its members in any state.

California was not one of the states which had adopted the NAIC Uniform Unauthorized Insurers Act. California Commissioner Roddis, in 1969, believed that the Insurance Laws of California already had enough teeth so that he could shut down unauthorized insurers. He contacted a large number of such insurers, among them TIAA and the Retirement Association, and ordered these insurers to obtain certificates of authority in California or to cease and desist from doing any further business in that state.

Early in 1969, Mr. Roddis resigned as California's commissioner. His successor, Richards D. Barger, a Los Angeles attorney, took a more sympathetic view of the status of the Retirement Association, the job it was trying to do, and the nature of its clientele. Commissioner Barger proposed that the Retirement Association make application for a certificate of authority as a "grants and annuities society." Although that classification did not fit squarely with what the Retirement Association was doing, it gave the regulatory authorities a legitimate justification for allowing the Retirement Association to continue to do business. Regulation under that section was minimal. There were no premium taxes, but there was an annual registration fee.

By 1975, the Retirement Association, acting in accordance with the policy adopted in 1971, was licensed as a grants and annuities society in California, as a Section 200 retirement system in New York, under statutory exceptions in about four states, and under a limited certificate in Rhode Island.

The most serious challenge to the Retirement Association in this area came from the state of Illinois. Learning that the Retirement Association was underwriting pension and death benefits for Illinois employers, the deputy director and general counsel of the Illinois Department of Insurance requested that a representative of the Retirement Association's law department visit Springfield to discuss the matter.

At the meeting, which involved several of the top deputies of the Illinois department, Mr. Robins was informed that the present situation was unsatisfactory, and that the Retirement Association would have to obtain a certificate of authority or cease doing business in Illinois. The sticking point was an admission by the Illinois department that NHWRA could not be licensed in its form as a Section 200 organization.

Although they took a tough line, the Illinois authorities were, in fact, patient. They refrained from taking action with the understanding that the Retirement Association would become a mutual life insurance company and would then seek a certificate of authority in Illinois.

In the July/August 1973 *NHWRA Report*, Mr. Flynn discussed the results of the Retirement Association's first questionnaire sent out to all the member agencies. "Yes, we're smiling," the president wrote, "thanks to the nice things so many said in response to our questionnaire."[2] Almost 80 percent of the responding agencies gave NHWRA a good rating in this regard, with 29 percent being very favorable.

Mr. Flynn did not ignore, however, the 20 percent who were less satisfied. He thanked the members for their candor, assured them that specific areas of difficulty had been pinpointed, and stated, "We are working to clear these problems now."[3] In later years, Mr. Flynn conducted surveys of NHWRA's own employees to gain their impressions of its service performance to clients, working conditions, and other pertinent information about total operations.

The *NHWRA Report* introduced a section called "The Manager's Corner," which became a regular feature. The summer 1973 edition of the publication ran an article in "The Manager's Corner" by North Central Manager Jack Harrigan. He contrasted fixed contribution and fixed benefit plans. In the beginning, the Retirement Association had offered only the former, known also as a money purchase plan, and had allocated accumulated contributions plus investment return to individual accounts for each participant. Later, NHWRA moved toward fixed benefit plans, which based retirement income upon final pay and maintained contributions and interest earnings in the employer's fund.

"The choice of the right benefit plan is a difficult one," Harrigan concluded. "An important part of our NHWRA consultant's job is to analyze for you the vehicle which will best accommodate the needs of your organization."[4]

That very summer, the Retirement Association itself improved the plan for its own employees by adopting a noncontributory, cost-of-living, final salary arrangement with an eligibility age of 25 years with one year's service.

The employee benefits have been a source of increasing pride to many in the company as they have been expanded over the years since Mr. Flynn joined the organization. Howard Lichtenstein, today executive vice president in charge of consulting services, remarked when talking about compensation comparisons of Mutual of America with other insurance companies: "I would say that our employee benefits rank right at the top of all employee benefits packages in the country" *(Howard Lichtenstein Interview, March 15, 1988)*.

On June 14, 1973, the Retirement Association sponsored its first executive conference at New York's Biltmore Hotel. More than one hundred agency executives and board members heard William Flynn say:

> Management needs your suggestions in order to operate your Association effectively. The exchange of viewpoints which takes place at meetings like this all over the country helps us to set meaningful objectives for NHWRA in response to your needs. We welcome, too, your candid evaluations of our shortcomings so that we can correct them promptly.[5]

Later in 1973, Dan McGill reported on the insurance committee's review of a management recommendation to change the reinsurance agreement with John Hancock Mutual Life. The recommendations incorporated ideas from the work of the special committee chaired by Eldon Wallingford and the results of numerous subsequent negotiations between the John Hancock and NHWRA.

The John Hancock accepted a Retirement Association proposal for a new agreement. Under this agreement, Group

Deferred Annuity and Deposit Administration contracts reinsured with the John Hancock would be converted to an immediate participation guarantee basis. This would permit the Retirement Association the option to withdraw excess funds under the immediate participation guarantee contract in excess of funds necessary to support benefits payable under deferred annuities and benefits being paid to retired employees. It would also allow immediate credit of full earnings to NHWRA, which would make approximately $3.5 million more available to the Retirement Association than it received the previous year as dividends. Furthermore, it would allow subsequent recapture of money deposited with the John Hancock after January 1, 1974, subject to an acceptable asset liquidation adjustment.

Then Dr. McGill presented another proposal from his committee that the NHWRA offer three new pension plans as part of what it called the National Retirement Program. The Cost of Living Plan had already been announced. Next would come a Tax-Deferred Annuity Plan (TDA) and a Flexible Annuity Plan. Within a few months, the Retirement Association sent members information about the tax-deferred annuity permitted by the Internal Revenue Service for employees of tax-exempt, not-for-profit organizations engaged in educational, charitable, religious, scientific, or social service fields.

In the September 1973 issue of *NHWRA Report*, the Retirement Association presented the essence of its Tax-Deferred Annuity Plan.[6] Contributions would be made through a reduction in salary income designated for that purpose, with only the reduced salary being subject to income tax, and with plan contributions to accumulate with investment income on a tax-deferred basis. Contributions could be placed in the Retirement Association's general asset account, or the pooled common stock account, or a combination of both.

That *NHWRA Report* included illustrative computations and suggested the Tax-Deferred Annuity Plan be considered as a voluntary supplement to an organization's non-contributory basic retirement plan. The Retirement Association promised that its Tax-Deferred Annuity Plan would be available before the end of 1973 and would be offered to social agencies whether or not they were NHWRA members.[7]

A participant could choose a fixed benefit annuity, a variable annuity, or a combination of the two. The NHWRA plan would be "no-load," and, therefore, a worker's contributions would not be reduced by sales or commission charges. Finally, the employee would own his Tax-Deferred Annuity Plan with the option of increasing or decreasing contributions or discontinuing them temporarily or permanently. The plan would be completely portable.

The "no-load" aspect of the Tax-Deferred Annuity Plan was immensely popular because a participant's contributions were credited without any deduction to the funds accumulated with interest under the contract. The contract further promised that the full accumulated amount, again without deduction, could be withdrawn by the participant. In other words, the contract had neither a "front end" nor a "back end" load. The contract could be offered without explicit loading for two major reasons. One was the Retirement Association's practice of having salaried sales and service personnel who received no commissions or other incentives for sales. The other reason was that administrative expenses were modest and could be covered by margins in the investment returns over the interest rates credited. The contract was simple to understand and very competitive when compared to the tax-deferred annuities offered by other insurance carriers.

Larry Gerring remarks on the place of this product in the company's history: "A lot of companies sold these TDA's. In fact, we came into the business late that way. Well, we had one, but we really didn't market it very much. Then in the mid-1970's, we came out with a TDA product that was unique and really attractive, and we sold a bundle of them because we were way ahead of the competition on this. It's a great way of saving, and that product which was started at this time has become, maybe, our principal product now" *(Lawrence H. Gerring Interview, April 22, 1988)*.

In contrast to the modest NHWRA plans of the early years, this tax-deferred annuity and the other plans that the Retirement Association began to offer in the early 1970's were generous indeed. As if in anticipation of reader skepticism, the September 1973 *NHWRA Report* headed a column with the question, "Where's the Catch?"—and then went on to explain how the IRS approved the rationale for this program to help not-for-profit workers and thus made it possible.

Service continued to be the company keynote, although in this case the design of the tax-deferred annuity product created an investment risk for NHWRA. The rights of the participant to withdraw without penalty the funds accumulated at interest caused problems when economic circumstances led to a rise in the interest rates. The Retirement Association initially credited the same interest rate to all funds, and it was necessary to increase interest rates not only to attract new policyholders but also to retain existing funds. A rise in interest rates also caused a decline in the value of the bonds in which the funds had been invested.

Withdrawals, therefore, could lead to investment losses because of the reduced investment values. If periods of rising interest rates were balanced by periods of falling interest rates, the situation could be managed over time. Another solution adopted later by NHWRA was to segment the policyholders' existing funds and use different interest rates for the different segments of funds. A still more satisfactory solution came even later when the tax-deferred annuity product offered separate account funds such as a bond fund, stock fund, money market fund, or a composite bond/stock fund. The separate account funds operated on a unit value basis (like a mutual fund) in handling deposits and withdrawals.

In order to be competitive and attract new money, NHWRA offered a rate that reflected current conditions in the capital markets. If interest rates rose, the rate credited on new contracts and new contributions under existing contracts had to be credited to accumulations under old contracts since knowledgeable contract holders would be tempted to withdraw their accu-

172

mulated contributions and invest them as "new money" at current rates with another insurer. This could be done without penalty since the contract did not provide for a deduction from withdrawn funds.

In the interest of equity, the Retirement Association later divided the accounting of its TDA investment portfolio into various segments, or investment generations, according to when the funds were received. It also began crediting the various segments of the TDA contracts with a rate of interest that was reflective of the rate at which the monies were invested and reinvested. This was a version of the new money, or investment generation method of crediting investment returns.

In the autumn of 1973, the Retirement Association focused renewed attention on its board of trustees. At the request of President Flynn, A. Crawford Greene chaired a special committee, composed of William Aramony, Richard C. Brockway, Lewis D. Cole, C. Virgil Martin, and the president himself, that studied the composition of the board. Meeting in Chicago, they prepared a report which included recommendations of two kinds: trustee tenure and committee organization.

A January 1969 resolution had limited board service to not more than two successive three-year terms, and this restriction, some trustees believed, could jeopardize the Retirement Association's continuity of governance. Ten of the sixteen trustees whose terms were to expire in 1974 and 1975 would be ineligible for renomination. After considerable discussion, the board retained the structure but resolved to review the matter again the following spring.

In response to the committee's recommendations, the Retirement Association reactivated the executive committee, changed the name of the finance committee to the investment committee, and established a law committee to function beside the board's audit and insurance committees.

After January 1, 1974, NHWRA enjoyed the advantages of a change in the John Hancock reinsurance contract to an immediate participation guarantee basis. Actuarial and investment gains were more promptly reflected in the transfers to the

Earl T. Helsel served as a trustee and as a special
consultant to William J. Flynn from 1974 to 1986.

Retirement Association. Also, expenses under the reinsurance contract were reduced because NHWRA took over from the John Hancock some of the administrative functions and eliminated duplications, which led to faster handling of pension and other benefit claims.

The National Health & Welfare Retirement Association moved ahead with a changing executive team. Vice President and Actuary Donald S. Grubbs, who came in 1972, left after only two years at NHWRA to become chief actuary for the Internal Revenue Service. Mr. Flynn brought Howard H. Hennington from the Equitable to replace Mr. Grubbs as the Retirement Association's vice president and chief actuary.

Mr. Hennington, the son of a surgeon, graduated from the University of Rochester in 1935, spent a year in Germany studying mathematics at Göttingen University, and then returned to the United States for further graduate work at Brown University in preparation for teaching mathematics. He left the academic world to take a job at the Equitable Life Assurance Society, where he remained for 37 years and became a vice president. He also became a fellow of the Society of Actuaries, the American Pension Conference, and the International Actuarial Association.

In 1974, Earl T. Helsel, formerly a senior vice president of the Equitable, was named a special consultant to President Flynn. He served in that capacity without compensation until his death in 1986, bringing to the company the benefit of his rich experience as an executive in the insurance industry. With a contagious enthusiasm, whenever and wherever possible, he encouraged Retirement Association officers to move from the comfort zone of doing what comes easily to the excitement that comes with innovations.

Mr. Flynn speaks of Earl Helsel as one of the most important of the many individuals whom he has brought in over the years from the Equitable and elsewhere. "Earl Helsel worked here for 12 years. He was a retired senior vice president of the Equitable, and he came into the office two or three days a week. He was an expert in administration who had brought the

Equitable into the computer age. He gave me all this time to perfect our administration and our computers and refused to take so much as one penny in compensation" *(William J. Flynn Interview, April 19, 1988)*.

Another colleague from the Equitable to whom Mr. Flynn has expressed a great debt of gratitude is Harrison Givens. Both William Flynn and Dan McGill considered Mr. Givens one of the most brilliant actuaries and important senior officers of the Equitable. Mr. Flynn consulted with him on every aspect of the company's operations and was greatly influenced by his views. Mr. Flynn remembers Harrison Givens as one of the greatest supporters of Mutual of America from the beginning.

During 1974, the Retirement Association presented its third new, innovative plan which was soon established as an important part of the new National Retirement Program. It was the Flexible Annuity Plan, which, combined with the Cost of Living Plan and the Tax-Deferred Annuity Plan, made up NHWRA's National Retirement Program.

The Flexible Annuity Plan was created as a non-contributory defined contribution plan in which employer contributions were "directly related to each employee's salary."[8] It was suggested that member agencies contribute 10 percent of the worker's annual earnings. At retirement, the accumulated contributions could be used to provide either a fixed or variable annuity or a combination of the two. The Flexible Annuity Plan also offered disability annuity credits that provided for a continuing buildup of retirement benefits during a period of an employee's disability without additional employer contributions. The plan also provided a return to the beneficiary of the account balance as a pre-retirement death benefit.

With eligibility at age 25, one year's service, and full and immediate vesting, the Retirement Association could say: "Smaller organizations, particularly those with younger personnel, find the Flexible Annuity Plan an exceptional solution to their need for a modern and substantial plan of benefits."[9]

Individual participants would also find the Flexible Annuity Plan highly attractive. Even though they contributed their money to the plan, they could chose among investment options and retirement income alternatives. The worker with coverage could direct that his employer's contribution be placed in either the NHWRA general account, or the NHWRA pooled common stock account, or both. In addition, the participant could choose between fixed or variable income at retirement or opt for both.

The National Retirement Program proved popular from the start. The Cost of Living Plan, NHWRA's most comprehensive benefit package, was designed to "bring the benefit plans for health, social service and hospital employees firmly into line with the scope and level of coverage available to employees of industrial corporations."[10]

The NHWRA led the way by announcing this plan for its own workers in July 1973. The first client agency to enroll was the United Way of America, Alexandria, Virginia, on May 1, 1974. Then came United Fund of Mobile County, Alabama, which adopted the Cost of Living Plan on a community-wide basis, making it available to all the affiliated agencies of that area.

In May 1974, Mr. Kaufman, as chairman, convened the sixth annual meeting of the president's council in Washington, D.C. During the two-day conclave, the council heard committee reports by members who discussed the needs and wishes of participant employees engaged in hospital, health, and welfare work.

President Flynn presented a detailed report of company operations. Trustee William Aramony warned that adequate benefits were necessary to attract and retain competent personnel, and Vice President and Chief Actuary Hennington addressed alternatives for retirees to combat inflation. Board Chairman C. Virgil Martin stressed the importance of agency heads giving pre-retirement counseling to older workers. It was a most productive gathering.[11]

The 29th fiscal year, which the president described as a "year of significant growth and progress for NHWRA," came to a close on June 30, 1974.[12] Effective January 1, 1974, the Girl Scouts of the USA had adopted an NHWRA pension plan specifically designed for the 350 councils of that national organization. For over a year NHWRA had worked closely with the executives of Girl Scouts of the USA to formulate the provisions for the new National Girl Scout Council Retirement Plan.

Frances R. Hesselbein, national executive director of the Girl Scouts of the USA and now a member of the board of directors of Mutual of America, made these remarks about the long relationship between the two organizations: "There are almost 5,000 employees and 335 Girl Scouts Councils. Almost all of these councils are covered by Mutual of America. We're very proud to be able to provide not just the retirement plan by Mutual of America, but we also provide their other products, including the Tax-Deferred Annuity Plan. We are very pleased with a partnership that began in 1972. Twice a year we meet with the Mutual of America representatives and look at the retirement plan to be sure that it is as positive as it should be, and there have been many changes along the way" *(Frances R. Hesselbein Interview, March 17, 1988)*.

On Labor Day 1974, President Gerald Ford signed a pension reform bill that had been passed overwhelmingly by both houses of Congress. The new act was ERISA, the Employee Retirement Income Security Act. Congress had debated the issues involved in this landmark legislation for seven years before its final passage. The final law included not only high fiduciary standards for investment and protection of assets, but also required detailed disclosure and reporting requirements. Furthermore, the Act created the Pension Benefit Guaranty Corporation (PBGC) to guarantee benefits up to a maximum of $750 per month if a private pension fund became financially incapable of meeting its pension liabilities.

The PBGC plays a role in the insurance industry similar to that of the Federal Deposit Insurance Corporation (FDIC) in banking. The PBGC was to be financed by employer-paid premiums of one dollar per year per participant in defined benefit plans and governed by a board of directors comprised of the secretaries of commerce, labor, and the treasury.

NHWRA summarized the long and complicated ERISA document in an issue of the *NHWRA Report* that included this editorial comment about the pension reform bill:

> It demonstrates the government's serious concern for the employee who can be stranded with no retirement income despite long years of plan participation and, on the other hand, it recognizes that since the majority of private pension plans have successfully lived up to their promise of a pension, the regulations should not risk discouraging employer initiative to set up new plans or to improve existing ones.[13]

The Retirement Association warned its members that many of their plans would have to be revised to comply with the new law. At the same time, NHWRA could proudly point out that, in some respects, it was ahead of ERISA; for example, NHWRA had always fostered a policy of full and immediate vesting. The Retirement Association's Cost of Living Program and Flexible Annuity Plan would, with only minor adjustments, comply with the new law.

At the end of 1974, the Retirement Association initiated important changes in operations and personnel: it retained new outside legal counsel, engaged additional investment consultants, and elected Lewis D. Cole as its new chairman.

The firm of Satterlee & Warfield had done the early legal work for NHWRA. In the late 1940's, Homer Wickenden brought in Breed, Abbott & Morgan, who represented the Retirement Association with distinction for the next 25 years. By 1975, however, the Retirement Association turned to Rogers & Wells for advice. That firm has remained as counsel.

For ten years, Morgan Guaranty Trust served as NHWRA's investment advisor with impressive results, but the growing complexity and size of NHWRA's holdings made more diversified expertise seem prudent. As a result, NHWRA continued to retain Morgan Guaranty Trust for common stock investments, but engaged Scudder, Stevens & Clark, Ltd., for the bond portfolio.

C. Virgil Martin resigned as chairman of the board after two years in office. Mr. Martin firmly believed in the principle of rotation of board positions. He had served more than two consecutive three-year terms, and when his second term was over, he believed it was time to go. When he left the board, he accepted the presidency of the Chicago Association of Commerce and Industry. Lewis D. Cole, a trustee since 1968, succeeded him.

The years 1973 and 1974 were largely successful ones for NHWRA. Operating efficiencies had produced higher earnings and lower costs. The new insurance plans were being accepted for their effectiveness and innovative value to social service agencies and hospitals and to their individual participants. The membership grew significantly, and the Retirement Association brought in new people with promise and promoted others already there. Paul R. Zwilling, who later rose to senior vice president, joined the Retirement Association. Stephanie J. Kopp became an assistant vice president, and Daniel J. Robins moved up to the officer position of vice president and secretary.

Chapter Fifteen

ERISA AND STANDARDIZATION

"The major product developments took place around ERISA time, which was 1974. It was actually prior to 1974 when we designed what have now become our Cost of Living and our Flexible Annuity Plans. It was a combination of fortune, timing, and truly gutsy management. Our entire customer base had to cope with the new ERISA law, and the decision was to go out and tell the customers that by a stroke of the pen, they could adopt either our Cost of Living or our Flexible Annuity Plan and thus be in compliance with ERISA. With very little loss of business, we were able to standardize into these two molds probably 85 percent of our business. That had the benefit of our then being able to put a major effort into computerization of the two standard products, and it has allowed us to get where we are today with the computerization of the company.

"Accompanying this was the changeover to non-contributory plans, and the result was the creation of our tax-deferred annuity product, which today has about $1 billion in assets" *(Howard Lichtenstein Interview, March 15, 1988)*.

Richard Brockway enlisted Lewis D. Cole as a Retirement Association trustee for the reorganized, smaller board in 1968. Mr. Cole brought to NHWRA a combination of business knowledge and extensive volunteer community experience. A former president of Colorcraft Corporation, Mr. Cole was a vice president of the Council of Jewish Federations and Welfare Funds and had served as chairman of the Louisville United Jewish Campaign and the Louisville Conference of Jewish Organizations. He had also been chairman of the Louisville Community Chest and the Health and Welfare Council.

As a trustee, Mr. Cole was a member of the executive committee and was familiar with the problems of the Retirement Association in that capacity. When C. Virgil Martin resigned,

Lewis D. Cole
Chairman, 1974–1979

William Flynn and the other trustees considered him the obvious choice to be the sixth chairman of the governing board. He held this office for five years and has stated that one of the toughest challenges facing the Retirement Association when he took the job was "correcting or improving significantly communications between the company and its individual clients."[1]

The *NHWRA Report*, first distributed to member agencies in March 1973, was a good start. The next phase of the "Keeping Informed" program involved a series of six pamphlets entitled *A Closer Look*. They undertook the task of posing and answering questions that participants might ask about their pension plans. In addition, NHWRA distributed a steady flow of information about the significance of ERISA to the employer members.

The enactment of the Employee Retirement Income Security Act in 1974 snarled insurance companies, their lawyers, and their clients in what the Retirement Association termed "a maze of new responsibilities and a welter of paperwork."[2] A phrase popular within the industry, coined by a newspaper, was that the insurance world was suffering from "pension tension."

President Flynn advised all concerned to take heart, have patience, and remember the goal of formulating and maintaining a quality standard for the nation's private pension plans. He formed a task force composed of vice presidents Daniel J. Robins, law division; Howard H. Hennington, actuarial division; and Frank P. Montgomery, administration division. He directed them to develop guidelines to help members implement the new and often confusing requirements and gave them a team of technicians to prepare special kits for plan administrators to be available by late March 1975.

NHWRA also recommended that employers file an application for postponement of the ERISA fiduciary responsibility provisions of the Act that were to go into effect January 1, 1975. In addition, the Retirement Association filed a blanket postponement request on behalf of all its members. A genuine need existed for this emphatic response because the ERISA compliance requirements erected a legal structure of employee rights and employer responsibilities that had not existed before. A book of that era spelled out the cold facts: "The employer who sponsors a pension plan is answerable in a court of law for a great many actions and decisions in the whole pension area."[3]

Early in 1975, Mr. Flynn described NHWRA's concerted effort to help members meet ERISA requirements. As a special service to participants, there would be a series of meetings in some 60 cities across the country to discuss implications of the new law and its effect on Retirement Association plans.

The Retirement Association program combined altruism with practicality. In the first place, the bulletins, kits, and meetings reflected the company's commitment to go beyond the strictly business relationship of insurer and policyholder. Mr. Flynn was committed to helping each client member in the same spirit displayed by Messrs. Glover, Blanchard, and Brockway. At the same time, however, the impact of ERISA was a decidedly positive one for NHWRA. The legislation made it easier to achieve the goal of making the products more uniform because the new standard plans were in compliance with ERISA.

For some time, the Retirement Association had worked toward a standardized product line of non-contributory plans that culminated in the Cost of Living and Flexible Annuity Plans. As these plans were fully compatible with ERISA, they had immediate appeal to both agencies and their employees.[4] Then, too, non-contributory plans required coverage of all eligible employees, which was not the case with the earlier contributory programs.

The conversion of plans from a contributory to a non-contributory basis was one of the most important and dramatic moves made by Mr. Flynn and the Retirement Association in these years. Thomas Gilliam, a senior vice president in consulting services, now in New York but then working in Chicago, describes this crossroad: "We changed over 95 percent of our plans from contributory to non-contributory. Employees who once had to contribute three, four or five percent of their salary in order to enter the program would no longer be required to contribute anything. It was not mandatory, but the agencies supported us because it was the right approach. They believed in the company, and they knew we were doing it in their best interest and in the best interests of their employees. The clients asked, 'Is that the way to do it?' and we said, 'Believe me, that's the best way to do it'" *(Thomas Gilliam Interview, March 3, 1988)*.

William J. Flynn comments on the same period: "The whole world went to the standardized product because it was so far superior to anything that any one of them had, and the cost of doing it was so much lower. The quality of our administration, and the booklets, and the legal work on the contracts...were geared to this one thing. So...in the course of a few years, and it always took a voluntary decision on the other side, [nearly] every single plan of insurance in force here was changed to the new basis. That's how we furthered the growth of Mutual of America.

"We said very nicely, 'Either you do it this way [non-contributory] or you're really going to have to find someone else to do it.' They really had to come to grips with this matter and make a decision. The truth of the matter is that the large percentage of clients we serve have no other alternative except at additional expense. It is not easy to duplicate what we do except at an increase in the expense of operations" *(William J. Flynn Interview, April 19, 1988)*.

For three days in early April 1975, a company task force and seven regional teams of vice presidents and managers met at the home office for a training session in preparation for the nationwide meetings to help members cope with the new pension law. A total of 37 men and women took part. Regional meetings were announced for cities from Atlanta, Georgia, to Augusta, Maine; from Pittsburgh, Pennsylvania, to Phoenix, Arizona; with many beyond and between these locations.

Howard Hennington remembers these meetings well: "We had regional meetings in different parts of the country, and we

Howard H. Hennington joined NHWRA as vice
president and chief actuary in February 1974 and
became the Retirement Association's first executive
vice president in 1975.

invited our clients from that region to come. We then talked to them about the success of the company, what we were succeeding in doing to get the records cleaned up and in better order, and we described the benefits of these new standard plans. We wanted the clients to adopt some of these new and better plans. We were moving away from an era in which we had great varieties of plans for individual customers. They were small customers, and yet they had tailored plans. These meetings were part of a strong effort to try and reverse that trend and get them to adopt the standardized plans.

"These were nice opportunities, and they were the way we did business in those days. We would have a program at some hotel and talk to our client representatives in the morning. Following lunch at the hotel, we would continue the session, either in one large group or in smaller groups in the afternoon. They weren't terribly large groups. There might be 50 or 60 people. Dan Robins, Clem McCormack, or sometimes Frank Montgomery would be part of it.

"We usually had slides. Bill Flynn was a great one for slides. We'd have our slide projector, and our talk would be patterned around those slides. It was all carefully worked out. We might go off for a week. Sometimes it wasn't the same three people who continued the trip. Sometimes I would give Bill's talk; sometimes he would give mine.

"I liked to travel. So did Bill, and it was a great opportunity to see clients and talk to them and get acquainted with them and understand their views" *(Howard H. Hennington Interview, March 22, 1988)*.

The response to the challenge of ERISA was NHWRA's main effort at this time, but it did not preclude emphasis upon other benefits for social workers. Member agencies, for example, were urged to consider long-term disability coverage for their workers.

Helmut Frick, Middle Atlantic regional vice president, in "The Manager's Corner" section of *NHWRA Report* described the distinctive features of the Retirement Association's plan for this particular protection—an assured benefit that would not decrease as Social Security disability income rose.

187

Mr. Frick pointed out that many insurers offered "continuous offset" policies that provided lower private benefits in direct proportion to greater benefit income from the government. This had the result of preventing disabled workers from ever realizing an increase in their income. When Social Security disability benefits increased, the insurers reduced benefits. This was not the case with the NHWRA plan once a participating employee started receiving disability benefits.

William Flynn's leadership experience was much in evidence during this period as he was assembling more members of an effective team of talented people to operate NHWRA. Arthur Malocsay, formerly with the Equitable, joined the Retirement Association staff and, based on his prior experience, helped organize and put into operation a first-class, professional underwriting department. In addition, the president actively encouraged employees to continue their education, since that would increase their job advancement opportunities.

Stephanie Kopp has for years dealt with, among many other things, the personnel policies of the company. She remarked upon the efforts to upgrade qualifications and the serious need to do so: "Before the changes under Mr. Flynn, it was as if you had a group of social workers running a social agency, and that wasn't what we were supposed to be. We should have been professionals who knew the insurance business.

"Later on, Mr. Flynn announced that all of the people who were in the sales division would have to enroll in the chartered life underwriting course, the CLU. It gives a background in basic insurance principles. For the home office people, he had then announced that they should enroll in LOMA, which is a basic life insurance course for people not necessarily involved in selling. Now when I look back, I can see that those were the sorts of things that we didn't have before. No one had ever thought of doing them" *(Stephanie J. Kopp Interview, March 24, 1988)*.

During this time, Mr Flynn's talents caught the community's eye and brought him opportunities for wider service. He joined the not-for-profit board of United Student Aid Funds and became president of the Life Insurance Council of New York, an organization of life companies domiciled in New York, more popularly known by the acronym LICONY. The Retirement Association had earlier encountered some resistance when applying for membership with LICONY. Its admission was accepted after a strong, favorable case was presented by J. Henry Smith, chairman of the board and chief executive officer of the Equitable.

Two NHWRA trustees achieved special recognition in the spring of 1975. Amid the excitement of preparation for the regional meetings, Sister Evelyn Schneider and Dan M. McGill made news. Sister Schneider, executive director of St. Vincent's Hospital and Medical Center, became the first woman president of the Greater New York Hospital Association.[5] President Gerald Ford named Dr. McGill chairman of the seven-person advisory committee to the Pension Benefit Guaranty Corporation created under ERISA.[6]

In May 1975, the NHWRA investment committee chairmanship changed. Thomas W. Keesee, Jr., relinquished the post and resigned from the board because of other commitments. Mr. Keesee had joined the board before its 1968 reorganization and continued as a trustee with the smaller group selected at that time. He had earned degrees from Duke University and Harvard Law School and had years of experience in the world of finance and investment. When named to the board, he was serving as vice president of the Bessemer Securities Corporation, New York. He later became president of that firm. Leland S. Brown had appointed him to the finance committee, and, within two years, he attained the chairmanship of the group. He served with distinction.

Dolores J. Morrissey, a trustee since 1972, took his place, becoming the first woman in the company's history to head a standing committee of the board. She was a vice president at the Bowery Savings Bank and had an M.B.A. from New York University. Both Dolores Morrissey and Sister Evelyn Schneider were honored at a special dinner at the annual meeting in December 1977.

189

The investment committee, originally called the finance committee, had been formed in 1964 to supervise investment of certain dividend and interest funds withdrawn from the reinsurer, John Hancock Mutual Life. After a decade during which its total assets jumped from slightly over $7.5 million in 1965 to $228 million in 1975, the Retirement Association decided to strengthen its investment capacity.

This impressive record came from a combination of increasing annuity considerations (premium income) and wise investment decisions. Common stock separate account holdings, which began with the Flexi-Fund Plan and later expanded through the Cost of Living and Flexible Annuity Plans, accounted for much of this growth.

To augment the previous year's retention of Scudder, Stevens & Clark as consultant for debt securities of the general account portfolio, supplementing Morgan Guaranty Trust supervision of equity holdings, Mr. Flynn brought in the company's first full-time investment officer, Arthur C. Brett, Jr., as vice president. As the head of the newly established investment division, Mr. Brett was responsible for coordinating and monitoring the activities of NHWRA's investment advisors.

To make the new pension products succeed, NHWRA needed an up-to-date investment capacity. Dan McGill feels strongly that this has been a key ingredient for the company. "A good investment group is absolutely crucial, and that has been an interesting development because in the beginning they were using outside people. But as the amount of money that they were actually investing grew, it became feasible to have an internal staff. That was a very big decision, a crucial decision, because that could have messed things up very badly if Bill Flynn hadn't chosen the right people.

"The investment record has been good, and I think that part of the credit goes to the staff he has assembled. But it's partly due to the very fine committee that he has made up of professionals; it provides good guidance and is a check, at least, on the thinking of the investment staff" *(Dan M. McGill Interview, April 13, 1988)*.

That the investment performance has been an essential factor in NHWRA's success may be seen through two perspectives within a common historical background. Both participating employees and member agencies possessed a vital stake in the process.

Life insurance company managements and insurance regulators have traditionally accorded a high priority to preservation of principal. Specifically, for decades the companies were not permitted to invest in common stock equities. This situation posed no problems for the Retirement Association. However, the insurance industry wished to improve investment returns, and the Insurance Laws were liberalized to permit limited common stock investments in the general account.

From 1906 to 1951, life insurers domiciled in the state of New York could not invest in common stocks to any extent. In 1951, the law was changed to permit a company to invest up to 3 percent of general account assets in common stocks. The percentage was increased in 1957 to 5 percent of assets or 50 percent of surplus, and in 1969 these limits were doubled to 10 percent of assets or 100 percent of surplus. NHWRA took advantage of this opportunity to invest in common stocks.

However, on the experienced advice of his personal friend Grant Keehn, the retired vice chairman of the Equitable, Mr. Flynn, with board approval, decided that common stocks were not suitable investments for the general account which stood behind the insurance company's guarantees. This decision was made by the insurance committee because of the relatively small NHWRA surplus. This was one of the numerous times that Mr. Flynn was fortunate to have the benefit of Mr. Keehn's expert counsel.

In June 1975, Howard H. Hennington was named NHWRA's first executive vice president. In addition to his duties as chief actuary, Mr. Hennington was responsible for all technical areas of NHWRA activities, as well as for all operations in the absence of the president. Mr. Hennington enjoyed a close, effective relationship with the chief executive.

In September 1975, Lewis D. Cole chaired what would be his

The Retirement Association moved the
home office to 666 Fifth Avenue in 1976.

last meeting under the then existing board tenure rule, which would also remove Trustees Richard C. Brockway, Harold Hinderer, Gerard M. Peterson, and Frank C. Sutton, M.D. The board took the matter under advisement.

At the annual meeting of the members two months later, Mr. Cole was re-elected chairman. The others whose terms had expired were replaced. Mr. Brockway, after five years as president and chief executive officer and more than four years as vice chairman of the board, retired. William Flynn noted his predecessor had been one of NHWRA's most active trustees.

Chairman Cole praised Mr. Brockway for his leadership in fostering the development of employee benefit programs for those engaged in our country's voluntary social service organizations and hospitals. Years later, Lewis Cole added these thoughts: "Dick Brockway came at exactly the right time because he was an administrator. He knew the intricacies of government and of funding, and he knew how to give the Retirement Association a strong continuing basis" *(Lewis D. Cole Interview, April 29, 1988)*.

In early 1976, the Retirement Association discontinued the major medical product line since it had not been a success. A series of losses confirmed the president's conviction that it was not a proper product for NHWRA. William J. Flynn believes "a company should offer complete health insurance or none of it."[7]

One of the most exciting developments in 1976 was the move to new company headquarters. NHWRA had moved twice in the 1940's, twice in the 1950's, and then again in 1970. After only six years at 360 Park Avenue South, the Retirement Association began to explore other locations. The changes in the Park Avenue neighborhood where they were located made it difficult to attract and retain staff, and the general physical conditions of the offices did not meet the needs of the company.

Management retained realty consultants to find a better site further uptown and to obtain a tenant for the Retirement Association's present space occupied under a lease which would not expire until March 1990. That firm conducted a search and suggested space at 666 Fifth Avenue, where the entire fourth floor could be leased for 15 years at the same rate paid for 360 Park Avenue South, with options to expand to other floors.

George Chave, a former officer of the Equitable, also selflessly devoted much of his time and effort to studying all aspects of the move and then advising officers of the company during the transition to new quarters on Fifth Avenue. At Mr. Chave's insistence, his extensive work was performed without remuneration of any kind.

Despite relocation costs and other significant outlays involved with the move, NHWRA was still able to strengthen its financial position. Greater operating efficiencies permitted adding $4.2 million to contingency reserves within the next two years ending June 1978, as well as maintaining approximately the same ratio of liabilities to contingency reserves.

In the winter of 1976, the Retirement Association conducted the first in a series of three-day pre-retirement counseling seminars in Seattle, Washington. The program, "Preparation for Retirement through Education and Planning" (PREP), was designed to help workers 55 years and older plan for their retirement.

Joan Lane, currently senior field vice president in charge of sales for New York City North, was the staff person involved with this program. "The program was trying to guide people on how best to utilize their time at retirement, how to eat well, how to plan their finances. And it helped them with their questions about Social Security and their pensions. It was based on a schedule put out by the federal government. We pulled it all together and had slides and literature. The seminar took three days for each client" *(Joan M. Lane Interview, March 24, 1988)*.

That same winter, Mr. Kaufman presided at the two-day session of the president's council in New Orleans, where agency representatives convened for an extensive discussion of future policy objectives. A consensus emerged from the discussions regarding the need for a thorough study of benefit trends as well as the obligation for the NHWRA to market its benefit programs to new clients. The representatives present agreed to promote retirement income protection coverage for all health and welfare workers. Once again, the attendance, response, and enthusiasm confirmed the value of the president's council concept.

In June 1976, William J. Flynn presented a summary of his five-year presidency. He was fully justified in taking pride in the income increase from $41 to almost $72 million and an increase in assets from almost $62 million to more than $305 million during the five-year period from 1971 to 1976. Furthermore, the ratio of operating expenses as a percentage of total income from considerations had not increased. Mr. Flynn went beyond these impressive figures to urge new directions of effort, including increased market emphasis in fiscal 1977. President Flynn never forgot the Retirement Association's primary objective which he described as "quality service to our member organizations."[8]

At the same time, Dan McGill reported the first income expenditure from the Ralph Blanchard Memorial Fund. Accumulated income of $10,000 would be spent to fund a symposium and a book about Social Security and private pensions.

In July 1976, NHWRA made important changes in the NHWRA benefit programs. On July 1, member agencies began to enjoy increased interest rates on their pension plan payments as well as gains from lower annuity purchase rates. While disability coverage premiums went up, long-term disability income benefits also rose substantially. The improved investment earnings made this overwhelmingly favorable situation possible. William Flynn expressed the hope that NHWRA's improved interest rates would enable it to attract major clients. The trustees enthusiastically commended and supported his actions as the president and CEO in the overall direction of the Retirement Association.

Chapter Sixteen

CONVERSION
TO A LIFE COMPANY

"This organization has been unique through all of its various changes and aspects. For example, there have been and still are a handful of retirement associations, yet none of them but us has ever changed to a life insurance company" *(Howard H. Hennington Interview, April 7, 1988).*

Leland S. Brown retired in the winter of 1977. He had joined the board in 1954 and served as chairman from 1962 to 1972. Mr. Brown had held the chairmanship longer than any man in the Retirement Association's history and for 23 years had a vital part in major company decisions. Alexander J. Thomson, a Citibank vice president with pension experience, filled the vacancy on the board. Mr. Thomson, a graduate of the United States Military Academy, had been recommended to Mr. Brown by Citibank Chairman Walter Wriston.

In February 1977, the president reported that income from considerations for the last six months of 1976 was up 16.3 percent over the same period in 1975, and assets in December 1976 had reached almost $350 million. President Flynn attributed a large part of the increase in considerations to the Tax-Deferred Annuity Program. While member agencies could now look forward to a "stabilization in their employee benefit operations,"[1] life would continue to be hectic at the home office. Both the administrative services and actuarial divisions were under great pressure from ERISA and had to employ more people to keep on top of the increasing workload.

The actuarial function was especially critical from both an operational and a service standpoint. Actuarial cost calculations involve long-term assumptions over the lifetime of individuals as to expected mortality rates, interest rates, expense rates, salary scales, and termination of employment rates. These are matters of judgment and can be influenced by the desires of companies, unions, actuaries, accountants, and investment experts. Insurance company actuaries and independent consulting actuaries often have conflicting concepts of conservatism. Before ERISA, actuaries had greater freedom and discretion. Under ERISA, they had certain reporting and certifying functions that imposed fiduciary obligations on them. NHWRA not only needed qualified actuaries to provide calculations for clients under ERISA regulations but also to assist clients in various reporting requirements. To fill this need, NHWRA had begun to augment its professional actuarial staff.

In March 1977, the U.S. Department of Labor proposed regulations under ERISA covering format, content, reporting, and disclosure of Summary Plan Descriptions (SPD) required by ERISA. The Retirement Association informed its member agencies:

> The SPD is the basic document required by ERISA to inform the more than 40 million participants or beneficiaries receiving benefits of the terms of their plans. It includes a statement of ERISA rights. It must be written in such a way that the average participant in the plan can understand his rights and obligations under the plan. The SPD must describe the benefits provided by the plan, how to qualify for those benefits and how they may be lost, in a manner that will not confuse or mislead the participant.[2]

A particularly helpful service was a series of executive conferences held around the country to bring executive directors and trustees of member organizations together with NHWRA officers. They held top-level discussions of employee benefit programs and paid special attention to the Retirement Association's investment policy and the performance of its general account and pooled common stock funds.

Members were also advised of further delays at the U.S.

Department of Labor. Despite the March 15, 1977, regulations which were to have become final May 3, the government agency was forced to announce that action would be deferred to an unspecified date. NHWRA decided to continue issuing "Summary Plan Descriptions to member organizations with recently adopted retirement plans"[3] based on available guidelines. This was a valuable and much appreciated service and bespoke both courage and efficiency on NHWRA's part.

Meanwhile, the Retirement Association achieved new levels for the fiscal year ending June 30, 1977. Total income increased more than 20 percent over the previous year and exceeded $100 million for the first time. Much of this advance came from the addition of company field offices throughout the nation.

As set up originally in 1972, policyholder service at the home office was apportioned between staff persons concentrating on queries from members and participants within the seven distinct geographical regions. This division of labor improved office efficiency but was not sufficient to deal with the dimensions of the task. To serve small agencies with few employees better, the professional staff had to come closer to understanding the local needs.

Field representatives, always called consultants, were compensated on a salaried rather than commission basis. This practice, reflecting a conscious policy decision to go counter to insurance industry practice, was intended to avoid the hard-sell approach associated with many commercial life insurance agents and to assure that field representatives would devote as much time as might be needed to assist clients. This meant that the clients recognized that recommended products were based on need rather than on personal gain for the sales consultant. Howard Lichtenstein, as executive vice president in charge of consulting services, commented on the frequently examined issue of field service compensation: "The reason that we call our people consultants or assistant managers is to make a clear distinction between the commission motive, which exists for most insurance companies, and a broad approach to pension services which, hopefully, drives our field force.

"I would say that paying salary without commission has been very successful for us. I would also say that in our group pension area, most of the giant companies will be coming around to our method of operation" *(Howard Lichtenstein Interview, March 15, 1988)*.

Since 1973, the Philadelphia office, under Helmut Frick, served the Middle Atlantic Region (later East and West Atlantic) and was a model for future regional offices. Within two years, NHWRA established offices in Chicago, Illinois (North Central Region), and Providence, Rhode Island (New England Region). These were followed in 1977 with offices in Los Angeles, California (Southwestern Region), Dearborn, Michigan (East Central Region), and Dallas, Texas (South Central Region). In 1978, additional offices were located in San Francisco, California (Northwestern Region), Albany, New York (Upstate New York Region), Atlanta, Georgia (Southeastern Region), Pittsburgh, Pennsylvania (Central Region), and St. Louis, Missouri (West Central Region).[4] With the expansion of the field operations later, the regional offices were assigned city designations rather than territory designations.

The leaders involved in developing the regional branch office system included, in addition to Vice President Helmut Frick, Vice President John H. Harrigan in the North Central Region, and Vice President Thomas J. Baker in the Greater New York Region. At the regional vice presidential level were: Lawrence H. Gerring, Southwestern Region; Charles E. Jennerjahn, West Atlantic Region; Raymond J. Kraft, East Atlantic Region; Joe McElroy, South Central Region; and Robert A. Swanke, New England Region.

By 1985, Messrs. McElroy and Swanke remained in these regions while Mr. Gerring moved to Seattle, Washington, and John Harrigan and Charles Jennerjahn went to West Palm Beach, Florida. A number of these men had begun their NHWRA careers in field work. Messrs. Jennerjahn, McElroy, and Swanke came to NHWRA from the Equitable.

Gerard P. Buckley, who joined NHRWA in 1973, is an interesting example of a man who arrived at the company with considerable related experience. He says: "Before coming to Mutual, I worked for consulting actuaries and later I was the staff actuary and secretary of the Savings Associations Retirement Fund, which was a multi-employer retirement fund for the savings and loan industry. Then, from 1962 to 1965, I worked for an agency of the Mutual Life Insurance Company of New York. The management of the agency moved to North Atlantic Life and I went there. I was director of pension sales. Altogether this is my 38th year in the pension business" *(Gerard P. Buckley Interview, April 1, 1988)*. Mr. Buckley served in the capacity of regional manager and since the mid-1980's has headed the Boston office as vice president and currently as senior field vice president.

The field consultants received new tools to use in working with present and prospective members. The Retirement Association sent the chief executive officer of each constituent agency a number of *Benefit Planning Kits*. The original 1974 edition gave information about the Retirement Association's Cost of Living Program and a *Field Consulting Services Directory*. The 1977 edition provided pooled common stock separate account data and emphasized the concept of "One Stop Service."

This key marketing approach was described by Stephanie Kopp: "At one time we even had a set of slides and presentations going out to our clients to tell them about the company. We were calling this approach 'One Stop Service.' It was like a stop sign saying 'in one stop, we'll give you all of this.' Even our very current brochures do this, showing all the services we can give, how we can bill you, how we can invest your money, how we have communication and administrative services for you, and so on" *(Stephanie J. Kopp Interview, April 15, 1988)*.

At the 32nd annual meeting of the members in December 1977, Mr. Flynn reported on company activity. The cost of complying with ERISA regulations had risen every year since 1974 with a consequent decrease in both operating gain before dividends and net operating gain. In the spring of 1978, the attention of the Retirement Association's management was still focused on the complexities of ERISA compliance. NHWRA held 90 executive conferences nationwide to stress the advantage of member agencies securing IRS 401(a) qualified plan determination letters. Without such a determination, certain undesirable tax consequences might result with respect to the participants.

William Flynn also sought some political backing for his positions on ERISA. The president wrote United States Senators Jacob Javits and Harrison Williams in support of their proposed legislation to simplify implementation of ERISA. Mr. Flynn noted ERISA's "praiseworthy intentions" but warned that the "proposed merger was no assurance of relief for the small employer from the blizzard of regulations and paperwork" that had driven "up the cost of plan administration and thwarted plan improvements." Mr. Flynn also pointed out that "the law that set out to achieve safer pension plans threatens to foster safer pension plans for fewer people."[5]

President Flynn praised the idea of a commission to absorb the functions then spread among several government departments but declared this step would not assure relief for the small employer. Finally, Mr. Flynn commended the senators' suggestion that master pension plans could be sponsored by insurance companies and made available to several participating employers. He felt that "adoption of a master plan would essentially confine the employer's obligations to providing the contributions required to support the pension benefit while shifting to the insurer the full obligation of compliance with ERISA."[6]

June 30, 1978, signaled the start of "System '78." Mr. Flynn explained the phrase as "the working title of a very complex and arduous series of projects that culminated in a highly advanced billing and record maintenance system."[7] The president added that the improved administrative services would produce "a comprehensive monthly statement that details employers' financial data applicable to every active participant under every line of coverage."[8]

The Retirement Association believed that this new computer system would solve the remaining problems connected with the verification of records. To be on the safe side, management decided to increase the staff by 21, bringing NHWRA's employee total to an all-time high of 370. Mr. Flynn was called upon to make a great number of decisions concerning the revised computer system. "The real question is, how do you make a decision in an area where your knowledge is very weak? Well, I'll tell you. You've got to trust the individual who claims to know and whom you have put in charge. In the computer area, that's the most difficult thing because it's hard to determine whether a person really knows and whether he can own up if something goes wrong. I've had more difficulty in that area than in any other.

"So, the first thing is trust, but you find out in other ways, you see? While you may not know programming, there's a basic logic to what they are proposing to do, and you've got to be completely satisfied that you understand the logic and that you buy it" *(William J. Flynn Interview, April 19, 1988)*.

The Retirement Association also made several investment division staff changes. Arthur C. Brett, Jr., became the Retirement Association's first full-time investment officer. Vice President and Chief Investment Officer Joan M. Casson joined NHWRA in 1978 from Scudder, Stevens & Clark. She had handled the Retirement Association account there when that firm served as the Retirement Association's investment counsel. Before the end of the year, Mr. Brett resigned to take a position at the East River Savings Bank. Two additional vice presidents were added to the department: John L. Moore, Jr., equity holdings, and G. Douglas McCarter, fixed-income investments.

Lewis Cole, then chairman, remembers the role he played in hiring Joan Casson: "The board as a whole had been talking about bringing these investments in-house. One of the biggest projects was to operate them with the right kind of staff and investment experts. I said to Bill, 'I've been tremendously impressed with the woman from Scudder who shares the management of our account.' And Bill said, 'I'll be damned. We're having conversations with that very woman now!' That was Joan Casson, and she came over and now is in charge of all of our fixed-income investments" *(Lewis D. Cole Interview, April 29, 1988)*.

In order to improve the field organization, Mr. Flynn consulted with Joseph L. Beesley, formerly a senior vice president at the Equitable who had been its chief marketing officer. Mr. Beesley provided recommendations to Mr. Flynn on how best to establish a nationwide field operation within the framework of the Retirement Association's limited market place and in consideration of its fiscal constraints.

The major management changes and the emphasis upon improving the field service were designed to support the Retirement Association's conversion to a mutual life insurance company on December 31, 1978. ERISA had become law on Labor Day 1974, and major portions of this landmark pension legislation became effective on January 1, 1975. One section of critical concern to the Retirement Association provided that pension plan assets could be held only by a life insurance company or a trust.

In the fall of 1974, Vice President and Secretary Daniel Robins formally requested the U.S. Department of Labor, the federal department responsible for regulating that section of ERISA, for an exemption that would permit NHWRA to continue to hold plan assets. Mr. Robins argued that the Retirement Association acted, with respect to plan assets, in every way like an insurance company, and that the Retirement Association was itself a creature of insurance law and was regulated by a state insurance body. The U.S. Department of Labor agreed with these arguments and in early 1975 ruled that the Retirement Association was to be considered an insurance company for the purpose of holding pension plan assets. This was an important victory for the company. A contrary ruling would have been a catastrophe for an organization whose primary business was pensions.

Mr. Flynn was eager to open a New England regional office in Boston. Any company wishing to establish a New England regional headquarters will naturally think of Boston since it is not only the largest city in New England but also a major transportation hub. Several years earlier, the Retirement Association had actually had an office in the United Way headquarters in Boston. In response to a complaint by a local agent, however, Massachusetts Commissioner of Insurance Eugene Farnam had requested the Retirement Association to close that office and remove the personnel from Massachusetts.

That is why the first New England office was opened in Providence, where the Rhode Island Insurance Law allowed the Retirement Association to obtain a limited certificate of authority. Mr. Flynn was not satisfied; he was convinced that the right place for the New England office was Boston.

These two situations have one common thread. The Retirement Association, by 1975 a growing force in the pension field, was at a disadvantage because it was not an insurance company. Its structure was unknown outside of New York and presented a perplexing problem to several state insurance departments. Mr. Flynn found this situation to be unacceptable. He devoted several weeks in the spring of 1975 to the study of the problems of the Retirement Association and its subsidiary, the Health & Welfare Life Insurance Association (HWLIA).

During this time the president consulted with some of his key advisers, both on the staff and from the outside. Among them was George Johnson, who was living in California at the time. Mr. Johnson recalls: "Bill did not deal with all the technical details, and he shouldn't. That's not his role. His job is to get good people as competent advisors, listen to them, and if they make sense, to bag them.

"Bill and Dan McGill and Howard Hennington came out to talk to me about the changeover from an association. We sat on my back patio by the swimming pool. The main thing that we discussed was whether this was the thing to do, to have a mutual life company. Bill thought, and I think he was right, that you could sell this thing better as an insurance company.

"Being an insurance company would give them much more latitude and make it easier when they were dealing in other states, and it made more sense to have it all in one big company. You have much more prestige if you've got a $300 million asset company than if you have a $300 thousand company. This life company [HWLIA] never did have many assets.

"They were pretty well convinced that this was what they wanted, but they needed to talk over whether there was something they hadn't thought about. We hashed it over and couldn't figure out any strong negative reasons as to why we shouldn't go ahead" *(George E. Johnson Interview, May 13, 1988)*.

For this strategy meeting, the president had called together three men whose outstanding qualifications have contributed much to the development of the company over the years. Due to his creative mind and his breadth of knowledge and vision in the field of insurance, George Johnson was a powerful influence on the committee on long-range objectives of the 1960's and on the organization's affairs in general for decades.

Dan McGill's unique combination of academic and intellectual prowess in insurance matters, combined with years of practical experience in the decision making of corporate boardrooms, made him a key figure in the history of the company. His work as chairman of the Long Range Planning Committee established in 1983 has been a steady support and guide for directions that Mutual of America is taking today.

Howard Hennington's forceful grasp of the intricacies of insurance policy and programs grew from a lifetime of experience and responsibility in the field. His knowledge and acumen, especially in actuarial science, were a critical addition to the search for sensible decisions about where the organization should go.

In June 1975, Mr. Flynn presented a powerful and persuasive report. He demonstrated that HWLIA had never achieved success principally because it had not had the resources to be able to go out and license itself in all states. Here was the dilemma. It was too small to afford to become licensed rapidly in all states, but unless it could be licensed in substantially all states and do business nationally, it could not hope to grow. He also pointed out that because of its failure to become a viable company, HWLIA had a morale problem among its staff and was unable to offer incentives for a professional staff to come on board. The problems of the Retirement Association, he noted, were mainly akin to those described earlier. It was operating very much like an insurance company, but, lacking that formal insurance company structure, it suffered in important respects.

Mr. Flynn's recommendation was an interesting one. It was that the two companies be consolidated, and the subsidiary life insurance company be the surviving entity. That would immediately give the life insurance company the volume and staff it needed to become viable. Conversely, it would give the Retirement Association the legal status it needed to progress in the insurance industry.

In June 1975, the Retirement Association and HWLIA accepted the Flynn recommendation to consolidate the two companies. But even before he presented his arguments to management, Mr. Flynn had arranged an exploratory meeting with top officials of the New York State Insurance Department to discuss the question. The Retirement Association's representatives at this meeting, in addition to Trustee Dan McGill and senior officers Flynn, Hennington, and Robins, included one outside counsel, the Retirement Association's first examiner, I. Murray Krowitz. On his retirement as chief of the life bureau in September 1973, Mr. Krowitz had become associated with the law firm of Rogers & Wells.

The Insurance Department representatives were well acquainted with the problems Mr. Flynn would bring to the board's attention in June 1975. They did, however, introduce a new factor. They strongly believed that the surviving company should be a mutual company, one owned by the policyholders, rather than a stock company. HWLIA, the subsidiary company, was a stock company. The Retirement Association, although not an insurance company, was operated on a "mutual" principle. Its policyholders were its contributing members.

207

The leadership of the New York State Insurance Department believed it to be more logical to transfer the business from the subsidiary to the parent rather than from the parent to the subsidiary. Some way would have to be found to convert the parent into an insurance company.

There is a section in the New York Insurance Law which allows a fraternal benefit society to convert itself into a mutual life insurance company. There was no provision in the law which would allow a similar conversion for a Section 200 retirement system, but the Retirement Association had success in the past in bringing about changes in the New York law.

Rogers & Wells was asked to develop legislation for introduction in the New York State Legislature in 1977. Mr. Fioravante Perrotta, an experienced attorney of the firm, gained the support of State Senator John Dunne, who was then chairman of the Senate Insurance Committee, and Assemblyman Vincent Nicolosi, then chairman of the Assembly Insurance Committee. The legislation introduced and passed in 1977 permitted the conversion of a Section 200 corporation into an insurance company upon a vote by a majority of the members of the association and ratification by the board of trustees. The action required consent of the superintendent of insurance after a hearing to determine whether the conversion would be fair to the current members.

During 1976 and 1977, the attorneys worked on a charter and by-laws for the insurance company which would be the successor to the National Health & Welfare Retirement Association. They persuaded the Association of New York State Insurance Companies to support the legislation.

The legal formalities were, however, not the only matters of concern. Mr. Flynn set up a conversion task force, under the leadership of Frank Montgomery, to coordinate the administrative and computer changes which would be necessary before the Retirement Association could become a life insurance company. One matter that consumed a considerable amount of time was programming the computer so that the separate account could be operated according to Securities and

Exchange Commission (SEC) standards. As the separate account of a not-for-profit retirement association, it was considered exempt from registration under the various federal securities laws. Management of the Retirement Association was concerned that those exemptions might not carry over to the separate account of a life insurance company.

The administrative and computer work was, therefore, completed as though the separate account would eventually have to be registered. John Jacobus, vice president and associate general counsel of the Equitable, provided President Flynn with helpful advice with respect to SEC-registered products and the strategy that would have to be employed for registration.

Another matter which delayed the final action of conversion was the question of whether the Retirement Association's tax exemption would be continued after the conversion of the company to a life insurance company. The only way to settle this question in a manner that would satisfy the Insurance Department and give the voting members an informed choice was to ask the IRS. The response of the IRS was that simply changing the corporate form of the Retirement Association would not in itself alter the tax status as long as the company did not change its basic method of operation.

The board was now ready to move ahead to convert the Retirement Association into a mutual life insurance company. A notice and explanation were sent to all members for a hearing on October 4, 1978, before the New York State superintendent of insurance. The Retirement Association was represented by President Flynn, Chairman Cole, Executive Vice President Hennington, and Vice Presidents McCormack and Robins. The hearing determined that the conversion would be fair to present policyholders. The final legal steps of the conversion were now ready for implementation.

At their last meeting before the New York State Insurance Department hearing, the board had decided that the company name after the conversion would be the National Health & Welfare Mutual Life Insurance Association, Inc. Aesthetically, that name was not an improvement over the old name,

National Health & Welfare Retirement Association, but it was descriptive and conveyed the idea that the nature of the business of the Retirement Association would continue in the same way.

The change of name, while seeming slight now, came only after a considerable amount of discussion and seeking of opinions from many quarters. Howard Hennington was very much involved with this: "I lived through that period of our first name change because we couldn't still call ourselves the National Health & Welfare Retirement Association when we weren't one anymore. We had to get the 'life insurance' and either 'company' or 'association' in the name. And since it was mutual, we had to get the 'mutual' in there too. We even had consultants who suggested names to us.

"There was, at that time, a series of executive meetings around the country, and we had our presentations basically by Bill Flynn, Clem McCormack, and me. We had a dinner in the evening with some of our key customers, and in order to entertain them and to learn ourselves, we discussed the new name with them. Some of us had pet names we were advocating. We learned a lot from these discussions and, ultimately, we decided to maintain the position with our clients that we were not really going to change the nature of the basic business very much. So the new name, which is a terrifically long name, was much like the old name but more complicated. That was recognized all along. It was right for the short-term but wrong for the long-term because fairly soon after that we changed the name again" *(Howard H. Hennington Interview, April 7, 1988).*

A proxy statement was prepared and sent out. This statement was a disclosure document every bit as detailed as a proxy statement for a securities offering. The recipients were advised that each was entitled to one vote, which could be exercised in person or by proxy. Trustees Charles Devine, United Way of King County, Seattle, Washington, and Sister Mary Maurita Sengelaub, R.S.M., Sisters of Mercy, Detroit, Michigan, were named proxies along with NHWRA Vice President and Secretary Daniel J. Robins.

During this time, G. Robert Parker, formerly of the Equitable, joined the Retirement Association staff. He was named a vice president in December 1978. During his period of service, Mr. Parker organized and headed a specialized department within the administrative services division that was responsible for handling the myriad details associated with the accounts of former clients.

On December 15, 1978, a meeting, principally by proxy, was held at the offices of the Retirement Association. Irene Alpert, senior examiner of the New York State Insurance Department, was present as an inspector of elections to ascertain that all formalities had been observed. The membership voted to convert the Retirement Association into a mutual life insurance company. So did the board. On December 31, 1978, the National Health & Welfare Mutual Life Insurance Association, Inc., was born. The reason for choosing that date rather than January 1, 1979, is that life insurance companies file their annual statements on a calendar year basis, and management wanted to file an annual statement as a life insurance company for the calendar year 1978 because that would give them a head start on the major project of licensing the company in all states.

Employees arriving at the office on January 2, 1979, the first working day of the new year, saw little physical difference to indicate the change that had occurred over the holiday weekend. On the wall behind the reception desk, there had been five capital letters spelling out NHWRA. On that Tuesday, three letters spelled out NHW, but to some there was a subtle difference in the air. The difficult-to-explain, unclassifiable Retirement Association no longer existed. In its place was a strong, mature member of the New York State community of life insurers. Already one of the larger members of that community, it would grow in a few years to ninth largest, then eighth, then seventh. No wonder Mr. Flynn and his associates could feel a swell of pride when they came in that Tuesday and saw "NHW" on the wall.

There was still work to be done. The conversion was completed, but the consolidation had yet to be accomplished. NHW entered into a "transfer and assumption" reinsurance agreement with its subsidiary, Health & Welfare Life Insurance Association, Inc. Every policyholder of HWLIA had to consent to this agreement. Within a few months, all policyholders had consented. It remained merely for HWLIA to be liquidated by court order, the only way in which a life insurance company can completely cease operation. On July 1, 1979, NHW assumed substantially all of the business of its subsidiary company.

NHW was now in a position to do anything that a New York mutual life insurance company could do. It could write a full line of insurance products and hold pension plan assets by right. The next step was to solve the "doing business" problem. Since NHW was an insurance company, it could apply for a certificate of authority in the other 50 jurisdictions outside New York State. That process took almost seven years. By the fall of 1985, the company was legally qualified to write insurance in jurisdictions representing almost the entire population of the United States.

Chapter Seventeen
NEW FREEDOM THROUGH NHW

"I describe Bill Flynn in the following way. Rarely do you have a situation where you've got a natural leader, a person who has a sense of the future, who can commit to it...and work through the mire to get there, to get it done. And rarely do you have such a person in a position where he can really do it.

"You've got that in Flynn. He is one of those rare people who's a natural leader in a position of leadership" *(William Aramony Interview, May 9, 1988).*

The National Health & Welfare Mutual Life Insurance Association, Inc. (NHW) began its new existence with a fine record of financial growth. For the six months between June 30, 1978, the end of the fiscal year, and January 1, 1979, the start of the next combined calendar-fiscal period, total assets rose more than $52 million to a new high of more than $517 million. These figures, combined with the John Hancock reinsured reserves of almost $255 million, brought the grand total of the resources supporting the company's benefit obligations to over $772 million.[1]

This success came during a climate of general uncertainty for life insurance companies due to the changes in the economy that threatened the stability of the industry. Many experts were far from sanguine about the future. The president of Tillinghast, Nelson & Warren, Inc., a leading insurance consulting firm, wrote: "Most observers expect higher rates of inflation than have prevailed in the past; inflation must undermine the value of all long-term money promises such as life insurance policies provide."[2]

C. Paul Hulten
Chairman, 1979–1982

The havoc of inflation and weakness in the stock market affected many insurance companies' investment programs. NHW's Pooled Common Stock Account unit value was lower on January 1, 1979, than it had been six years before. Despite this situation, the company had big plans for the future and moved ahead with confidence.

The January-February 1979 edition of the *NHW Report* to member agency directors appeared with a new masthead and several pages of specific comments for the executives of member organizations. They read: "NHWRA has shed the confinements of its status as a retirement system to pursue broader horizons as a mutual insurance carrier."[3]

The report also noted that "numerous changes are in store as we effect the transition to a mutual insurance carrier." Social work leaders were assured, however, that "the major policies of NHWRA, those responsible for its identity and very considerable success, are certain to be preserved." The Retirement Association enumerated a number of practices that would be continued, declaring, "We are not dismantling NHWRA; we are enlarging its mission. The greater underwriting flexibility gained by the corporate conversion admits a bolder concept of employee benefit programs, further improving our capacity to serve the not-for-profit community."[4]

The first board meeting of 1979 brought a new role for Trustee C. Paul Hulten, a lifelong California resident and senior executive vice president of Western Bancorporation, Los Angeles. Mr. Hulten, "prominently known to human services professionals,"[5] had come to the NHWRA board in 1975, and this was his first meeting as chairman of the board. Because of the high esteem in which he was held by the other board members, he was chosen as chairman after only four years on the board.

Two other men merit special mention in connection with that board meeting: Dan M. McGill and Lisle C. Carter, Jr. Dr. McGill served on the board from 1972 to 1979 and was retained as a consultant to the board in 1979. Dr. Carter, an NHW trustee and attorney, now associated with the United

Way of America, had just received an appointment to the President's Commission on Pension Policy. To recognize this honor, William Flynn volunteered full NHW resources in support of Dr. Carter as a commission member.

Political change and economic uncertainty at the end of the decade were revamping the attitudes and opinions of people toward their personal and financial future. A survey sponsored by NHW entitled "American Attitudes Toward Pensions and Retirement" revealed opinions that the new mutual life insurance company believed were valuable for the not-for-profit community.

Inflation emerged as the most critical concern. Many respondents expressed an erosion of confidence in Social Security, although most voiced positive sentiments about employer-sponsored retirement plans. A good number favored employer-provided cost-of-living supplements to cope with the upward price spiral. However, 68 percent of those still working indicated a willingness to contribute toward their pension benefits if it meant larger and earlier retirement income. The company not only gave these findings careful study but also shared them with its membership.[6]

The conversion of the Retirement Association to a mutual life insurance company necessarily caused a number of internal changes, one concerning the election of trustees. In April 1979, the company decided to move the election process from December to April, beginning in 1981, because of the shift from a June 30 fiscal year to the calendar year basis required for all life insurance companies. One class of trustees would serve until April 1981, a second group until April 1982, and the remaining third of the board until April 1983. Also, partly influenced by the views of Mr. Flynn, the trustees would be more involved with the company's planning process.

From the time of his arrival, Mr. Flynn made the board and his relations with it a high priority. Stephanie Kopp, among whose jobs has been the secretary to the board for several years, says: "I remember that he always took great pains and detail with the board. He made a great effort to get to know personally all the members of this 24-person board. He also took a very keen interest in material sent to the board. He feels that his key responsibility as the top executive is of a planning nature, one of positioning the company by working with the board" *(Stephanie J. Kopp Interview, April 15, 1988).*

As a mutual life insurance company, NHW was in a better position to serve the health and welfare community because it was now able to obtain licensing in every state. In addition to having additional field offices, NHW could introduce a more diversified product line and expand administrative and communications services.

Mr. Flynn told member agency executives that the company was "...prepared to accommodate clients with more flexible underwriting policies and a broader range of provisions for strengthening and improving existing programs as necessary" and would increase its "present complement of coverages in order to offer plans conforming to the more specialized needs of many employers."[7]

In the summer of 1979, NHW decided to bid on a non-participating, guaranteed-interest group annuity contract for the Board of Pensions of the United Presbyterian Church in the United States of America. The transaction would have involved a single-sum payment on October 1, 1979, of between $80 million and $90 million, with specific NHW annual payments to the Board of Pensions over a 15- to 25-year period. This ambitious venture could be contemplated because of the new freedom of action enjoyed by NHW. The company now eagerly sought new accounts—particularly large ones—but before long, President Flynn began to feel that the size of the Presbyterian transaction might be out of proportion to the capacities of NHW at that time. The Presbyterian Church offer was, therefore, not vigorously pursued, and the case was awarded to another insurance company.

Once again, Dan McGill played a part: "Mutual was very, very competitive. They probably could have gotten that contract, but they would have had, first of all, to strain very hard on the interest rate because they were in competition with

Travelers and Aetna and John Hancock and others. It would have been quite a surplus strain, and Bill, I think to his great credit, with all the desire for the company to grow and to show the increase in assets, just felt that it was too great a risk to take. It would have been a big, big thing for them. It was too early for it. He would do it now, I'm almost sure" *(Dan M. McGill Interview, April 13, 1988).*

NHW experienced consistent growth during 1979. Furthermore, this record of expansion applied not only to clients but also to money. Assets under management had risen from $12 million in June 1964 to over $500 million in December 1978. Clearly, NHW's investment capacity had become more sophisticated. Not only had there been consistent and even dramatic growth in the volume of assets under in-house management, but the periodic investment reports were more analytical and informative.

In 1978, the company published its first separate *Investment Report* for distribution to all the clients. The first was for the fiscal year ending June 30, 1978, for NHWRA, and the second was for the period ending December 31, 1978, for NHW. The latter included "Overview of the Economy." This was an analysis of the nation's financial markets, a forecast of the future, and investment particulars for both the general account and the pooled common stock separate account of NHW.

At the end of 1979, Mr. Flynn had good news to share with member agencies. Despite double-digit inflation, the company kept operating costs within 9.4 percent of the prior year's figure. Nearly 1,100 new plans had been sold within the 12-month period, 600 of which were the popular Tax-Deferred Annuity and Voluntary Employee Contribution Plans.

Mr. Flynn confirmed that more than 3,500 hospitals and human service organizations had adopted the Tax-Deferred Annuity, which the president asserted was "the most liberal offered by any insurer. It is free of any administrative charges or penalties upon withdrawal—thus assuring participants that 100% of their contributions and interest earnings are credited to their accounts."[8]

The importance of public relations was recognized ever more clearly at NHW. Advertising and promotion were making NHW known throughout the community service and health field and could influence public opinion, shaping the climate in which NHW did business. There was an increase in the publicity department's budget from the modest $40,000 in 1971 to $187,000 in 1979. The allocation was $350,000 for 1980.

Paid advertisements in trade publications and an occasional piece in national newspapers like the *Wall Street Journal* were part of the promotional program. There was also more intensive outreach within the family of clients. In this connection, the president inaugurated *NHW Participant News* in January 1980, as a supplement to the 1979 "Benefit Statement" sent to each member agency employee.

A letter from Mr. Flynn on the front page of the first issue explained: "I believe it will prove informative and helpful whether you are a young householder new to the responsibilities of family life or a senior employee anticipating a rewarding retirement to cap a satisfying career."[9]

Since the 1960's, most large American corporations have had a board audit committee. The New York Stock Exchange made it mandatory for all domestic companies listed on the Exchange to have such a committee by June 30, 1978; NHWRA had done so as early as 1955. A board audit committee serves as an instrument "to protect trustees; stimulate management performance; and assist the independent auditor by providing an institutional safeguard that reinforces his independence."[10]

In early 1980, a series of personnel and organizational changes led by Mr. Flynn were designed to reinforce the company's capacities for the increasingly competitive struggle that lay ahead. On February 28, 1980, Allen J. Bruckheimer was appointed director of internal audit. With this appointment, Mr. Flynn created a facility that he had sought and that he felt was necessary to further the company's goals. Frank P. Montgomery and Clement R. McCormack became executive vice presidents. At this juncture, NHW had nearly 35 officers of vice presidential rank or higher.

William Kaufman was the chairman of the president's council from 1972 to 1981.

Richard F. Huegli served as chairman of the president's council from 1981 to 1982 and of the chairman's council from 1982 to 1985.

The next day, the trustees honored departing colleagues. Recently retired Trustees Lewis D. Cole, A. Crawford Greene, and Richard F. Huegli received farewell tributes for their conscientious service. Executive Vice President and Chief Actuary Howard H. Hennington, who planned to retire on March 31, 1980, was cited for his professional excellence, his wise counsel, and great loyalty.

That spring, the president reported that the insurance consulting firm of Milliman & Robertson, Inc., would again evaluate group insurance rates, dividends, and underwriting procedures as they had the previous year. Mr. Flynn indicated that the figures from January to March 1980 were not only impressive but counter to industry trends, which reflected stiff competition with other financial institutions for funds in a high interest environment. Premium income rose nearly 20 percent over the same period in 1979, and general account assets increased at a 34 percent annual rate.

In June 1980, the president's council met for the 12th time since its organization in 1969. The occasion was climaxed by a dinner at the Waldorf-Astoria with more than 75 guests, including New York City's Mayor Edward I. Koch and former New York Governor Malcolm Wilson. Board Chairman C. Paul Hulten presented the first NHW Distinguished Community Service Award to Sister Evelyn Schneider, president of St. Vincent's Hospital and Medical Center in New York City, for "her exceptional work on behalf of the underprivileged, and her delivery of meaningful health care services to those in need."[11]

Council business concluded with an announcement of a change of leadership as William Kaufman became chairman emeritus and Richard F. Huegli, executive vice president, United Community Services of Metropolitan Detroit, became chairman-elect of the council. Three new positions were also created within that council—that of "vice chairperson" and filled by member representatives Calvin E. Green, president, Tri-State United Way Services (New York City); Frances R.

Hesselbein, national executive director, Girl Scouts of the USA (New York City); and Woodrow Lee, administrator, Levering Hospital (Hannibal, Missouri).

In September 1980, President Flynn announced that the Catholic Archdiocese of New York had endorsed the offering of the company's Tax-Deferred Annuity Plan to some 18,000 employees affiliated with that religious body. NHW had also recently negotiated several other large cases. Mr. Flynn thanked council members, especially former Trustee William Aramony, the national executive of the United Way of America, for their help in placing the company before prospective clients throughout the health and welfare field for the purpose of enrolling them in benefit programs.

Ralph Waldo Emerson once wrote that the hard-beaten path to the door of achievement must be earned by quality products, superior to those of anybody else.[12] William Flynn and his predecessors gave contemporary meaning to this adage by developing retirement programs second to none.

Beginning with Ralph Blanchard's initial efforts and building through three and a half decades, NHW grew to serve thousands of not-for-profit social agencies. It attained this response by giving close, unflagging attention to the principle of providing the best possible retirement income protection to those men and women whose careers were spent in serving others.

It was fitting that William Flynn received the 1980 Brandeis University Distinguished Community Service Award in recognition of his respected leadership in the insurance industry and his "uncommon devotion to the wider community in the fields of health care, higher education and medical research."[13]

Chapter Eighteen

INDEPENDENCE
AND STEADY GROWTH

"Mr. Flynn has laid out what he wants for the company, and he is always thinking of what the next step should be, and he has kept his board informed. He's committed to what he does, and he's very motivated to succeed" *(Stephanie J. Kopp Interview, April 15, 1988).*

On December 31, 1980, the National Health & Welfare Mutual Life Insurance Association, Inc., drastically amended its reinsurance agreement with the John Hancock Company. In 1980, with the concurrence of the New York State Insurance Department, termination of the reinsurance contract was negotiated between NHW and the John Hancock. The reinsurance reserves with the John Hancock then amounted to about $245 million; additional funds with the John Hancock amounted to about $85 million. The termination value would be paid to NHW over a period matching the years over which the associated annuity payments would have been paid. No further premium payments would be made to the John Hancock. The contract would continue on a participating or dividend paying basis during the pay-out period.

This major transaction required an enabling amendment to the New York State Insurance Law. This amendment also made it clear that the recapturing insurer could take the present value of the payments as an admitted asset. With this change, the NHW assets as of December 31, 1980, would be, for the first time, more than $1 billion.

The company vigorously expanded its products to offer additional coverage for its clients. As of January 1, 1981, NHW offered Accidental Death and Dismemberment (AD&D) insurance to group policyholders. AD&D protection moved

William J. Flynn
Chairman, 1982–Present

the health and welfare company closer to a long-held goal of providing clients with benefit programs comparable to those available in the profit-making sector. In the first year, over 75 percent of the group life clients accepted this extra insurance.

Greater assets and wider protection necessarily meant augmenting the staff. Soon NHW needed additional home office space as well. President Flynn secured board approval on February 19, 1981, to rent an additional floor, the 10th floor at 666 Fifth Avenue. Speaking of this expansion, Paul Hulten, who was chairman of the board at the time says: "One of the best deals that we ever made was acquiring the additional space at 666 Fifth Avenue. We got a very good price. The real estate market in New York was really depressed then so we got in there at just the right time" *(C. Paul Hulten Interview, April 25, 1988).*

Mr. Flynn also announced plans to increase the number of field offices from 13 to 21 in response to intense competition that was being felt on several fronts, particularly from major insurance companies, independent actuarial consulting firms, and bank trust departments.

The first board meeting in 1981 was the last for six trustees, including Earl T. Helsel. The forthright Helsel, with 43 years of experience at the Equitable, had rendered NHW invaluable service, and his colleagues acknowledged his commitment to the affairs of the organization, his term as chairman of the insurance committee, and his years of day-to-day involvement. They praised the generous manner in which he had made available the benefit of his distinguished insurance background and executive talent. He had made an enduring contribution to the company's progress.

Among the new trustees elected two months later were: Dolores J. Morrissey, senior vice president, Bowery Savings Bank, and Frances R. Hesselbein, national executive director, Girl Scouts of the USA. Miss Morrissey had served as a trustee for six years ending in 1978 and was one of the few to rejoin the board after an absence. Mrs. Hesselbein moved on to the board from the president's council.

The president's council had first met January 16, 1969, and had held sessions about that time for a number of years. Later meetings were convened in June, and the council came together for an especially interesting assembly on June 17, 1981. Three persons stood out: William Kaufman, Richard Huegli, and William Aramony. After addresses by Dr. Robert J. Myers, chief actuary of the Social Security Administration, and Dr. Lisle C. Carter, Jr., president, University of the District of Columbia (both former Retirement Association trustees), the first three occupied center stage.

Mr. Kaufman, executive director of the Community Foundation of Mobile, Alabama, had retired from the council chairmanship the previous year. Mr. Huegli, executive vice president, United Community Services of Metropolitan Detroit, Michigan, had succeeded him in that role. Mr. Aramony, president, United Way of America, received NHW's Distinguished Community Service Award for 1981.

William Aramony, a leading professional in American social work, had also been a Retirement Association trustee and was later re-elected to the board. At the dinner during which he received the Distinguished Community Service Award, keynote speaker Frank E. Sullivan, president of Mutual Benefit Life Insurance Company, extolled Mr. Aramony by including him "among some of the best minds in America."[1]

Dan McGill commented upon William Aramony and his ongoing role with the company: "That relationship between United Way and Mutual of America has been unique, and it's invaluable. Bill Aramony just sparks with ideas and they're good ones. He has been quite a stimulant to the company. He and Bill Flynn operate at a very high level and for the good of the cause" *(Dan M. McGill Interview, April 13, 1988)*.

Congress passed the Economic Recovery Tax Act (ERTA) of 1981 in the summer of that year. One of the purposes of this legislation was to expand the opportunities of wage earners to establish individual retirement arrangements. It did this by permitting persons already participating in an employer-sponsored pension plan to establish an Individual Retirement

Annuity (IRA). Under the original provision in ERISA, only persons not participating in an employer pension plan could establish such an account. ERTA "excited attention, but also caused confusion for many employers and their employees."[2]

As had been the case with ERISA, this most recent legislative effort raised questions from NHW policyholders, including: "Are employee contributions to a retirement plan tax deductible?" and "How does the law affect Tax-Deferred Annuity (TDA) plans?" NHW prepared a review of the subject and sent it to all agency heads to alert them to the implications of the new law. The company recommended client consideration of the IRA, which could be offered as an additional savings plan to employees who were already eligible for a TDA Plan.[3]

William Flynn continued to maintain a two-way relationship with policyholders and, for the second time in eight years, asked them for answers to questions of his own. The company retained a consulting firm to conduct a survey of client attitudes. Once again, the response to all questions "was better than 80 percent positive." Mr. Flynn was especially gratified to learn that the area of greatest weakness in 1973, effective communications, was now NHW's strongest point. More than 90 percent agreed that field consultants were accessible when advice or assistance was needed.[4]

During the final quarter of 1981, two executives joined the NHW at the home office at 666 Fifth Avenue, and one departed. Dwight K. Bartlett, III, former chief actuary of the Social Security Administration, joined NHW in October as executive vice president and chief actuary. George M. Lingua came to the company at the same time from Citibank, where he had been a senior vice president in their investment management group. Mr. Lingua was responsible for NHW's field consulting services division. Clement R. McCormack retired as executive vice president and treasurer in December 1981 after sixteen years of service.[5] The trustees noted that his eminent career with NHW exhibited a special combination of sound business acumen with a faithful commitment to the health and human services community.

Mr. Bartlett succeeded Howard H. Hennington, who had retired and was elected a trustee. Before his Social Security Administration days, the new executive vice president had been senior vice president and chief actuary of the Monumental Life Insurance Company, Baltimore, Maryland. At the time he joined NHW, Mr. Bartlett was also vice president of the Society of Actuaries. Dwight Bartlett remembers his thoughts about taking the new job: "I did not know Howard Hennington, but Dan McGill said that the chief actuary had retired and that there was an opening here. So I came up and visited several times with Bill Flynn and was enormously impressed with him as well as with the mission of the company. It is a unique company with a strong social service flavor to it, and I think that gave it the same kind of appeal that drew me to the Social Security Administration" *(Dwight K. Bartlett, III, Interview, March 29, 1988).* The same year Mr. Bartlett joined NHW he received the Social Security Administration Commissioner's Citation for distinguished service to that agency.[6]

The twelve months of 1981 proved to be a time of steady expansion for NHW, both geographically and statistically. New field offices were opened in Akron, Ohio; Boston, Massachusetts; Denver, Colorado; Fort Lee, New Jersey; Hartford, Connecticut; Lake Success, New York; Milwaukee, Wisconsin; Seattle, Washington; and West Palm Beach, Florida. The 23 regional offices now employed 90 men and women spread over most of the metropolitan areas in the nation. They were needed to serve the thousands of clients who paid 1981 premiums of $163.3 million. Assets neared $1.3 billion.[7]

President Flynn sought to get the greatest benefit from these field offices by urging the NHW people on the scene to expand their local contacts and increase the client base. Also, he kept in continual contact with policyholders through successive issues of the *NHW Report* and maintained direct communication with individual insured workers through the more recently created *NHW Participant News.* The *NHW Report,* started in March 1973, was issued eleven times in 1982.

The first issue of *NHW Participant News* to appear in 1982 contained a personal message from Mr. Flynn:

> At this time of year people take a close look at the benefits employers provide. I hope NHW Participant News will help you in making wise decisions about the future...whether you are but recently started in a career or nearing that long-sought goal of retirement.[8]

NHW Participant News was distributed with benefit statements containing personalized information for the person named about benefits, the employee's contributions, if any, and other factors in the benefit picture.

The new legislation that expanded eligibility for IRA's was to become effective January 1, 1982, and the company moved quickly to place this information before its clients and their employees. Four successive issues of the *NHW Report* featured the new provision of the law and its applicability to the health and welfare organization family. The December 1981 issue announced the wider IRA availability, and the January 1982 issue noted the IRA relationship to NHW's Tax-Deferred Annuity (TDA) and Voluntary Employee Contribution Plan (VEC).

The March edition of the *NHW Report* focused upon the necessity for all Americans to do hard, advance retirement planning. This was necessary in order to cope with the devastating increase in the cost of living during the decade beginning June 1971. NHW posed such questions as: "Where is the retirement money coming from?" and "How much will you need in retirement?" It suggested methods for an individual to make these necessary calculations through the application of a "Do-It-Yourself" procedure offered in the report.[9]

In February 1982, William Flynn was appointed chairman of the board. This advancement represented more than a promotion; it marked the end of one era and the beginning of another. For the first time, the board chairman would be a salaried employee of the company rather than a volunteer.

Chairman Flynn was the eighth man to hold that title, but the first to combine it with two other designations, chief executive officer and president. The trustees resolved, as permitted in the By-Laws, that William Flynn could continue to be designated chief executive officer and also function as president until the 1982 annual meeting.

Chairman C. Paul Hulten left the board with the praise of his colleagues for his dedicated commitment to the affairs of NHW. Mr. Hulten, who had retired as senior executive vice president of Western Bancorporation in 1980, felt the time had come to sever his Retirement Association ties as well. He strongly believed the chairmanship should be vested in a person who was paid and employed on a full-time basis.

Paul Hulten remembers feeling strongly about this development: "I think that I was the driving force behind Bill Flynn's becoming chairman. It didn't seem to me that it was proper in the business environment of those days that a person who was considered to be an officer of the corporation could only give it part-time attention. So I was the force behind the change of making the chairman of the board a full-time, paid employee of the company.

"The other thing the directors always worried about was what if something happens to Bill Flynn? They went for years without having really dynamic leadership. I thought they should have the chairman of the board be the chief executive officer and also have an active president" *(C. Paul Hulten Interview, April 25, 1988).*

Despite the new executive titles held by William Flynn, he was still the man who had come to NHWRA from The Equitable Life Assurance Society in 1971. He had more experience, but he continued to emphasize those elements of his consistent business style that had marked his direction of the company from the beginning. It might be described as a blend of mission, vigor, and self-discipline. Mr. Flynn never forgot a company credo: "Commitment to the not-for-profit community—to make available for their employees the absolute best in benefit programs and all associated services."[10]

The new chairman found a special opportunity in the spring of 1982 for personal involvement in public affairs for the benefit of his company's future. This was through his connection with the New York State Executive Advisory Commission on Insurance Industry Regulatory Reform, known as the Heimann Commission. Governor Hugh L. Carey had appointed a group of nine men and one woman on November 17, 1981

> To identify and evaluate existing provisions of the New York State Insurance Law relating to investments, practices and permitted operations of New York insurance companies, and to recommend to the Governor necessary changes in such provisions and regulation policies consistent with protection of policyholders and the economic well-being of New York insurance companies and the State.[11]

One member of the commission was Laura D. Blackburne, an attorney who headed the Institute for Mediation and Conflict Resolution, Inc., in New York City. Ms. Blackburne later became a trustee of NHW.

In March 1982, Mr. Flynn presented a LICONY (Life Insurance Council of New York) "White Paper" to the Heimann Commission entitled "Economic Aspects of Life Insurance Operation in the State of New York." In this paper he stressed the need for new investment strategies and vehicles to permit life insurance companies "to manage, rather than merely react to, the sweeping changes forced on financial institutions over the last fifteen years as a result of inflation, high interest rates, and a high-risk environment."[12] John Heimann gave the governor his group's report two months later.[13]

William Flynn was then named by LICONY to serve on its special committee to monitor the future developments and legislative follow-through of the Heimann Commission recommendations. At stake were the careers of more than 169,000 men and women employed by the Empire State's insurance industry, whose life companies accounted for more than 60 percent of aggregate premiums in the United States. Also at stake was the viability of policyholder pensions and life insurance in a time of drastic inflation and shrinking dollars.

Before long the report brought legislative results. The complex, restrictive, detailed limitations on investments in the law were eliminated and replaced by general standards. The Insurance Law was amended to grant greater discretion to management to manage with new, carefully-defined guidelines designed to enforce prudence and protect the solvency of the company.

By September 1982, William Flynn and Dwight Bartlett were ready with details of the revised deferred annuity product used with the TDA, IRA, and Voluntary Employee Contribution (VEC) plans. They proposed a radical change in the company's funding of its TDA, VEC, and IRA products. Under the new system, participants would be able to keep their investment in the general account or select from several funds in a separate account, including a money market fund, a stock fund, a bond fund, and/or a composite fund with no guarantee of investment experience. Participants using these funds would bear the entire investment risk, along with the greater opportunity for investment income and capital gains or losses.

The proposal would permit employees to protect their retirement purchasing power and keep up with inflation. Second, it would enable NHW to cope with competition from banks already offering such options. Third, it would help protect NHW, and particularly its general account, from disintermediation. During periods of rising interest rates, disintermediation is likely to result in the loss of the difference between the guaranteed transfer value and the market value of funds being withdrawn.

Joan Casson, who has been the chief investment officer at the company for many years, comments on the realities of client investment: "The separate account effort includes the stock funds, the composite fund, the bond fund, and the money market fund. In addition to these four funds, we have a general account fund option. For the individual clients in this block of business, which is roughly one billion dollars now, the preference is overwhelmingly to put their money in the general account fixed rate fund.

"Our clients, except for some of the larger, more sophisticated pension clients, just seem to favor having more money in the fixed income than in the stock side. It reflects the underlying conservative nature of the participants, the individuals in this business" *(Joan M. Casson Interview, May 18, 1988).*

Throughout the remainder of 1982 and continuing into the next year, NHW sponsored a number of meetings with participants to explain the potential of tax-deferred annuities and their relationship to the individual retirement accounts, which were being highly publicized by the media throughout the nation. One such successful meeting was organized by Regional Vice President Gertrude Wilkinson, Milwaukee, Wisconsin. She directed the presentation of a useful session for the employees of St. Alexius Hospital in Bismarck, North Dakota.

In the fourth quarter of 1982, NHW celebrated its 37th anniversary and was gratified by a report of favorable statistics for operations up to that time. Total assets had exceeded $1.6 billion by year end.

Three additional field offices had been opened during the year, giving the National Health & Welfare Mutual Life Insurance Association physical presence in White Plains, New York; Richmond, Virginia; and Washington, D.C. This brought the total number of field offices to 26.

The year also brought a sad event, Milton H. Glover died in October 1982. The trustees applauded the dedication, spirit, and entrepreneurial vision of this man who had served successively as president, vice chairman, and chairman. He was one of the pioneers among business executives, who nearly four decades previously had foreseen the need for a special organization to provide pension and ancillary benefits to employees of the not-for-profit health and welfare community.

Chapter Nineteen
FOUR DECADES AND ONWARD

"It's perfectly clear, from the success of this company that our strong commitment to social service does not conflict with sound financial principles. As the company has grown in size and capacity, it has become possible for us to become active and supportive, in a financial as well as a human sense, in many kinds of activity" *(Dwight K. Bartlett, III, Interview, March 29, 1988).*

The years 1983 to 1985 were the culmination of the first four decades of the company's existence. The energies geared toward expansion that had been building from the moment that Mr. Flynn joined the company were finding outlets in many important areas.

One of the most significant efforts of these years was the work done by the Long Range Planning Committee established in 1983. Its impact on the thinking and planning of management helped the company to engage the future. The close of 1983 ushered in a new era when NHW became Mutual of America.

A major reorganization of the company, as great or greater in consequence than the one completed in the past two decades, was under way. The story of this new enterprise is beyond the scope of this history, but its roots lie in the period now being discussed. The trends of this time toward expanded markets, increasingly improved services and administration, continual upgrading and selection of talented personnel, and new directions in policy and product will be in evidence for years to come. Mutual of America has created a momentum of growth that retains the humanitarian origins and purposes of its founding, and this clearly will not change.

Dwight K. Bartlett, III
President, 1984–1989

As the 40th anniversary approached, the client base still continued to grow. From the original 400 member agencies in 1945, the number had risen to nearly 8,000 in 1985. From the original loans of $25,000 in 1945, assets had soared to almost $2.9 billion in 1985. From the handful of workers in 1945, some of them sitting on boxes for lack of chairs, the payroll had grown to nearly 600 people four decades later.

In February 1984, Dwight K. Bartlett, III, became the fifth president of the organization that had begun with the earnest, but unpoetic name of the National Health & Welfare Retirement Association. Now it is Mutual of America, a more modern and arresting title, and yet the principal responsibility of providing pension, retirement plans, and insurance for the not-for-profit sector remains constant. Mr. Bartlett's task has been to share in the formulation of policy and direct the operations of an increasingly complex and varied business venture.

William Flynn, working with the board of directors, has provided the leadership that has ultimately made the dramatic success of Mutual of America possible. His dedication and decisive approach to challenges has given the corporation a positive attitude that is constantly strengthened by its achievements.

Mr. Flynn and his staff have expanded effective insurance coverage to many thousands of individuals in the past two decades. His principles of conducting business and dealing with people have been creative, equitable, and humane. In these crucial factors he has shown himself to be a splendid successor to Ralph H. Blanchard, a great figure in the company's history.

Nevertheless, beyond the accomplishments of any individual, these final years of the first four decades witnessed an organization that was coming together and achieving a sense of purpose and the conviction that problems can be solved and challenges overcome. The spirit of professionalism and dedication that had been so carefully nurtured over the previous twenty years was making the work of Mutual of America both effective and enjoyable.

In 1983, the American Cancer Society, "...the nation's largest voluntary agency,...fighting what is clearly America's most devastating health problem,"[1] became a major policyholder. Lane W. Adams, then its executive vice president and chief executive officer, joined the company's board of trustees.

Mr. Adams, previously a banker in Salt Lake City, Utah, was also a trustee of United Way International. Through this affiliation he got to know William Aramony, now president of the United Way of America and United Way International, who introduced him to William Flynn.

As Lane Adams remembers it: "Bill Aramony was very enthusiastic and supportive about making the change and felt it was good for the not-for-profit sector. We represented a major segment of that, and it would be good for us and good for the institution; all would benefit. Mr. Flynn and his people worked out the arrangements in order to attract our business and make the agreement palatable.

"I have a vivid recollection of the impact of Bill Flynn's personality at our first gathering. He was very impressive and different from what might have been considered the usual insurance executive. He came on very positively, very upbeat, and he proved himself to be a 'helluva' salesman. Along with his Irish wit and charm, he had an amazingly impressive knowledge of the facts" *(Lane W. Adams Interview, March 16, 1988).*

Mr. Flynn demonstrated good reasons for the American Cancer Society to adopt an NHW retirement program. The health organization, with 2,300 employees, was not satisfied with its existing coverage. The National Health & Welfare Mutual Life Insurance Association, Inc., was able to provide a number of financial alternatives. The company was able to make available competitive products for the same number of dollars that the American Cancer Society was allocating to its present plan. Furthermore, NHW was able to "offer them a bundling of the required services together with a nationwide field network to work with their local divisions, at a cost of approximately one-half of what they were accustomed to spending."[2]

Other considerations played a part, too. When the American Cancer Society amended its plan and changed carriers, it opted for a broad-based retirement system committed to the not-for-profit community. This new system was, according to a communication from Dwight Bartlett and Howard Lichtenstein, resolutely oriented toward service. They told Lane Adams that NHW was exceptional in providing every service that is necessary for the successful operation of a modern retirement program.

Howard Lichtenstein describes this significant time: "I was involved in bringing the American Cancer Society into Mutual of America. That acquisition was, in my opinion, one of the major turning points for this organization, and the effort was undertaken primarily by Bill Flynn and myself. He had the very strong sales and personal contacts, and I was a key architect of the plan design.

"We presented a creative solution to a problem they had. The American Cancer Society management and board were so impressed that they then offered us a look at their pension plan to see if there were ways of redesigning it" *(Howard Lichtenstein Interview, March 15, 1988)*. The head of the American Cancer Society then undertook the transfer of more than $20 million to NHW and declared with enthusiasm, "ACS employees are more secure today and look forward to a more attractive retirement tomorrow because of William Flynn's enlightened and resourceful leadership."[3]

After this impressive start for 1983, the trustees endorsed the chairman's latest outline of priorities. They recognized the tremendous growth of NHW and the increased responsibilities of the board members by initiating a policy of compensation for those who did work for the company but who were not on a salary basis of remuneration. An extra-budgetary appropriation for the management information systems division enabled that department to acquire hardware, software, and additional programmers to support the greatly increased separate account business.

The Retirement Association had established its first separate account in 1967. This account was to be used as a depository for some employer contributions in connection with the Flexi-Fund Program. The company was faced with the question of whether to register the separate account under the various federal Securities Laws. The opinion of outside counsel was immediately sought. The advice that the company followed was that securities issued by the not-for-profit Retirement Association were exempt from the 1933 Act registration and that the Retirement Association itself was exempt from the 1940 Act registration.

When the Retirement Association management was working toward the conversion of the company to a mutual life insurance company, it confronted the question again. There was a real concern that the successor company, as a life insurance company, could no longer take advantage of the 1933 Act and 1940 Act exemptive provisions.

This time, after exhaustive consideration, it was decided again that registration of that separate account (Pooled Common Stock Separate Account No. 1) was not necessary. Separate accounts need not be registered under the Securities Laws if they are used exclusively for the funding of qualified pension profit sharing and savings plans. To assure the correctness of its decision, the Retirement Association in 1976 and 1977 made a strong effort to obtain from each employer making use of that separate account a copy of its letter from the IRS, determining that its plan met the requirements of Section 401(a) of the Internal Revenue Code of 1954.

On June 4, 1984, the company established a second separate account. This account was to be used, not for pension products, but for basically individual products such as IRA's and Section 403(b) tax-deferred annuities. It was a four-part account consisting of a stock, a bond, a money market, and a composite fund. Such a separate account for individual products had to be registered under the federal acts. On January 1, 1985, the new account (Mutual of America Separate Account No. 2) commenced operations with respect to the public. The company registered as an investment company under the 1940 Act; it also registered as a broker dealer and as an investment advisor.

The company had not only pioneered pensions for health and welfare employees but had also consistently enriched the scope of such plans through careful management practices and skilled investment capacity. Dwight Bartlett highlighted these qualities with a study of the company surplus level policy which he completed early in September 1983.

Mr. Bartlett observed that NHW had maintained a surplus, or statutory net worth, in the range of 3 to 6 percent of general account assets since September 25, 1978. He confirmed 3 percent as a minimum surplus ratio and declared a higher maximum figure might become appropriate, subject to the statutory limit of 10 percent, which would exclude the Mandatory Security Valuation Reserve. Mr. Bartlett wanted to be certain the company accumulated sufficient reserves to remain solvent in the face of any changes in the relation between assets and liabilities that could be caused by inflation's bringing higher interest rates and lower security values.

During 1983, management responded to a new external challenge. The 1982 Tax Equity and Fiscal Responsibility Act (TEFRA) had inadvertently hurt many NHW clients because of a rule that had been intended to prevent unreasonable concentration of employee benefits in favor of top officers to the detriment of workers who were paid less.

The Act's definition of "key employee" did not take into consideration the special circumstances of the not-for-profit agencies. In them, any employee who functioned as an officer could be termed "key," although he might be paid less in comparison to his or her counterpart in the business sector. The result of this situation was that client agencies were finding that their plans were deemed "top heavy" under TEFRA rules. NHW decided to seek a class exemption from these requirements for not-for-profit health and welfare employers and retained former Trustee Lisle C. Carter, Jr., a Washington, D.C., attorney with the firm of Verner, Liipfert, Bernhard & McPherson as counsel for this purpose. The Treasury Department officials were receptive to efforts by NHW, the United Way of America, and outside counsel to secure the exemption for pension contributions made by or for key employees of not-for-profit, tax-exempt organizations, and by the following year substantial relief had been obtained for those unreasonably impacted by the rules.

On January 1, 1984, National Health & Welfare Mutual Life Insurance Association became Mutual of America Life Insurance Company. The change had been considered for some time. Two factors were involved. The first was the need for a more manageable company name, and the second had to do with the meaning of the name. The various letter designations used in the decades since the National Health & Welfare Retirement Association's founding in 1945 seemed cumbersome. The 1978 conversion of the company into a life insurance company compounded the problem with an even longer name, National Health & Welfare Mutual Life Insurance Association. "Mutual of America" clearly projected a more contemporary image with which clients could easily identify.[4]

In addition, this name resolved the confusion that had been caused by the previous designations and had come up repeatedly over the years. No longer would people wonder if "National" connoted a government relationship, nor would they speculate on the medical ramifications of "Health." The change took place January 1, 1984, with assurances sent to each client that all guarantees, commitments, products, and services of NHW would continue in full force and effect under the new name. The name change would have no effect on employers' plans or on plan participants or their beneficiaries.[5]

The trustees of Mutual of America were renamed directors in September 1984. Since 1945, board members had been known as trustees, a designation considered apt for Ralph Blanchard's National Health & Welfare Retirement Association. With the great expansion of the business, however, and the change of the corporate name to Mutual of America, the original term became less accurate. "Director" conformed to contemporary life insurance industry practice.

In 1985, the company took action to restore flexibility to director tenure. This freedom had been somewhat restricted since the 1968 reorganization of the board when it had been decided that no member could serve more than two consecutive terms of three years each, and that no director could be elected after reaching age 70.

These confining limitations were self-imposed, not required by law, nor contained in the Charter or By-Laws. What had seemed to be a good idea 17 years before had become an impediment to wise and experienced board guidance. Company assets had jumped from less than $10 million in 1967 to almost $3 billion in 1985, and the demands upon directors had multiplied as well. The board voted to eliminate any limitations on tenure.

A. Crawford Greene, who has been, except for a period in 1980 and 1981, a board member since 1968, remarks: "It just didn't make any sense to have a one three-year term or two three-year terms and then rotate off the board because, with the complexity of the operation, it really takes quite a while before you know what's going on" *(A. Crawford Greene Interview, April 26, 1988).*

Mutual of America acted upon the conviction that "no business strategy is good forever."[6] It had always been the chairman's policy to set objectives annually and then strive to meet them. However, Mr. Flynn was flexible and willing to qualify goals and methods when the situation required it, for he believed that "growth in and of itself is not enough. We intend to continue to utilize the strength and experience that come with growth to serve our clients."[7]

The need to discipline growth and direct it to the best advantage had brought the Long Range Planning Committee into existence in 1983, when the chairman's recommendation to reestablish it met with enthusiastic approval. Dan M. McGill, chairman of the Insurance Department of the Wharton School of the University of Pennsylvania, was named head of the group. Serving with him were former Trustee Earl T. Helsel and current board members William Aramony, Eugene J. Callan, Howard H. Hennington, and William J. Flynn. James

J. Needham, a former commissioner of the Securities and Exchange Commission and the chairman and chief executive officer of the New York Stock Exchange, served on the committee until his resignation from the NHW board in November 1983.

The committee's task was to examine the company's products, services, markets to be served, and the related possibilities for expansion and/or change, and to develop a set of recommendations to guide the company's business strategy over the next five to ten years.

In April 1984, Dr. McGill presented the recommendations. The committee had been created in a climate of a financial services industry revolution influenced by technological advances, inflation, increased consumer sophistication, and deregulation of financial institutions. The report contained a note of urgency and stressed that Mutual of America could not ignore these changes and the great challenges they placed in the path to an expanding future. The company was searching for the best ways to do what E. James Morton, the John Hancock president, could foresee as the future of the insurance industry: "filling niches, such as target markets or specialty products, or diversifying to offer clients more services than they have in the past."[8]

Despite the risk of new ventures, greater danger could come from doing nothing. The company had to expand its markets and products. It could benefit its contract holders through improved pricing and better service attributed to the economies of scale and by the convenience of offering (either directly or through related organizations) the products and financial services that its current and prospective customers need and want, thereby saving clients from having to seek several different suppliers for such services. The committee concluded that Mutual of America should, for the present, confine its operations to the not-for-profit field. The long-term interests of Mutual of America would best be served by the company's continuing its close identification with the not-for-profit field, both symbolically and substantively.

The company had to consider making changes in the corporate charter to permit service to extended markets. Howard Lichtenstein studied the question and concluded that the revised charter would enhance market potential by more than 660,000 institutions. In 1982, there were 1.2 million not-for-profit institutions in the United States, and 6.5 million people were employed in the philanthropic sector. Philanthropic organizations, overwhelmingly, were employers of small numbers of people: 96 percent of all organizations in that sector employed fewer than 100 people. In fact, 97 percent of the company's clients were employers of under 100 people.[9]

The first phase of implementation was completed in 1984 when the corporate charter was amended to enable Mutual of America to provide its products and services to an expanded market of federal, state, and local governmental employees, not-for-profit educational organizations at all levels, unions engaged in the field of social welfare, religious organizations, and others generally classed as social welfare organizations by the Internal Revenue Code and Income Tax Regulations. The amended charter also permitted the company to offer additional insurance and related services.

In this vein, a general description of the company was presented in a special brochure published in September 1984, entitled *A Company Dedicated to Serving the Not-for-Profit Community*. The booklet introduced Mutual of America to prospective clients, emphasizing the company's "one unified program," with "true portability" of benefits. It cited the "integrated intelligence" of board members intimately associated with client agencies, and the "expert insight" gained from the involvement of such national industry figures as Dan M. McGill, chairman of the Insurance Department of the Wharton School; Robert J. Myers, former deputy commissioner, Social Security Administration; and Donald S. Grubbs, former director of the actuarial division of the Internal Revenue Service.

Also, following the recommendations of the Long Range Planning Committee, Mutual of America sought professional advice on how best to continue preparing for the future. The company retained a consulting actuarial firm to determine if Mutual of America should enter the property-casualty business. Its June 1985 report recommended that the company not enter that business at that time, and the advice was heeded.

Implementation of the charter changes dealing with market expansion began in 1985. Director William MacDonald had this to say: "This company is really dedicated to service and to having a good product, a product better than anyone else's, priced better than anyone else's. Now, I think that it is imperative, as we move into other areas, that we protect our not-for-profit status because it is an advantage, no question about it. As we get into other things and have subsidiaries that are going to be for profit, we have to be careful. Of course, we have had the kind of legal talent that has enabled us to take it step by step and protect that not-for-profit status" *(William E. MacDonald Interview, April 21, 1988).*

Mutual of America showed its support for the not-for-profit organizations in other ways. In 1983, guidelines were established for a company matching gifts program, whereby it agreed, within certain limits, to match employee charitable contributions, and by June of that year the company had extended its program of corporate philanthropy by making a gift to the Girl Scouts of the USA for its Edith Macy Conference Center in Briarcliff Manor, New York. A newly-formed contributions committee composed of William E. MacDonald, chairman, William Aramony, and Eugene Callan began to formulate a policy for future corporate giving.

In confirmation of its long-standing commitment to the not-for-profit field, the company voted a contribution to the United States Holocaust Memorial Council in support of a Washington, D.C.,conference to be held in September 1984 to recognize the righteous people who helped nearly one million Jews escape the atrocities of the Holocaust. William Flynn chaired the conference, and Trustee Sister Mary Maurita Sengelaub, R.S.M., participated and later reported to the board.

The company had established an award for community service in 1980. The 1983 Distinguished Community Service Award was presented to Robert J. Myers on May 19, 1983, during a dinner at the Waldorf-Astoria Hotel. Hundreds of government and human service organization leaders were present to honor the former chief actuary of the Social Security Administration. William Flynn praised Dr. Myers for his significant commitment to Social Security and his contributions to numerous voluntary institutions on whose boards he had served.[10]

The following month, the company paid tribute to Trustee George A. (Gus) Shea, executive vice president of United Way of America. Since the reorganization of the board 15 years earlier, some 55 men and women had been elected to it. Most served six years, a few, including A. Crawford Greene, Richard F. Huegli, and Lewis D. Cole, remained active for a longer period. Others, such as Wilmer A. Jenkins, Thomas C. Edwards, and Flaxie M. Pinkett, experienced short tenure. Although Gus Shea, who died in May 1983, was one of these, his surviving colleagues praised his thoughtful counsel, which had contributed so significantly to the effectiveness of the board.

On February 14, 1984, the company paid tribute to Grace G. Blanchard for her indomitable spirit and continued support of Mutual of America. The noble work of her late husband, Ralph Blanchard, universally recognized as the founder of Mutual of America, was also praised.

In early 1984, Mutual of America chose a new president and promoted four officers. Stephanie J. Kopp was appointed senior vice president and secretary-elect; Howard Lichtenstein became senior vice president with responsibility for the consulting services division; Manfred Altstadt was named vice president and treasurer; and Paul R. Zwilling rose to the position of senior vice president and chief actuary.

Mr. Zwilling's predecessor in that role, Dwight K. Bartlett, III, became president in February 1984. The position had been vacant for two years. William J. Flynn had become chairman and chief executive officer in February 1982 and had relinquished the presidency at the annual meeting in the fall of that year. Mr. Bartlett was the fifth man in the company's history to hold this title, following Milton H. Glover, Ralph H. Blanchard, Richard C. Brockway, and William J. Flynn.

Mr. Bartlett's promotion reflected burgeoning corporate growth on the one hand, and executive vision on the other. As assets surged close to the $2 billion mark and annual income neared $440 million, Mr. Flynn needed a top-level management colleague. At the same time, the continuity of leadership benefited from an active presidency to complement the chairmanship. Mr. Bartlett's elevation provided Mr. Flynn with the opportunity to achieve both goals, while retaining the ultimate management role as chief executive officer.

Mutual of America continued to assume its share of responsibility for industry concerns. In November 1983, William Flynn, in his capacity as chairman of the Life Insurance Council of New York, appeared before the New York State Temporary State Commission on Insurance, Banking, and Financial Services. That body, referred to as the DeWind Commission, had been formed, in part, to examine the question of banks owning insurance companies and insurance companies owning banks. At that appearance, Mr. Flynn recommended that insurance and banking should remain separate enterprises until much greater study has been given to the question.

President Bartlett later testified before the House of Representatives Subcommittee on Labor-Management Relations. Speaking for the company, Mr. Bartlett noted the need for "a national retirement policy" and stated that "the development of such a policy is long overdue. The accelerated adoption of piecemeal legislation, such as DEFRA, ERTA, REACT, TEFRA, etc., has created a volatile environment in the pension field...."[11]

For the 39th anniversary on October 1, 1984, Chairman Flynn and President Bartlett announced that more than 320,000 active participants were covered under 22,000 benefit plans in force for the not-for-profit human services organizations the company served.[12] These men and women were Mutual of America's share of the total employee benefit industry, which at the end of 1983 had reached an estimated annual cost level of $510 billion, up over 7.8 percent from the previous year.[13]

The growth in clients meant not only more employee participant accounts to service but an expanded staff to administer the increased number of plans. Mutual of America employed 214 workers when Mr. Flynn became president in 1971. After a decade, 451 persons were on the payroll. By the end of 1985, there were 651 employees.

With the greater size and experience came increased managerial sophistication. The early decades of the company were characterized by relative informality in hiring and job supervision. Later, the company developed a more formal personnel program with official forms for almost every phase of office life, from hiring through performance reviews to promotion or termination.

Stephanie Kopp describes the change in personnel policy: "What has happened now is that there is more refinement and more specialization. The personnel department sends out, on an annual basis for all employees, review sheets to the operating divisions explaining the procedures and policies of evaluating employees. We now have a structured type of operation, very formalized, but, hopefully, one that has not lost contact with the people, and I don't think it has" *(Stephanie J. Kopp Interview, April 15, 1988).*

In July 1973, Stephanie Kopp was appointed personnel manager. She was succeeded in that position by Second Vice President Vivian P. Giacini, who later became a senior vice president. Employment opportunities kept opening for both high school and college level jobs. Job posting made it easier for employees to broaden their experience by alerting them to positions open throughout the company. There were ample opportunities for advancement, too, with promotion from within the ranks being followed whenever possible.

More than 40 employees had come to Mutual of America from The Equitable Life Assurance Society of the United States. Some of them had been recruited by William Flynn, others came later, and still others joined after retirement. William Flynn is the first to acknowledge the debt of Mutual of America to former and current employees of the Equitable. This help has been on many levels, from the highest policy advice to specific office details. For example, Mr. Flynn says: "Every stick of furniture that we use is what we call 'Equitable Standard.' Every piece out there is the quality the Equitable insisted on when they put up their building" *(William J. Flynn Interview, April 19, 1988)*.

From the beginning, employees have expressed a sense of purpose and a certain caring for each other that stems from the company's original commitment to social welfare organizations. There is also an underlying sense of family, a closeness that surfaces whenever joy or sadness is shared. On April 27, 1985, Vice President G. Douglas McCarter of the investment division, who had made a major contribution to the financial growth of the company, died quite suddenly. William Flynn had just reached California that day en route to a long-planned trip to the Orient. He flew back to New York to comfort McCarter's family before resuming his journey overseas.

Mutual of America reached the summer of 1985 with an impressive list of recent achievements in its service to not-for-profit organizations across the country. It enjoyed an average annual compound growth in assets of 18.6 percent over the previous ten years compared to an industry average of 10.9 percent for that period. The ratio of expense to revenue was only 6.5 percent, which meant 93.5 cents of every revenue dollar was put aside for the payment of benefits.[14]

Fortune magazine included Mutual of America in its "Service 500" list of the "Top Fifty" life insurance companies, ranking it 48th in asset size among more than 2,000 life insurance companies in the United States.[15] In New York, Mutual of America advanced to seventh rank in asset size among a total of 86 life insurance companies domiciled in that state.

There was more favorable news in 1985. A. M. Best Company gave Mutual of America its highest rating, A + (Excellent). More than 260 life companies had gone out of business, merged or changed name as recently as 1980 to 1982, but the successor to the innovative NHWRA grew larger and stronger. A. M. Best noted: "The majority of the principal officers have spent their entire careers in the life insurance business."[16]

The company's 40th anniversary was observed with four days of meetings and celebrations at the Waldorf-Astoria Hotel in New York City. Varied activities for different parts of the Mutual of America family were scheduled in sequence. They began with a dinner for the field force on September 17 and concluded with the anniversary banquet on September 20, 1985.

William Flynn and Dwight Bartlett used the opening dinner to introduce a new sales award named for former Vice President Thomas J. Baker, who had died in 1982. Regional Vice President Sidney H. Spector and Field Consultant Teresa Gwiazda, both of the Philadelphia office, jointly received the first award and were honored for "superior achievement and professionalism."[17]

When President Bartlett spoke at the sales meeting the next day, he emphasized to his audience that clients expected more than reactive service, and that the company should take the initiative regarding their needs.

During the evening of September 18, company officers and representatives of the chairman's council and selected client agencies attended a dinner to honor Elie Wiesel, the future Nobel laureate, then chairman of the U.S. Holocaust Memorial Council. On that occasion *The Courage to Care,* a film sponsored by Mutual of America about those who risked their lives to save Jews during the Holocaust, was shown for the first time. Later it was to be shown before many influential groups and nominated for an Academy Award as the best short documentary that year. Robert Gardner won an Emmy for Best Director when the film was broadcast. William Flynn presented Dr. Wiesel with Mutual of America's 1985 Distinguished

William Aramony, Lane Adams, and William J. Flynn
at the dinner celebrating Mutual of America's 40th anniversary
(In the background, left to right: Richard C. Brockway,
Mrs. George E. Johnson, George E. Johnson, Mrs. John Dunne)

Community Service Award because he embodied the values of caring for humankind, which Mutual of America exists to help and serve.

The chairman's council, with Richard F. Huegli presiding, met throughout the following day and a half. Mr. Huegli led the group through a number of plenary sessions interspersed with several workshops. Mr. Flynn informed the council that Mutual of America would continue to serve only the not-for-profit world, but, in serving that world, it might create for-profit subsidiaries to provide additional services. That evening, September 19, the council members, directors, and other guests enjoyed dinner aboard the Empress of New York as the chartered craft cruised the harbor under evening skies. The next morning, the council reconvened for the final session. At the conclusion, Richard Huegli relinquished the chairmanship of the council to Howard Nolan, executive vice president, United Way of San Antonio and Bexar County, Texas.

The entire program concluded with the dinner on September 20, attended by the directors, members of the chairman's council, home office employees, and many employees of Mutual of America from across the country. Among the honored guests were James P. Corcoran, New York State superintendent of insurance; John Carter, president and CEO of the Equitable; and Peter Flanagan, president of the Life Insurance Council of New York. The keynote address was given by William Aramony. Distinguished Community Service Awards (in addition to the one given to Elie Wiesel) were presented to the American Cancer Society's chief executive officer, Lane W. Adams; Frances R. Hesselbein, national executive director of the Girl Scouts of the USA; and Sister Cecilia Schneider, executive director of the New York Foundling Hospital.

There were many distinguished associates and employees, past and present, as well as good friends of Mutual of America, on the dais that evening. Some of these members and friends of the Mutual of America family were: Grace Blanchard, widow of Ralph Blanchard, acknowledged founder of the Retirement

Recipients of Mutual of America's Distinguished Community Service Awards:

Sister Evelyn Schneider (1980)

William Aramony (1981)

Robert J. Myers (1983)

Lane W. Adams (1985)

Frances R. Hesselbein (1985)   Sister Cecilia Schneider (1985)

Elie Wiesel (1985)   Sister Mary Maurita Sengelaub,
R.S.M. (1987)

Association; Mary Stander, one of the company's very first employees; Mr. and Mrs. Lane W. Adams; Mr. William Aramony; Mr. and Mrs. Dwight K. Bartlett, III; Mr. Richard C. Brockway; Mr. and Mrs. Leland S. Brown; Mr. and Mrs. Lewis D. Cole; The Honorable James P. Corcoran; Mr. and Mrs. John R. Dunne; Mrs. Frances R. Hesselbein; Mr. and Mrs. Richard F. Huegli; Mr. and Mrs. George E. Johnson; Mr. and Mrs. William Kaufman; Mr. and Mrs. William E. MacDonald; and Sister Cecilia Schneider.

William Flynn was described by New York State Senator John R. Dunne as a combination of "priest, police inspector and politician." When he delivered the closing remarks, Mr. Flynn told the crowd gathered in the grand ballroom that "Institutions don't care. People care. It's the people on the dais behind me who represent the caring which built this company. Our future will make our past pale."

> The history of Mutual of America is a history of caring. From its inception, the organization has been dedicated to serving those who work in the not-for-profit field. From its founding in 1945, the mission of Mutual of America has remained constant:
>
> To provide men and women in the not-for-profit field with an organized capacity for ensuring their financial security.
>
> *(from the 40th Anniversary Dinner Program)*

Chapter Twenty

EPILOGUE
1985 TO PRESENT

The years following the 40th anniversary have been ones of sustained growth and expansion in Mutual of America's regular insurance operations. This noteworthy continuity has been achieved through the marketing and selling of coverages developed and proven successful during the company's long experience with the needs of not-for-profit clients. At the same time, an extensive range of products has been added that include structured settlements, funding agreements, thrift plans, and many new financial services.

The customer base has been enlarged in accordance with the strategies presented in the Long Range Planning Committee's report in 1984. This document called for new methods of creating greater direct contact and relationships with clients. It urged the company to be responsive to the rapid changes occurring in the nation's financial services industry. In line with this, the committee recommended that the one-stop shopping concept be further developed and the products made more competitive and attractive to an increasing variety of new clients.

The commitment to increase Mutual of America's overall market share also was clearly expressed in the company's Charter that was amended in January 1985. That document empowered the corporation to transact insurance business with people involved in new types of not-for-profit activities, such as employees of federal or state or local government organizations engaged in educational, health or social welfare work.

Coordinated endeavors toward realizing these new goals have been successful. Dwight Bartlett observed that: "The pace of change has accelerated. We've broadened our product line and our market very substantially" *(Dwight K. Bartlett, III, Interview, March 29, 1988).*

In these past few years, Mutual of America has been maturing as a major force in the American insurance industry. The company moved to the 39th rank overall in American life insurance companies in 1987, according to *Fortune* magazine. Its assets were recorded as $4.2 billion for that year, and this upward climb is continuing.[1] In 1988, assets of Mutual of America and its subsidiaries exceeded $4.8 billion.

Expansion and increased operating size always require streamlining and creative readjustment in a healthy, imaginative corporation. One such path taken by Mutual of America has been the establishment of a National Telecommunications Center at Boca Raton, Florida.

In the near future, most of the company's computer operations will be directed and performed there. The center will also provide instantaneous communication between the home and regional offices to ensure swifter and more efficient service of numerous types to clients old and new. Furthermore, it will enable direct computer connections between the company and terminals located in the offices of many clients throughout the country.

This completely modern facility is a matter of pride to William Flynn. He said: "You'd have no idea how incredibly important our telecommunications project is. All that hardware and software will make the difference between a really viable institution and one that is not adjusting to new challenges. Telecommunications is a key to our whole future" *(William J. Flynn Interview, April 19, 1988)*.

On July 1, 1988, Mutual of America underwent a corporate restructuring as major as any that has come before in the era of William Flynn's leadership. Once again, it stems from the recommendations made in the 1984 Long Range Planning Committee report, which counseled management to create an integrated corporate entity that would be appropriate to the changing economic and social environment.

Therefore, Mutual of America has recently been reorganized to operate in the best way to fulfill its fundamental goal, which is to serve its not-for-profit policyholders by utilizing personnel and resources in the most productive and cost effective manner. To achieve this, the corporation has established or acquired additional subsidiaries to provide services other than pension related services to not-for-profit clients.

One of these is The American Life Insurance Company of New York, which will do business in group life insurance, disability insurance, individual life insurance, and other related insurance activities. The Mutual of America Financial Services Corporation, an important subsidiary whose task is to provide clients with a highly competitive and encompassing range of financial credit services, has also been formed. This reinforces the basic commitment to bring one-stop services of all types to the customer. As an important additional convenience, these services will be offered to policyholders through their place of work rather than having them deal with different carriers.

Another subsidiary is The Mutual of America Foundation which seeks to promote volunteer action as the most effective method of improving communities and social welfare. The foundation will also alert not-for-profit organizations to the various methods of organizing and following through on planned giving programs to raise funds for important causes.

Meanwhile, most of the fundamental pension and insurance activities that deal directly with the clients are now consolidated in one operation, the consulting services division. The unified leadership offered by this group will do much to ensure the highest quality of dependable service to clients.

While under the authority of this division, the field offices, which numbered 33 in 1988, will be expanded, and the service functions deployed to the local offices. This will decentralize the home office and bring the company's presence closer to the customer in the field through immediate contact with regional offices. This development derives from the tradition of making programs and services more immediately and personally available, which has been a goal of the company from its beginning.

The future of Mutual of America is positive and flexible, as promising as the outlook for the nation itself. The company thrives on change, on reexamining itself, and constantly adapting to handle new challenges and demands. It is determined to be always prepared to fulfill the obligations of its growing business to greater numbers of clients.

In seeking, first of all, health, welfare and retirement security for its not-for-profit workers, it has utilized the entrepreneurial spirit that is the essence of American industry. By uniquely meshing the imperatives of social responsibility and awareness with the exacting demands of competition in the market place, Mutual of America continues to progress in the spirit of its founders.

ASSETS

(In Millions [M] and Billions [B])

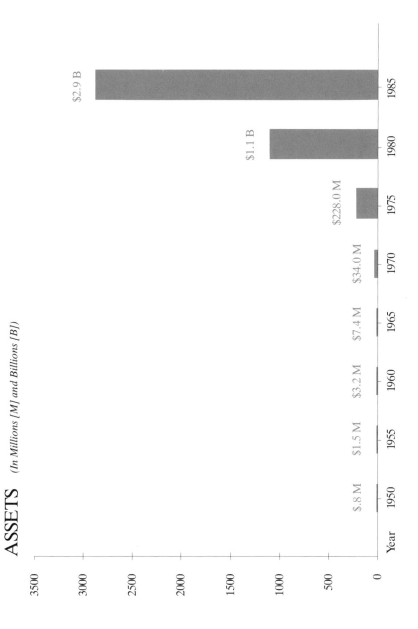

| | 3500 | 3000 | 2500 | 2000 | 1500 | 1000 | 500 | 0 |

| Year | 1950 | 1955 | 1960 | 1965 | 1970 | 1975 | 1980 | 1985 |

$.8 M $1.5 M $3.2 M $7.4 M $34.0 M $228.0 M $1.1 B $2.9 B

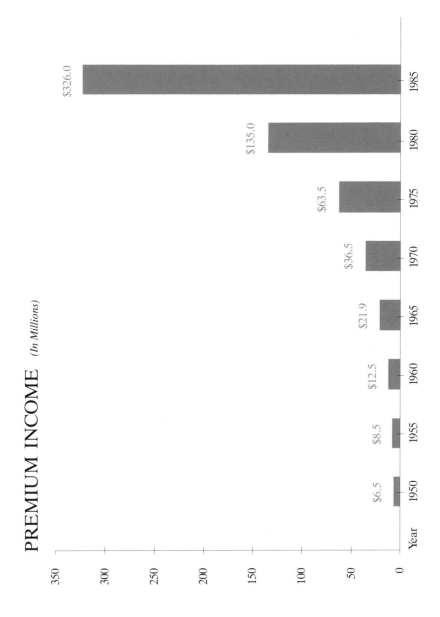

PREMIUM INCOME *(In Millions)*

Year	Value
1950	$6.5
1955	$8.5
1960	$12.5
1965	$21.9
1970	$36.5
1975	$63.5
1980	$135.0
1985	$326.0

BENADITS PAID *(In Millions)*

Important Dates
in Mutual of America's History

National Health & Welfare Retirement Association, Inc. (NHWRA)

September 1943	Community Chests and Councils (CCC) received committee report recommending that CCC develop a retirement plan for health and welfare workers.
January 1945	NHWRA chartered and licensed under Section 200 of the New York State Insurance Law as a retirement system and authorized to transact business. Gerard Swope named Chairman of the Board and Milton H. Glover named President. Ralph H. Blanchard, Executive Director of CCC, key to these arrangements and board member. Agreements with the John Hancock Mutual Life Insurance Company to reinsure all benefits provided by the Retirement Association.
May 1945	NHWRA incorporated as a not-for-profit corporation.
June 1945	NHWRA received federal income tax exemption under Section 101(8), later known as Section 501(c)(4).
October 1945	NHWRA achieved enrollment of 400 agencies with 5,000 participants and qualified under New York State requirements to begin operations. NHWRA offered Plan A, a standard contributory defined contribution plan calling for an

October 1945 (continued)	employee and employer contribution rate equal to 5% of each employee's salary, plus an additional employer contribution of 2% of payroll for past service pension benefits. The plan also provided supplemental death benefits of 10 months salary.
October 1946	Announcement of Plan C for American Hospital Association.
June 1947	Henry Bruère elected Chairman.
November 1947	Plan B benefit program superseded Plan A and provided past service benefits only by specific arrangement.
January 1951	Social Security Act amended to include, on optional basis, employees of not-for-profit religious and charitable organizations.
July 1951	Plans D and E adopted to complement Plans A and B and developed with lower employee and employer contribution rates to coordinate with Social Security contributions and provide supplemental death benefits of 7 months salary.
September 1951	Ralph H. Blanchard named President, succeeding Milton H. Glover.
October 1955	Milton H. Glover became Chairman, succeeding Henry Bruère.
July 1957	Article III of By-Laws introduced new flexible plans tailor-made for each agency and added defined benefit plans for the first time as an alternative to the Plans A, B, C, D, and E defined contribution plans.
March 1960	A committee on long-range objectives established, chaired by Ralph Blanchard.

March 1960 (continued)	George E. Johnson retained to advise committee.
November 1960	Ralph H. Blanchard became President on full-time basis, i.e., no longer a volunteer.
November 1962	Leland S. Brown elected Chairman, succeeding Milton H. Glover who became Honorary Chairman.
October 1963	NHWRA announced that New York State Law had been amended to permit retirement associations to write deposit administration plans and that it had received approval to offer group disability income insurance.
June 1965	George E. Johnson, Vice President and Trustee, was authorized as Acting President in the absence of Ralph H. Blanchard due to illness.
August 1965	NHWRA acquired its first high capacity computer.
November 1965	Richard C. Brockway elected President effective January 1966.
May 1966	Health & Welfare Life Insurance Association, Inc. (HWLIA) licensed in New York as a wholly-owned subsidiary life insurance company.
January 1967	NHWRA Flexi-Fund Program introduced involving a common stock separate account and deposit administration contracts. Contracts not reinsured with any other insurance company.
May 1968	Change in size of board of trustees approved by New York State Insurance Department.

October 1968	First meeting of the 24-person board of trustees.
January 1969	President's Council met for first time, chaired by Terrance L. Webster.
June 1971	William J. Flynn elected President. Richard C. Brockway named Vice Chairman and CEO.
February 1972	William J. Flynn named CEO.
June 1972	William Kaufman became chairman of President's Council.
November 1972	C. Virgil Martin elected Chairman of the Board.
March 1973	NHWRA's Cost of Living Retirement Plan announced as the first of several standardized plans called the National Retirement Program. Tax-Deferred Annuity Plan and Flexible Annuity Plan introduced later as part of this program.
June 1973	NHWRA's first branch field office opened in Philadelphia, Pennsylvania.
January 1974	John Hancock reinsurance contract effective for change to immediate participation guarantee basis.
November 1974	Lewis D. Cole elected Chairman of the Board.
January 1978	NHWRA brings responsibility for the investment operation in-house.
June 1978	Initiation of "System '78," a computerized, comprehensive monthly billing system detailing employers' financial data.

National Health & Welfare Mutual Life Insurance Association, Inc. (NHW)

December 1978	NHWRA converts from a retirement association to a mutual life insurance company named National Health & Welfare Mutual Life Insurance Association, Inc. (NHW). Fiscal reporting period changed to calendar year basis.
February 1979	C. Paul Hulten elected Chairman of the Board.
July 1979	NHW consolidates with HWLIA by taking over the business of HWLIA, then liquidating the subsidiary.
December 1980	Reinsurance contract with the John Hancock terminated with agreement to transfer funds in specified amounts over a period matching the years over which the annuity payments would have been made. No further payments were made to John Hancock. The NHW reserves held by John Hancock became an NHW asset, making the total NHW assets over $1 billion.
June 1981	Richard F. Huegli named chairman of President's Council.
February 1982	William J. Flynn elected Chairman of the Board, President, and Chief Executive Officer. President's Council renamed Chairman's Council.
April 1983	Long Range Planning Committee consisting of current and former board members established, chaired by Dan M. McGill.

Mutual of America Life Insurance Company (Mutual of America)

January 1984	Name changed to Mutual of America Life Insurance Company.
February 1984	Dwight K. Bartlett, III, named President.
April 1984	Long Range Planning Committee recommendations: Mutual of America expand its market and its products; provide broad financial services to current and prospective clients either directly or through related organizations; continue close identification with the not-for-profit field.
February 1985	Mutual America Corporation established as holding company of the parent; incorporated in the state of Delaware.
September 1985	Mutual of America celebrated its 40th anniversary.

271

James W. Bartrop
Edmund J. Beazley
Philip Bernstein
Roger E. Birk
Laura D. Blackburne
Ralph H. Blanchard
Robert E. Bondy
C. M. Bookman
Harry Boyer
Mabel H. Brandon
Howard S. Braucher
Richard C. Brockway
Mrs. Charles S. Brown
Edward H. Brown
Leland S. Brown
The Reverend Robert Brown
Henry Bruère
The Most Reverend Joseph Brunini
George Bugbee
Fred M. Butzel

Charles C. Cabot
Eugene J. Callan
Harry Carey
Winslow Carlton
The Right Reverend Howard J. Carroll
Lisle C. Carter, Jr.
Dede W. Casad
J. Herbert Case
Jacques Chabrier
Robert X. Chandler
Clarence R. Chaney
Richard J. Ciecka
Jacob Clayman
Lewis D. Cole
J. Douglas Colman
William R. Consedine
Lawrence T. Cooper

Lester B. Granger
M. E. Grant
A. Crawford Greene, Sr.
A. Crawford Greene
Frederick Greenwood
James A. Greer, II

James A. Hamilton
Robert M. Hanes
Shelby M. Harrison
Mrs. Samuel C. Harvey
John H. Hayes
John S. Hayes
Howard J. Heinz, II
Earl T. Helsel
Howard H. Hennington
Frances R. Hesselbein
Clarence E. Hill
Harold Hinderer
Sidney Hollander
Richard F. Huegli
C. Paul Hulten
Jane Hurd
Peter H. Husch

Aaron L. Jacoby
Wilmer A. Jenkins
George E. Johnson
Holgar J. Johnson
J. Harold Johnston
Eugene Kinckle Jones
Mrs. Lee Jordan

William Kahn
Frank W. Karr, Jr.
William Kaufman
Thomas W. Keesee, Jr.
Clarence King
Donald J. Kingsley

The Right Reverend Monsignor John O'Grady
Jack Owen
Theodor Oxholm

James R. Page
Philip A. Palese
Augustin H. Parker, Jr.
Eugene J. Patton
Michael A. Pelavin
Donald A. Pels
Leo Perlis
Walter Perry, Jr.
Gerard M. Peterson
C. Whit Pfeffer
Delmont K. Pfeffer
Dean Phillips
Flaxie Madison Pinkett
Jerome Pollack

Laurence E. Richardson
Stanley Richman
Benjamin B. Rosenberg
Lessing J. Rosenwald
Anthony J. J. Rourke, M.D.
Mary E. Ruddy
Edward L. Ryerson

George M. Saunders
Sister Evelyn Schneider
Edgar Scott, Jr.
Ramon S. Scruggs
Sister Mary Maurita Sengelaub, R.S.M.
Mrs. Victor Shaw
George A. Shea
Howard C. Sheperd
Samuel J. Silberman
John S. Sinclair
Raymond P. Sloan
Charles Warren Smith

Executive Vice Presidents of Mutual of America, 1988

Manfred Altstadt

Patrick A. Burns

Joan M. Casson

Stephanie J. Kopp

Howard Lichtenstein

Thomas J. Moran

Thomas J. Roach

Vice President Isadore Feferman joined the administrative staff of the Retirement Association in September 1947.

Vice President Sarah W. Belle began as a roving clerk on the administrative staff in March 1953.

Company Officers
1945–1988

Staff Officers

Chairman & Chief Executive Officer: William J. Flynn

Presidents: Dwight K. Bartlett, III
Ralph H. Blanchard
Richard C. Brockway
William J. Flynn
Milton H. Glover

Acting President: George E. Johnson

Executive Vice Presidents: Manfred Altstadt
Patrick A. Burns
Joan M. Casson
Howard H. Hennington
Stephanie J. Kopp
Howard Lichtenstein
George M. Lingua
Kenneth J. Ludwig
Clement R. McCormack
Frank P. Montgomery
Thomas J. Moran
Thomas J. Roach

Senior Vice Presidents: Liane Bronstein
Allen J. Bruckheimer
John Cerrato, Jr.
Rita Conyers
William A. DeMilt

Senior Vice Presidents: Roger C. Ferrara
Vivian P. Giacini
Thomas Gilliam
Raymond J. Hayes
Alan Jacobs
Gregory A. Kleva, Jr.
Joel Levine
Kenneth J. McCaffrey
Paul E. Mais
John E. Manley
Dolores J. Morrissey
Timothy J. O'Keefe
Daniel J. Robins
Marilyn A. Sloane
John F. Wells, Jr.
Joseph D. Williams
Paul R. Zwilling

Vice Presidents: Robert W. Allmang
Diane M. Aramony
Thomas J. Baker
Sarah W. Belle
Nicholas A. Branchina
Arthur C. Brett, Jr.
J. Thomas Burkard
Saul Chandler
George Cherlin
Edward Cole
J. Douglas Colman
Walter Curti
Linda DeHooge
Alma Delfino
Isadore Feferman
Victor Fried
Joyce W. Gardiner
Robert Giaquinto
Donald S. Grubbs
William H. Hackett

Vice Presidents: Thomas A. Harwood
John H. Hayes
Sandra W. Hersko
George E. Johnson
Darrel Johnston
Jack H. Kleinmann
Raymond J. Kraft
Nancy McAvey
G. Douglas McCarter
R. Donald McCarter
Robert C. MacFarlane
Francis J. McGuire
James T. McGuire
Janet Malek
Robert G. Malm
Robert W. Maull
Frank W. Miller
John L. Moore
Roger F. Napoleon
Joan O'Donnell
Samuel H. Ourbacker
G. Robert Parker
Eugene J. Patton
Raymond C. Peterson
Alvin Prichard
Antonio Quesada
Anna M. Ridolfo
Sam Rosen
Burton Ross
Guy A. Shane
William G. Shannon
Walter W. Siegel
Gerald S. Silva
Robert Somelofske
Joan Squires
Teresita StaCruz
Christopher W. Stanwood

Vice Presidents: Jane E. Sullivan
Frank C. Sutton
Robert Trawinski
James D. Trevett
Neil Waldman
Hae Soo Whang
William R. White
Homer Wickenden
Donald E. Wissell
Thomas C. Woodruff

Second Vice Presidents: Marion Amrhein
Richard Bamonte
Leonard Brown
Charles Jennerjahn
Jenny Jones
Grace I. Luce
Gordon McCoun
Lynn Nadler
Ralph Paladino
Joanne Spinner
Eugene Thomas
John B. Walthausen
M. Elaine White

Assistant Treasurers: C. Henry Evensen
Richard Montgomery

Secretary: Harold Porton

Comptroller: Michael Reape

Field Officers

Senior Field Vice Presidents: Gerard P. Buckley
Fiske Field
Helmut Frick
John H. Harrigan
Joan M. Lane
Joe A. McElroy
Nicholas Moccia
Robert D. Sadler
Sidney H. Spector
Edward Wenzel

Vice Presidents: Leo Ahola
William S. Conway
Charles Craig
Arthur Dalessandro
Mary Donovan
Gerald M. Leonard
Patrick McNulty
John B. Nilson
Richard Pelchat
William Rose

Regional Vice Presidents: Norris Andersen
John Austin
Mary Cafferty
William Carson
Joseph Ceccacci
Lawrence H. Gerring
Bernard Hynes
Jody Jurica
Robert Kordecki
Manuel R. Lopez

Regional Vice Presidents: James McKendrick
Thomas E. MacMurray
Michael Melnick
Joseph A. Oganda
Norman Sokoloff
Robert A. Swanke
Jacqueline Van Zant
Gertrude Wilkinson
Donald J. Wise

Second Vice President: Paul Lorenti

Council Chairmen

President's Council
Chairmen: Terrance L. Webster, 1968-1972
William Kaufman, 1972-1981
Richard F. Huegli, 1981-1982

Chairman's Council
Chairmen: Richard F. Huegli, 1982-1985
Howard J. Nolan, 1985-Present

Interviews

Lane W. Adams, Current Member of the Board of Directors, Mutual of America, March 16, 1988.

William Aramony, Current Member of the Board of Directors, Mutual of America, May 9, 1988.

Dwight K. Bartlett, III, President, Mutual of America, 1984 to 1989, March 29, 1988.

Sarah W. Belle, Vice President, Administrative Services, Mutual of America, March 3, 1988.

Grace Blanchard, wife of Ralph Blanchard, founder of the National Health & Welfare Retirement Association, April 13, 1988.

Richard C. Brockway, President, NHWRA, 1966 to 1971, and former Vice Chairman of the Board of Trustees, NHWRA, March 25, 1988.

Leland S. Brown, Chairman of the Board of Trustees, NHWRA, 1962 to 1972, April 6, 1988.

Gerard P. Buckley, Senior Field Vice President, Boston, Massachusetts, Mutual of America, April 1, 1988.

Joan M. Casson, Executive Vice President and Chief Investment Officer, General Account Investments, Mutual of America, May 18, 1988.

John Cerrato, Jr., Senior Vice President, Consulting Services, Mutual of America, May 7, 1988.

Lewis D. Cole, Chairman of the Board of Trustees, NHW, 1974 to 1979, April 29, 1988.

Linda DeHooge, Vice President and Assistant to the Chairman, Mutual of America, March 3, 1988.

Isadore Feferman, Vice President, Corporate Communications, Mutual of America, March 1, 1988.

William J. Flynn, Chairman of the Board of Directors and Chief Executive Officer, Mutual of America, March 21, 1988 and April 19, 1988.

Helmut Frick, Senior Field Vice President, Consulting Services, Mutual of America, March 10, 1988.

Lawrence H. Gerring, Regional Vice President, Seattle, Washington, Mutual of America, April 22, 1988.

Thomas Gilliam, Senior Vice President, Consulting Services, Mutual of America, March 3, 1988.

A. Crawford Greene, Current Member of the Board of Directors and Chairperson of the Compensation Committee, Mutual of America, April 26, 1988.

John H. Harrigan, Senior Field Vice President, West Palm Beach, Florida, Mutual of America, Deceased, May 12, 1988.

Howard H. Hennington, Executive Vice President, NHW, Retired, and Member of the Board of Directors, Mutual of America, March 22, 1988 and April 7, 1988.

Frances R. Hesselbein, Current Member of the Board of Directors and Chairperson of the Audit and Nominating Committees, Mutual of America, March 17, 1988.

C. Paul Hulten, Chairman of the Board of Trustees, NHW, 1979 to 1982, April 25, 1988.

George E. Johnson, Member of the Board of Trustees, Acting President, 1965, Consultant, and advisor on insurance, NHWRA, May 13, 1988.

William Kaufman, Member of the Board of Trustees and Chairman of the President's Council, NHWRA, April 28, 1988.

Stephanie J. Kopp, Executive Vice President and Secretary, Mutual of America, March 24, 1988 and April 15, 1988.

I. Murray Krowitz, Inspector, New York State Department of Insurance, Retired, May 10, 1988.

Joan M. Lane, Senior Field Vice President, New York, NY-North, Mutual of America, March 24, 1988.

Howard Lichtenstein, Executive Vice President, Consulting Services, Mutual of America, March 8, 1988 and March 15, 1988.

Clement R. McCormack, Executive Vice President and Treasurer, NHW, Retired, March 30, 1988.

William E. MacDonald, Current Member of the Board of Directors, Mutual of America, April 21, 1988.

Dan M. McGill, Member of the Board of Trustees, NHWRA, and Consultant to the Board of Directors, Mutual of America, April 13, 1988.

C. Virgil Martin, Chairman of the Board of Trustees, NHWRA, 1972 to 1974, April 5, 1988.

Frank P. Montgomery, Executive Vice President, Mutual of America, Retired, March 18, 1988 and April 18, 1988.

Daniel J. Robins, Senior Vice President and General Counsel, Mutual of America, Retired, March 15, 1988, March 29, 1988, and April 12, 1988.

Araxe Sookikian, Office Staff, Mutual of America, Retired, March 16, 1988.

Mary D. Stander, Office Staff, NHWRA, Retired, May 10, 1988.

Christopher W. Stanwood, Vice President, Field Director, NHWRA, Retired, March 31, 1988.

Notes

Chapter One

1. *Information Please Almanac* (Boston: Houghton Mifflin Company, 1985), p. 65.
2. "Social Security: United States," *Encyclopaedia Britannica* (Chicago, 1954), Vol. 20, p. 900.
3. *People & Events* (Alexandria, Va.: United Way of America, 1977), p. 75.
4. Ibid., p. 76.
5. Ibid., p. 81.
6. *People & Events,* p. 92 (quoting *Community,* UCFCA, January 1943, pp. 66-74).
7. *People & Events,* p. 94.

Chapter Two

1. *New York Times,* January 18, 1945.
2. *New York World Telegram,* January 17, 1945.
3. *Vindicator* (Youngstown, Ohio), January 20, 1945.
4. *Chronicle* (Spokane, Washington), January 17, 1945.
5. Letter from Arthur J. Altmeyer to Ralph H. Blanchard, December 12, 1944.
6. P. N. Eckman, second vice president, The John Hancock Mutual Life Insurance Company, in a letter to Milton H. Glover, January 4, 1945.
7. NHWRA By-Laws, Article I, Paragraph 18.
8. "Report of the Pension Committee," Pension Plans for Hospital Employees, American Hospital Association, excerpts from the *Hospital Review*, 1945, p. 17.
9. Milton H. Glover and Gerard Swope booklet, "To You in Health and Welfare Work," August 1, 1945.
10. "Announcement of Effective Date," letter and flyer dated October 17, 1945.
11. "Says Hospital Must Boost Wages to Hold Basic Working Force," *Boston Globe,* March 11, 1946.

Chapter Three

1. "Retirement Program for Hospital Employees," *New England Journal of Medicine,* February 13, 1947.
2. "Parley to View Hospitals from Experts' Angle," *Milwaukee Star,* February 20, 1947.
3. "Pensions for 50 Hospitals," *Hospitals,* May 1947 (Reprint).
4. Letter from Franklin D. Roosevelt to The Bowery Savings Bank trustees, December 11, 1933.
5. John H. Hayes, "Retirement payments for hospital employees," *Hospitals,* August 1949, Vol. 23, p. 62.
6. "First Retirement Benefit Check Received from National Consultant," *St. Mary's Extra* (Rochester, New York), November 21, 1949, Vol. 2, No. 5, p. 1.
7. "Social Security: United States," *Encyclopaedia Britannica* (Chicago, 1954), Vol. 20, p. 901.

Chapter Four

1. "Welfare Retirement Covers Nearly 24,000," *Eastern Underwriter,* November 7, 1952.
2. *Benefits,* No. 4, August 1952, Versions for Plans A and B and Plans C and D.
3. *Annual Report,* October 30, 1953, p. 5.
4. Ibid., p. 7.
5. Ibid., p. 10.
6. New York State Insurance Department, Report on Examination of NHWRA, June 30, 1953 (February 1, 1955) by Israel M. Krowitz.
7. *Annual Report,* October 30, 1953, p. 5.
8. Ibid., p. 11.
9. *Annual Report,* October 28, 1954.

Chapter Five

1. *Annual Report,* October 27, 1955.
2. Author's Interview with Earl B. Schwulst, Henry Bruère's successor, Bowery Savings Bank, December 30, 1985.
3. *Annual Report,* October 24, 1957, p. 2.
4. Ibid.

Chapter Six

1. *Annual Report,* October 24, 1957, p. 2.
2. *Annual Report,* October 30, 1958, p. 1.
3. Ibid., p. 3.

4. Ibid., p. 2.
5. Ibid., p. 3.
6. Ibid. (Wilbur J. Cohen, *Hospitals,* quoted by Ralph Blanchard).
7. *Annual Report,* October 29, 1959, pp. 5 and 10.
8. Ibid., pp. 2-3.
9. Ibid., p. 2.
10. Author's interview with Grace Godolphin Blanchard.

Chapter Seven

1. *Annual Report,* November 2, 1962, p. 10.
2. Ibid., p. 19.
3. Ibid., p. 9.
4. Ibid.

Chapter Eight

1. *Annual Report,* October 30, 1963, p. 1.
2. Ibid., p. 13.
3. Ibid.
4. Ibid., p. 12.
5. *Annual Report,* October 29, 1964, pp. 5-6.
6. Ibid., pp. 4-6.

Chapter Nine

1. *Annual Report,* October 1, 1965, pp. 6-9.
2. Ibid.
3. Letter from C. Virgil Martin to Ralph H. Blanchard, February 16, 1972.
4. NHWRA "Schedule of Investments," June 30, 1965.

Chapter Ten

1. *Annual Report,* October 1, 1965, p. 9.
2. Ibid., pp. 10-11.
3. *Annual Report,* 1966, p. 7.
4. "Announcing the Flexible Funding Program of NHWRA," December 1966.
5. Ibid.
6. *Annual Report,* 1967, p. 7.
7. *Pension and Welfare News,* September 1967.
8. *Annual Report,* 1967, p. 8.
9. Ibid.

Chapter Eleven

1. *Annual Report,* 1968, p. 5.
2. Ibid., pp. 2-3, 7.
3. Ibid., p. 6.
4. Ibid.
5. "A Matter of Some Importance...to the Member Agencies of National Health & Welfare Association, Inc.," 1968.
6. Ibid.
7. *Annual Report,* 1968, p. 8.
8. *Annual Report,* 1969, p. 3.
9. Ibid., p. 4.

Chapter Twelve

1. John Naisbitt, *Megatrends* (New York: Warner Books, 1982), p. 22.
2. William H. Carr, *From Three Cents A Week* (Englewood Cliffs, N.J.: Prentice-Hall, Inc., 1975), p. 196.
3. *Annual Report,* 1969, p. 5.
4. *Annual Report,* 1970, pp. 5-6.
5. "Retirement, Death and Long-Term Disability Plan Objectives," 1970, p. 1.
6. Ibid., p. 2.
7. NHWRA By-Laws, Article VII, Section 10.

Chapter Thirteen

1. *Annual Report,* 1971, p. 5.
2. *Annual Report,* 1972, p. 4.
3. Ibid., p. 3.
4. Author's interview with Leland S. Brown, September 15, 1986.

Chapter Fourteen

1. *NHWRA Report,* Vol. 1, No. 1, March 23, 1973, p. 1.
2. *NHWRA Report,* Vol. 1, No. 3, July/August, 1973, p. 1.
3. Ibid.
4. Ibid., p. 2.
5. Ibid., p. 3.
6. *NHWRA Report,* Vol. 1, No. 4, September 27, 1973.
7. Ibid., p. 2.
8. *Annual Report,* 1973, p. 15.
9. *NHWRA Report,* Vol. 2, No. 5, July/August 1974, p. 1.
10. *NHWRA Report,* Vol. 2, No. 3, May 28, 1974, p. 1.
11. *NHWRA Report,* Vol. 2, No. 4, June 28, 1974, pp. 3-4.
12. *Annual Report,* 1974, p. 4.
13. *NHWRA Report,* Vol. 2, No. 6, September 1974, p. 1.

Chapter Fifteen

1. Author's correspondence with Lewis D. Cole, July 31, 1985.
2. *NHWRA Report,* Vol. 3, No. 1, January 28, 1975, p. 1.
3. Dan M. McGill, ed., *Social Security and Private Pension Plans: Competitive or Complementary?* (Homewood, Illinois: Richard D. Irwin, Inc., 1977), p. 22.
4. Howard Lichtenstein memorandum of May 5, 1986, to author.
5. *NHWRA Report,* Vol. 3, No. 4, April 28, 1975, p. 2.
6. *NHWRA Report,* Vol. 3, No. 3, March 28, 1975, p. 4.
7. Author's interview with William J. Flynn, October 6, 1986.
8. *Annual Report,* 1976, p. 4.

Chapter Sixteen

1. *NHWRA Report,* Vol. 5, No. 1, January/February 1977, p. 1.
2. *NHWRA Report,* Vol. 5, No. 2, March 1977, p. 1.
3. *NHWRA Report,* Vol. 5, No. 3, April/May 1977, p. 1.
4. *Annual Report,* 1977, p. 5; *Annual Report*, 1978, p. 4.
5. *NHWRA Report,* Vol. 6, No. 2, May 1978, p. 1.
6. Ibid.
7. *Annual Report,* 1978, p. 5.
8. Ibid.

Chapter Seventeen

1. *NHW Report,* Vol. 1, No. 2, April 1979, p. 2.
2. James C. H. Anderson, "Alternative Futures of The Life Insurance Industry," *Insurance Marketing,* September 1977, p. 28.
3. *NHW Report,* Vol. 1, No. 1, January/February 1979, p. 1.
4. Ibid.
5. Ibid., p. 3.
6. *NHW Report,* Vol. 1, No. 2, April 1979, p. 4.
7. *Annual Report,* 1979, p. 7.
8. Ibid., p. 5.
9. *NHW Participant News,* January 1980.
10. *The Audit Committee: Concept and Practice* (New York: Main, LaFrentz & Co., 1976), p. 1.
11. *NHW Report,* Vol. 2, No. 3, July/August, 1980, p. 3.
12. Ralph Waldo Emerson, *Journal,* February 1855.
13. *NHW Report,* Vol. 2, No. 5, November 1980, p. 1.

Chapter Eighteen

1. *NHW Report,* Vol. 3, No. 6, July 1981, p. 1.
2. *NHW Report,* Vol. 3, No. 10, November 1981, p. 1.
3. Ibid.

4. *NHW Report,* Vol. 3, No. 8, September 1981, p. 1.
5. *Annual Report,* 1981, p. 11.
6. *NHW Report,* Vol. 3, No. 11, December 1981, p. 3.
7. *Annual Report,* 1981, p. 1.
8. *NHW Participant News,* January 1982, p. 1.
9. *NHW Report,* Vol. 4, No. 3, March 1982, pp. 1-2.
10. *Annual Report,* 1982, p. 12.
11. Letter from John G. Heimann ("Report of the Executive Advisory Commission on Insurance Industry Regulatory Reform") to Honorable Hugh L. Carey, May 6, 1982, p. 2.
12. *NHW Report,* Vol. 5, No. 8, September 1983, p. 1.
13. "Heimann Commission Report," May 6, 1982.

Chapter Nineteen

1. Speech by Lane W. Adams, "The Vital Connection," Brigham Young University, April 12, 1978, p. 4.
2. Memorandum from Howard Lichtenstein to Stephanie J. Kopp, September 12, 1985.
3. Memorandum from Lane W. Adams to the author, August 1985.
4. *Mutual of America Report,* Vol. 6, No. 1, January 1984, p. 1.
5. Ibid.
6. James C. Worthy, *Shaping an American Institution: Robert E. Wood and Sears, Roebuck* (Urbana and Chicago: University of Illinois Press, 1984), p. 267.
7. *Annual Report,* March 1983, p. 3.
8. Thomas S. Campbell, "Interview E. James Morton: Loma's New Chairman Shares His Views," *LOMA Resource,* Vol. 9, No. 6, September/October 1984, p. 6.
9. "Prospective Markets for Mutual of America," September 11, 1984.
10. *NHW Report,* Vol. 5, No. 6, June 1983, p. 1.
11. *Mutual of America Report,* Vol. 7, No. 6, p. 1.
12. *Mutual of America Report,* Vol. 6, No. 10, October 1984, p. 1.
13. Mary Jane Fisher, "Benefits Payments Cost Employers $550 Billion in 1983, Says Chamber," *National Underwriter,* Life & Health Insurance Edition, 89th Year, No. 4, January 26, 1985, p. 1.
14. *Annual Report,* 1985, p. 2.
15. *Fortune,* Vol. 111, No. 12, June 10, 1985, pp. 188-189.
16. *Best's Insurance Reports: Life-Health, 1985,* 80th Annual Edition (Oldwick, N.J.: A.M. Best Company, 1985), p. 1601.
17. Thomas J. Baker Award Program, September 17, 1985.

Epilogue

1. *Fortune,* Vol. 115, No. 12, June 8, 1987, pp. 208-9.

Bibliography

Primary Sources

COMPANY MATERIALS
Annual Reports
Annual Statements and Schedules
Investment Reports
Mutual of America Reports
NHW Participant News
NHW Reports
NHWRA Bulletin
NHWRA Reports

Miscellaneous brochures; correspondence; interviews; memoranda; speeches.

NEWSPAPERS AND JOURNALS
Boston Globe. 1946.
Chronicle. 1945.
Eastern Underwriter. 1952.
Fortune. 1985, 1987.
Hospitals. 1947, 1949, 1958.
Insurance Marketing. 1977.
Milwaukee Star. 1947.
National Underwriter. 1985.
New England Journal of Medicine. 1947.
New York Times. 1945.
New York World Telegram. 1945.
Pensions and Welfare News. 1967.
St. Mary's Extra. 1949.
Vindicator. 1945.

PUBLIC DOCUMENTS
New York State Insurance Department Reports of Examinations

Secondary Sources

Bartell, H. Robert, Jr., and Simpson, Elizabeth T. *Pension Funds of Multi-Employer Industrial Groups: Unions, and Non-Profit Organizations*. New York: National Bureau of Economic Research, 1968.

Best's Insurance Reports: Life-Health 1985. 80th Annual Edition. Oldwick, N.J.: A. M. Best Company, 1985.

Blumenfeld, Samuel L., ed. *Property in a Humane Economy*. La Salle, Illinois: Open Court Publishing Company, 1974.

Boorstin, Daniel J. *The Decline of Radicalism: Reflections on America Today*. New York: Random House, 1963.

Brown, J. Douglas. *The Human Nature of Organizations*. New York: American Management Association, 1973.

Buck, Wendell. *From Quill Pen to Computers: An Account of the First One Hundred and Twenty-five Years of the Manhattan Life Insurance Company of New York*. New York, 1975.

Buley, R. Carlyle. *The Equitable Life Assurance Society of the United States, 1859-1964*. New York: Appleton-Century-Crofts, 1967.

Burns, James MacGregor. *Leadership*. New York: Harper & Row, 1978.

Cahn, William. *A Matter of Life and Death: The Connecticut Mutual Story*. New York: Random House, 1970.

Carr, William H. A. *From Three Cents a Week...: The Story of the Prudential Life Insurance Company of America*. Englewood Cliffs, N.J.: Prentice-Hall, 1975.

Chamberlain, Neil W. *Remaking American Values: Challenge to a Business Society*. New York: Basic Books, 1977.

Christensen, Burke A. "Law and Life Insurance: 'New Wave' Life Insurance May Cause Shake Out of Less Efficient Insurers." *Trusts and Estates* 124, no. 5 (May 1985): 58-60.

Cochran, Thomas C. *Challenge to American Values: Society, Business and Religion*. New York and Oxford: Oxford University Press, 1985.

The Consumer's Union Report on Life Insurance. New York: Holt, Rinehart & Winston, 1980.

Cornuelle, Richard C. *Reclaiming the American Dream*. New York: Random House, 1965.

Dun and Bradstreet. *What the Manager Should Know About the Computer*. New York: Dun and Bradstreet, 1968.

Encyclopaedia Britannica. Volume 20. Chicago: Encyclopaedia Britannica, 1954.

Epstein, Joseph. *Ambition: the Secret Passion*. New York: E. P. Dutton, 1980.

Greenewalt, Crawford. *The Uncommon Man: The Individual in the Organization*. New York: McGraw-Hill, 1959.

Gregg, Davis W. *Group Life Insurance: An Analysis of Concepts, Contracts, Costs, and Company Practices*. Homewood, Illinois: Richard D. Irwin, 1957.

Gudmundsen, John. *The Great Provider: The Dramatic Story of Life Insurance in America*. South Norwalk, Connecticut: Industrial Publications Company, 1959.

Hannah, Leslie. *Inventing Retirement: The Development of Occupational Pensions in Britain*. Cambridge and New York: Cambridge University Press, 1986.

Hayakawa, S. J. *Language in Thought and Action*. 4th ed. New York: Harcourt, Brace and Jovanovich, 1978.

Hodgkinson, Virginia Ann, and Weitzman, Murray S. *Dimensions of the Independent Sector, A Statistical Profile*. Washington, D.C.: Independent Sector, 1984.

Hooker, Richard. *A Century of Service: The Massachusetts Mutual Story*. Springfield, Massachusetts: R. J. Holden, 1951.

Hurley, Dunlea. *Panorama of a Century, 1847-1947*. Philadelphia: The Penn Mutual Life Insurance Company, 1947.

Information Please Almanac: Atlas and Yearbook. 38th ed. Boston: Houghton Mifflin Company, 1985.

James, Marquis. *Biography of a Business, 1792-1942: Insurance Company of North America*. Indianapolis and New York: The Bobbs-Merrill Company, 1942.

James, Ollie M. *Splendid Century, 1867-1967*. Cincinnati: The Union Central Life Insurance Company, 1967.

Kleiler, Frank M. *Can We Afford Early Retirement?* Baltimore: The Johns Hopkins University Press, 1978.

Kleinmann, Jack H. *Fringe Benefits for Public School Personnel*. ...New York: Teachers College, Columbia University, 1962.

Lasch, Christopher. *The Culture of Narcissism: American Life in an Age of Diminishing Expectation*. New York: W. W. Norton, 1978.

McGill, Dan M. *Fulfilling Pension Expectations*. Homewood, Illinois: Richard D. Irwin, 1962.
——. *Fundamentals of Private Pensions*. Homewood, Illinois: Richard D. Irwin, 1955.

McGill, Dan Mays, ed. *Social Security and Private Pension Plans: Competitive or Complementary?* Ralph H. Blanchard Memorial Endowment Series Volume 1. Published for the Pension Research Council. Homewood, Illinois: Richard D. Irwin, 1977.

Magee, John H. *General Insurance*. Chicago: Richard D. Irwin, 1946.

Mason, Alpheus Thomas. *Brandeis, A Free Man's Life*. New York: The Viking Press, 1946.

Naisbitt, John. *Megatrends*. New York: Warner Books, 1982.

Novak, Michael. *The Spirit of Democratic Capitalism*. New York: Simon and Schuster, 1982.

Novak, Michael, and Cooper, John W. *The Corporation: A Theological Inquiry*. Washington D.C.: American Enterprise Institute for Public Policy Research, 1981.

Pease, George Sexton. *Patriarch of the Prairie: The Story of Equitable of Iowa, 1867-1967*. New York: Appleton-Century-Crofts, 1967.

People & Events. Alexandria, Virginia: The United Way of America, 1977.

Salisbury, Dallas L., ed. *Economic Survival in Retirement: Which Pension is for You?* Washington D.C.: Employee Benefit Research Institute, 1982.

Schultz, James H. *The Economics of Aging*. Belmont, California: Wadsworth Publishing Company, 1976.

Shulman, Richard. *The Billion Dollar Bookies*. New York: Harper's Magazine Press, 1976.

Silk, Leonard, and Vogel, David. *Ethics and Profits, The Crisis of Confidence in American Business*. New York: Simon and Schuster, 1976.

Stamper, Powell. *The National Life Story: A History of the National Life and Accident Insurance Company of Nashville, Tennessee*. New York: Appleton-Century-Crofts, 1968.

Stone, Mildred F. *A Calling and Its Colleges: A History of the American College of Life Underwriters*. Homewood, Illinois: Richard D. Irwin, 1963.

Strange, Georgianne. *From Days of Knights*. Indianapolis: American United Life Insurance Company, 1977.

Trowbridge, Charles L. and Norma. *Characteristics and Concerns of Old Age*. Privately printed, 1983.

Wall, Joseph Frazier. *Policies and People, The First Hundred Years of the Bankers Life*. Englewood Cliffs, N.J.: Prentice-Hall, 1979.

Warner, W. Lloyd. *The Corporation in the Emergent American Society*. New York: Harper and Brothers, 1962.

Worthy, James C. *Shaping an American Institution: Robert E. Wood and Sears, Roebuck*. Urbana and Chicago: University of Illinois Press, 1984.

Index

Washington, D.C. *(cont)*
regional office, 233; part of Middle Atlantic Region, 163, 165
Webster, Terrance L., 118, 122–23, 153, 155
West Atlantic Region, 200
West Central Region (St. Louis, Missouri), 200
West Palm Beach (Florida): field/regional office, 200, 228
Western Region, 163
Whang, Hae Soo, 132
Wharton School of The University of Pennsylvania, Insurance Department: Chairman Dan McGill, 149, 243, 245; Pension Research Council, 157
White Plains (New York): field/regional office, 233
Wickenden, Homer: career, 13, 15, 19, 21, 24, 28, 29, 33, 38, 61, 84, 179; member CCC organizing committee, 12; secretary of provisional board, 13
Wiesel, Elie, 251, 253
Wilkinson, Gertrude, 233
Williams, Harrison, 202
Wilson, Malcolm, 221
Winston, Ellen, 121
Wisconsin Hospital Association, 33
Wright, Bp. John, 117
Wriston, Walter, 197
Wyatt, Clarence W., 34

York Hospital (York, Pennsylvania), 162–63
Young Men's Christian Association (YMCA) pension fund, 76, 86
Young Women's Christian Association (YWCA) pension fund, 76

Zavatt, Theodore V., 13
Zwilling, Paul R., 180, 247

PROMISES TO KEEP
The Mutual of America Story

Project Coordinator,
Pamela Lehrer, Mutual of America

Designed by Sue Koch in association with
Pamlyn Smith Design, Inc.

Copyedited and indexed by Barbara A. Porter
in association with Pamlyn Smith Design, Inc.

Printed by the L. P. Thebault Company,
Parsippany, New Jersey